TOWARD ADOLESCENCE:
THE MIDDLE SCHOOL YEARS

Seventy-ninth Yearbook of the
National Society for the Study of Education

PART I

By

THE YEARBOOK COMMITTEE

and

ASSOCIATED CONTRIBUTORS

Edited by

MAURITZ JOHNSON

Editor for the Society

KENNETH J. REHAGE

19 | NSSE | 80

Distributed by THE UNIVERSITY OF CHICAGO PRESS • CHICAGO, ILLINOIS

The National Society for the Study of Education

Founded in 1901 as successor to the National Herbart Society, the National Society for the Study of Education has provided a means by which the results of serious study of educational issues could become a basis for informed discussion of those issues. The Society's two-volume yearbooks, now in their seventy-ninth year of publication, reflect the thoughtful attention given to a wide range of educational problems during those years. A recently inaugurated series on Contemporary Educational Issues includes substantial publications in paperback that supplement the yearbooks. Each year, the Society's publications contain contributions to the literature of education from more than a hundred scholars and practitioners who are doing significant work in their respective fields.

An elected Board of Directors selects the subjects with which volumes in the yearbook series are to deal, appropriates funds to meet necessary expenses in the preparation of a given volume, and appoints a committee to oversee the preparation of manuscripts for that volume. A special committee created by the Board performs similar functions for the Society's paperback series.

The Society's publications are distributed each year without charge to approximately 4,500 members in the United States, Canada, and elsewhere throughout the world. The Society welcomes as members all individuals who desire to receive its publications. For information about membership and current dues, see the back pages of this volume or write to the Secretary-Treasurer, 5835 Kimbark Avenue, Chicago, Illinois 60637.

The Seventy-ninth Yearbook includes the following two volumes:

A complete listing of the Society's previous publications, together with information as to how earlier publications still in print may be obtained, is found in the back pages of this volume.

Library of Congress Catalog Number: 79-91183
ISSN: 0077-5762

Published 1980 by
THE NATIONAL SOCIETY FOR THE STUDY OF EDUCATION

5835 Kimbark Avenue, Chicago, Illinois 60637
© 1980 by the National Society for the Study of Education

First Printing, 8,000 Copies

Printed in the United States of America

iv

Officers of the Society
1979-80

(Term of office expires March 1 of the year indicated.)

JEANNE CHALL

(1981)
Harvard University, Cambridge, Massachusetts

MARGARET J. EARLY

(1982)
Syracuse University, Syracuse, New York

JOHN I. GOODLAD

(1980)
University of California, Los Angeles, California

PHILIP W. JACKSON

(1982)
University of Chicago, Chicago, Illinois

A. HARRY PASSOW

(1981)
Teachers College, Columbia University, New York, New York

KENNETH J. REHAGE

(Ex-officio)
University of Chicago, Chicago, Illinois

RALPH W. TYLER

(1980)
Director Emeritus, Center for Advanced Study in the Behavioral Sciences
Stanford, California

Secretary-Treasurer

KENNETH J. REHAGE

5835 Kimbark Avenue, Chicago, Illinois 60637

v

The Society's Committee on the Middle School Years

MAURITZ JOHNSON

(Chairman)
Professor of Education
State University of New York
Albany, New York

DONALD H. EICHHORN

Superintendent of Schools
Lewisburg, Pennsylvania

DAVID ELKIND

Chairman, Eliot-Pearson Department of Child Study
Tufts University
Medford, Massachusetts

A. HARRY PASSOW

Professor of Education
Teachers College, Columbia University
New York, New York

GORDON F. VARS

Professor of Curriculum and Instruction
Kent State University
Kent, Ohio

Associated Contributors

THOMAS M. ACHENBACH

Research Psychologist, National Institute of Mental Health
Bethesda, Maryland

DAVID P. AUSUBEL

Distinguished Professor Emeritus
Graduate School and University Center
City University of New York
New York, New York

vii

ASSOCIATED CONTRIBUTORS

STEFANIE M. BARTH

Research Associate, National Council on Crime and Delinquency
Hackensack, New Jersey

DAVID BROMBERG

Assistant Professor of Pediatrics
University of Maryland
Baltimore, Maryland

STEPHEN COMMINS

Assistant Professor of Pediatrics
State University of New York
Buffalo, New York

MORRIS E. ESON

Professor of Psychology
State University of New York
Albany, New York

STANFORD B. FRIEDMAN

Professor of Psychiatry and Human Development
University of Maryland
Baltimore, Maryland

JOHN P. HILL

Fellow, Center for the Study of Youth Development
Boys Town, Nebraska

MARTIN L. HOFFMAN

Professor of Psychology
University of Michigan (Ann Arbor)

and

Visiting Professor of Psychology
Graduate School, City University of New York
New York, New York

GWEN INGRAM

Director, Youth Center
National Council on Crime and Delinquency
Hackensack, New Jersey

JOAN SCHEFF LIPSITZ

Director, Center for Early Adolescence
University of North Carolina
Chapel Hill, North Carolina

JEAN V. MARANI

State Coordinator, Florida Right to Read Program
Florida Department of Education
Tallahassee, Florida

EDITH BLAKESLEE PHELPS

Executive Director, Girls Clubs of America, Inc.
New York, New York

MILTON G. RECTOR

President, National Council on Crime and Delinquency
Hackensack, New Jersey

STEVEN SELDEN

Assistant Professor of Education
University of Maryland
College Park, Maryland

H. GORDON STEVENSON

Associate Professor of Library Science
State University of New York
Albany, New York

CAROL KEHR TITTLE

Professor of Education
University of North Carolina
Greensboro, North Carolina

CONRAD F. TOEPFER, JR.

Associate Professor of Education
University of Georgia
Athens, Georgia

SEAN A. WALMSLEY

Assistant Professor of Reading
State University of New York
Albany, New York

Editor's Preface

In 1976, A. Harry Passow, a member of the Board of Directors of the National Society for the Study of Education, surveyed a sampling of educational leaders concerned with the middle school years to probe the extent of interest in a yearbook pertaining to that period. He subsequently approached me, on behalf of the Board, regarding the possibility of my chairing a yearbook committee on this topic, which had been my major area of professional interest during the 1950s and 1960s. Unaware of the intricacies of such an assignment, I accepted it.

In forming the committee, I considered it essential that the members should be people with whom I knew I could work, who could work together, and who would have a distinctive contribution to make to the project. Professor Passow, whom I had known for forty years, provided both recent experience in editing a NSSE yearbook and liaison with the Board of Directors of the Society. David Elkind, whom I knew through his work in the "World of Inquiry" school in Rochester, N.Y., gave us the invaluable insights of a highly respected psychologist. Gorden Vars, my former colleague in the Junior High School Project of Cornell University, is widely known for his writing and leadership within both the junior high/middle school community and the National Core Conference. Donald Eichhorn is well known as an outstanding middle-grades administrator. Early in our work, D. Bob Gowin, of Cornell University, found it necessary to resign from the committee, to our great loss, as his ideas had strongly influenced the format adopted for the yearbook.

At its first meeting, the committee engaged in wide-ranging discussion of the assigned topic: education and socialization during pre- and early adolescence. It soon became apparent that the yearbook could not address such specific school concerns as grouping, curriculum content, and activities programs. Instead, the focus would have to be on the young people themselves who make up this age group. Three questions arose: What do we know about them? How are we intervening in their lives? How can we learn more about them and learn how to help them?

Analysis of these three questions gave rise to potential chapters for two yearbooks. Through compromises and with an eye toward balance, the committee settled on something close to the final table of contents and generated a list of potential contributors best qualified to put some prime meat on the skeleton we had created.

To the remarkable group of authorities in various professional and scholarly fields who have contributed to this volume is due the credit for the actual content of the yearbook. Most of them had more to say on their topics than we could possible accommodate and consequently had to endure painful tightening and cutting of their creations. The reader should also know that the authors were caught up in the only real controversy the committee faced, namely, whether or not to employ the term "transescence" in the text and title. We finally decided to use that term throughout the text but not in the title. Many authors graciously accepted its inclusion in their chapters, even though the term was one that would not ordinarily be found in their writing. Only time will tell if this controversial word is destined to disappear or to become widely accepted in the literature pertaining to the age group.

Thus was the yearbook brought into being. We have received great satisfaction from our work on it and we take a certain amount of pride in the volume. The catholicity of its contents virtually assures that there is something in it for everyone—educators and noneducators, practitioners and scholars. The committee is hopeful, however, that the yearbook will serve a sort of "ecumenical" function, that all who deal in some way with the age group will view *all* of its content as having significance to them, not just selected chapters that pertain most directly to their particular professional concerns. If this hope is realized and the volume turns out to have a positive influence on the way we treat our young at a critical period in their lives, then the contributors and the committee will have to share the credit with those readers who were astute enough to fuse the insights gained from the volume's disparate perspectives into a deeper and firmer understanding on which to base their intervention efforts.

MAURITZ JOHNSON
Albany, December 1979

Acknowledgements

It is with great appreciation that we acknowledge here the contributions made to this volume by the several authors. The National Society for the Study of Education is most grateful to them for their help in enabling us to get out a book that is a substantial addition to the literature pertaining to the period of early adolescence. Our special thanks go to the committee responsible for developing the plan for the volume and for seeing it through to completion. Donald H. Eichhorn, David Elkind, A. Harry Passow, and Gordon F. Vars, as members of that committee, gave generously of their time and talent at all stages in the project. Mauritz Johnson, as chairman of the committee and editor of the book, has performed all the functions required by those roles with great skill, incredible patience, and a deep understanding of what the Society hopes to accomplish through its publications. The dedicated services of all who have had a part in this work are greatly appreciated, for it is only through such services that the Society can continue to bring publications of quality in the field of education to its members.

KENNETH J. REHAGE
Editor for the Society

Table of Contents

CHAPTER I

Prologue

GORDON F. VARS

Young people between the ages of ten and fourteen go through some of the most dramatic life changes that they will ever experience. It is during these years that puberty transforms the child into a young adult, and achievement of the biological capacity to reproduce has profound repercussions on all other aspects of development—intellectual, moral, social, and emotional.

Yet this period is one of the least understood and most understudied in the entire span of human life. Joan Lipsitz, after reviewing existing research on this age group, chose a very apt title for her book: *Growing Up Forgotten.*[1] She also documented the special vulnerability of the age group and the epidemic proportions of such problems as teen-age pregnancy, venereal disease, drug and alcohol addiction, runaways, and the like.

As a social institution that serves all young people, the school is in a pivotal position with respect to both the problems and the promises of the young. Transition from elementary school to either a junior high or a middle school takes place during these years. It is often a traumatic change, bringing new problems and concerns to compound those connected with growing up. The middle school, like the junior high school before it, has been promoted as an educational institution specifically designed in terms of the characteristics and needs of the ten- to fourteen-year-old. Yet few educators in any school have had either preservice or in-service preparation for dealing with students of this age. Like their counterparts in other institutions, including the family, they may fail to serve the age group adequately because of widespread myths and misinformation.

1. Joan Lipsitz, *Growing Up Forgotten: A Review of Research and Programs Concerning Early Adolescence* (Lexington, Mass.: D. C. Heath, 1977).

I

One factor that contributes to the neglect of this age group is the lack, until recently, of a convenient label for this period in life. The years immediately preceding puberty are referred to as "late childhood" or "preadolescence." The years immediately following puberty are called "early adolescence," and the young person at this stage may be referred to as a "young adolescent," an "early adolescent," or even an "emerging adolescent." Thus, to talk about the time span that *bridges* childhood and adolescence has required cumbersome phrases such as "pre- and early adolescence." Fortunately, Donald H. Eichhorn has coined the word "transescence," defining it as follows in his pioneering book on the middle school and its clientele:

Transescence: the stage of development which begins prior to the onset of puberty and extends through the early stages of adolescence.[2]

This definition can be further operationalized by considering how the social relations within an age group change when the first of its members reaches puberty. From that time on, the thoughts of many are focused on that anticipated event, even though it may be several years before others reach that magical moment. Transescent preoccupation with the personal and social events surrounding puberty are vividly portrayed in the novels of Judy Blume, such as *Are You There, God? It's Me, Margaret.*[3] Indeed, the phenomenal popularity of her books stems largely from her sensitivity to the concerns of young people in this period of life.

The beginning of transescence in any particular group of young people is relatively easy to determine. The lack of privacy in most school showers and locker rooms makes it almost impossible to hide budding breasts or darkening pubic hair. The first menstruation or ejaculation merely confirms what is already obvious to one's peers. Transescence fades into adolescence when the majority of one's age mates have entered puberty and have turned their attention to the social concerns about rating and dating that are typical of high school students.

The concept of transescence has proved especially useful to

2. Donald H. Eichhorn, *The Middle School* (New York: Center for Applied Research in Education, 1966), p. 3.

3. Judy Blume, *Are You There, God? It's Me, Margaret* (Scarsdale, N.Y.: Bradbury Press, 1970).

educators in the junior high/middle-school movement. An annual publication of the Educational Leadership Institute in Springfield, Massachusetts, is called *Transescence*, and the term appears with increasing frequency in books and periodicals on the middle school. On the other hand, the term has not yet found widespread acceptance in other fields, hence the use of the older terminology in many chapters of this book. The need for a simple, widely accepted term for the age group is acute. Edgar Z. Friedenberg says that if people have no word for something, either it means nothing to them or it matters too much to talk about.[4] When we have a commonly accepted name for this age group—marked by such growth, change, and therefore promise—it will be an indication that we have taken a first step toward providing for them purposefully.

This yearbook brings much needed attention to young people in this transitional age. Section One, edited by Gordon Vars, describes their place in contemporary society. Section Two, edited by Donald Eichhorn, indicates some ways to promote their development and welfare. Section Three, for which David Elkind served as editor, suggests ways to learn more about them. Just as the transescent years are crucial to the health and welfare of the individual, so may our society's treatment of young people during these critical years determine the future of our way of life.

4. Edgar Z. Friedenberg, *The Vanishing Adolescent* (New York: Dell Publishing Co., 1959), p. 19.

SECTION ONE

THE AGE GROUP IN ITS MILIEU

CHAPTER II

The Age Group

JOAN SCHEFF LIPSITZ

Every age clamors for our attention. What are the claims that early adolescence makes? At this point, we are not sure. We are less informed about this stage of development than about any other among minors in America.[1]

We hold contradictory tenets to be true about this period of life. On the one hand, we see this as a quiescent stage marked by the latency period, with little that is compelling in terms of growth and development; on the other hand, we see it as marked by the onset of puberty, a time when hormones riotously dictate the distasteful behavior of previously personable children. On the one hand, we see this as a healthy time in life, and therefore safe to ignore; on the other hand, we see it as a time of serious crises, and therefore demanding vigorous legal intervention.

Since the 1960s we have paid an unusual amount of attention to early childhood and mid- to later adolescence. It was our conviction that, were all children equal at the starting line, they would have equal capacities to share in America's dreams. We therefore channeled many of our resources into early childhood education and health programs. We took a second look at our "products"—those young people ready to enter the labor market—and therefore placed some emphasis on programs to prevent dropouts, on vocational training, and on remediation. It was a question of inputs and outputs, although marked by streaks of nonmechanistic political ideology and social conviction. We placed little emphasis, however, on the years between the starting and the finishing lines. Too old to be cute, too young to stage protests, young adolescents received

1. Joan Lipsitz, *Growing Up Forgotten: A Review of Research and Programs Concerning Early Adolescence*, A Report to the Ford Foundation (Lexington, Mass.: Lexington Books, D. C. Heath, 1977), p. 124.

7

little of our attention. Why are we paying attention now?

If there is such a thing in the world of academic and public policy as a "critical mass" that is a prerequisite for heeding the claims of an age group, then early adolescence has finally attained that critical level. There are two independent areas of concern leading us to take a new look. First, the trend in the social sciences is toward a holistic or life-span perspective of human development. It is a trend with which observers familiar with research from the 1930s and 1940s will be comfortable: only through an analytical framework that embraces each stage of life within a context of the entire life-span can coherence be brought to developmental literature. Since early adolescence has been sorely slighted in our research efforts, there is a gap that some life-span researchers see the need to close.

Second, and apparently unrelated, several categories of concern are converging that alert us to early adolescence as an increasingly troubled time. School violence reaches its height during the junior high school years. The most dangerous place for a seventh grader to be is in school. The only age group for which the birth rate is not decreasing is that of fifteen-year-olds and under. The average age of runaways is fourteen and a half. The average age of children in foster care is twelve. Juvenile crime appears to "blossom" around age fourteen. Somewhere between 20 percent and 30 percent of eighth graders drink excessively. Drug abuse soars in the junior high years. The suicide rate among young adolescents, while lower than for youth aged sixteen to twenty-two, is rising rapidly, and may have doubled in the past twenty years. (See chapter 8.) Our tendency is to become specialists in categories of behavior, like teenage pregnancy, drug and alcohol abuse, or juvenile crime, and to be unaware of possible broader trends; but there have been so many categories of concern about young adolescents that it has become harder to avoid taking a cross-categorical view and questioning the possible meanings of these very troubling statistics.

While policy analysts question whether we have a youth crisis among young adolescents, life-span researchers ask how we can help facilitate the healthy development of this age group. There are few people doing the questioning, and they rarely converse with each other. Nonetheless, these parallel activities from two different perspectives have led to a heightened level of interest in early adolescence.

But what is an "age group"? Are we contributing to the fragmentation and categorization of human beings by insisting upon the importance of early adolescence? Again, there are two perspectives from which this question can be answered.

First, developmentally, there are "centers of similarities" when we look at the characteristics of physical, emotional, social, and intellectual growth of boys and girls in kindergarten through grade four and then in grades five through eight. Similarly, there appear to be fewer differences among pupils in grades six and seven and then again in grades nine and ten.[2] From a developmental perspective, we are not creating an age group, but rather recognizing several years in the life-span that have many developmental tasks and characteristics in common.[3]

Second, we can argue that we are not creating a *new* fragmentation. We are rather acknowledging that through our laws and social institutions we have already created early adolescence as an age group. Because so much of what constitutes the adolescent experience in America has been institutionally determined (for example, by age segregation in middle and junior high schools), an artificial fragmentation already exists. It is only by acknowledging this segregation, determining the extent to which it is developmentally meaningful, and the extent to which it is a destructive imposition, that we can determine what it means to be a member of this age group.

In order to make this determination, we must take an extremely broad developmental and social-institutional perspective, looking at the universal aspects of puberty and at the socially created institutions that in large measure define what it means to be a young

2. George E. Mills, "The How and Why of Middle Schools," *Nation's Schools* 68 (December 1961): 43-53, as cited in William M. Alexander et al., *The Emergent Middle School* (New York: Holt, Rinehart and Winston, 1978), pp. 14-15; Wilfred P. Dacus, "A Study of the Grade Organizational Structure of the Junior High School as Measured by Social Maturity, Emotional Maturity, Physical Maturity, and Opposite Sex Choices" (doct. diss., University of Houston, 1963).

3. Peter Blos, "The Child Analyst Looks at the Young Adolescent," in *Twelve to Sixteen: Early Adolescence*, ed. Jerome Kagan and Robert Coles (New York: W. W. Norton and Co., 1972), pp. 55-72.

adolescent. Thus, we must look not only at socio-emotional, cognitive, and physical development, but also at the family, the school, youth groups, the juvenile justice system, health care, and the media.

What are the claims that early adolescence makes upon society? This yearbook attempts to answer that question from a variety of perspectives. This chapter provides an overview of the renewed dialogue about pre- and early adolescence in America.

The Youth Cohort

"Epidemic" is a word that comes to mind when we think about adolescents in America. We have a pregnancy "epidemic," a dropout "epidemic," a suicide "epidemic." Underlying this medical terminology is our sense that we have an epidemic of adolescents, "an outbreak," according to Webster's, "or product of sudden rapid spread, growth, or development, *specif:* a natural population suddenly and greatly enlarged."

During the 1960s, the youth cohort (ages fourteen to twenty-four) expanded by 52 percent and the number of students in that cohort increased by 82 percent.[4] We are still reacting to this unprecedented leap in the number and proportion of school-aged and school-attending youth in America.

Our reactions take several misshapen forms. First, we ascribe to adolescence per se characteristics that were endemic to youth in a specific era only (for example, protests, rebellion, alienation). Second, we generalize to all adolescents characteristics that were true of a small proportion of middle-class youth. Third, in our concern with "youth problems" that we perceive as beginning in high school, we overlook the importance of the pre- and early adolescent years. Fourth, we retain our embattled mentality beyond the baby boom years, despite evidence of declining school enrollments and an aging society.

At present, there are 19.8 million ten- to fourteen-year-olds, representing 7.7 percent of the population. In 1976, there were substantially fewer persons under seventeen than there were in 1970. The largest increases during these years were for ages eighteen

4. Michael Timpane et al., *Youth Policy in Transition*, Report No. R-2006-HEW (Santa Monica, Calif.: Rand Corp., June 1976), p. 4.

to twenty-four and twenty-five to thirty-four, reflecting the aging of the baby boom population. There is a steady decrease in the number of adolescents of each age group under fifteen years of age. There are, for example, 4.2 million fourteen-year-olds, but only 3.7 million ten-year olds. According to demographers, this trend will continue if there is no upward change in fertility trends and rates.[5] We need to be dealing now with a shrinking youth cohort, even though we have not yet recovered from being overwhelmed by the sheer numbers of the previous cohort. We are, in other words, vulnerable to adolescents, to their demographic characteristics, as well as to their individual personalities.

Definitions of Adolescence

At the same time, the vulnerability of adolescents to society is exquisite. Adolescence is in such great measure a construct of social legislation and norms that there is little consensus about how to define the term "adolescence." Konopka adopts a biological definition: "that span of a young person's life between the obvious onset of puberty and the completion of bone growth."[6] There are certain phenomena, like the adolescent growth spurt, the appearance of secondary sex characteristics, and menstruation/ejaculation that are the universal biological marker events of early adolescence.

Once we leave the area of universal endocrine changes, however, adolescence is culturally determined and defined. Sociologically, adolescence is sometimes defined by social markers, such as entry into junior high or middle school and complete independence from the family of origin,[7] or the period between dependent childhood and self-sufficient adulthood.[8]

5. Kurt J. Snapper and JoAnne S. Ohms, *The Status of Children 1977*, DHEW Publication No. (ODHS)78-30133 (Washington, D.C.: Office of Human Development Services, Administration for Children, Youth, and Families, U.S. Department of Health, Education, and Welfare, 1978), p. 17.

6. Gisela Konopka, "Requirements for Healthy Development of Adolescent Youth," *Adolescence* 8 (Fall 1973): 2.

7. Glen H. Elder, Jr., "Adolescence in the Life Cycle: An Introduction," in *Adolescence in the Life Cycle: Psychological Change and Social Context,* ed. Sigmund E. Dragastin and Glen H. Elder, Jr. (Washington, D.C.: Hemisphere Publishing Corp., 1975), pp. 1-22.

8. Rolf E. Muuss, *Theories of Adolescence*, 2d ed. (New York: Random House, 1962), p. 4.

We grow up in historical contexts and in particular communities. Becoming an adolescent during the Depression had a different meaning from growing up during the expanding economy of the 1950s, which was different from entering adolescence during the 1970s, with shrinking job markets and growing inflation. Thus, Elder says that it is not possible to discuss adolescence outside a socio-historical perspective.[9]

Bakan argues that adolescence has been created and defined by legislation, specifically compulsory education, child labor laws, and special legal procedures for juveniles. He sees adolescence as socially defined by the marker events of pubescence and the legal ages for termination of compulsory education, child labor restrictions, and juvenile court procedures.[10]

Definitions become even less clarifying when we turn to the psychological literature. The best "conceptual umbrella" we have, according to Gallatin, is given to us by Erikson, who emphasizes the integration of past experience, the development of a sense of individuality, and a growing awareness of personal destiny. It is a decisive period for identity formation. As Gallatin points out, the traditional textbook in adolescent development gives us a catalogue of the events of adolescence without a unifying definition.[11]

Efforts at definition become still more difficult when we consider the middle school years, which span pre- and early adolescence. Cohen and Frank point out that we tend to extend "middle childhood" upward and adolescence downward to cover an embarrassing lack of knowledge and theory about the eleven- and twelve-year-old, whom they call "preadolescent" and others call the "young adolescent" or "transescent." (See chapter 1.) "The 'preadolescent' of eleven or twelve years is neither the ideal-typical middle child of nine nor the archetypal adolescent of sixteen. We may still prefer to think of him *in transition* from childhood to adolescence, but we have begun to recognize more clearly that

9. Elder, "Adolescence in the Life Cycle: An Introduction," p. 13.

10. David Bakan, "Adolescence in America: From Ideal to Social Fact," in *Twelve to Sixteen: Early Adolescence*, ed. Kagan and Coles, pp. 73-89.

11. Judith E. Gallatin, *Adolescence and Individuality: A Conceptual Approach to Adolescent Psychology* (New York: Harper and Row, 1975), pp. 16, 194; Erik Erikson, *Identity: Youth and Crisis* (New York: W. W. Norton, 1968), p. 91.

the 'preadolescent' deserves a period of his own." [12] Cohen and
Frank argue, as do most other contemporary observers, that it is
the conjunction of rapid biological, social, cognitive, and emotional
changes that lends special significance to pre- and early adolescence.

Given our difficulty in defining adolescence, early adolescence,
and preadolescence, and our lack of consensus about their delimit-
ing marker events and their origins, we are often tempted to ask
whether there is such a stage in the life span as adolescence, or
whether it is so strongly determined by social views and contexts
that efforts at definition are useless. Whatever our difficulties,
caused by and leading to our continuing search for explanatory
theories, there is growing consensus that the resolution of biological, cognitive, and socio-emotional changes during early adolescence, changes unique in the life span in intensity, helps determine
the quality of one's adult life. The years from ten to fourteen form
a critical time in human development.

Psychosocial Tasks of Early Adolescent Development

The growth events of adolescence are in large measure determined by what has happened before and they determine much of
what follows.[13] Adolescence occupies a "pivotal position in Eriksonian theory—as the period that simultaneously recapitulates all
the earlier stages of development and anticipates all those to
come"[14] The psychosocial "tasks" of early adolescence reflect a
continuum of events during a crucial period that is part of the life
span. They are not isolated phenomena.

IDENTITY AND INDIVIDUATION

During early adolescence, we consciously explore our uniqueness as individuals and our relatedness to other human beings. We
seek continuity of experience in two ways: continuity between
our experience of our *selves* from one moment to the next, and

12. Donald Cohen and Richard Frank, "Preadolescence: A Critical Phase
of Biological and Psychological Development," in *Mental Health in Children*,
ed. D. V. Siva (Westbury, N.Y.: PJD Publications, Ltd., 1975). Page numbers
cited in this chapter are from the prepublication manuscript.

13. Erikson, *Identity: Youth and Crisis*, p. 23.

14. Gallatin, *Adolescence and Individuality*, p. 174.

continuity between the way we perceive ourselves and others perceive us. Thus we achieve a sense of identity. It is one paradox of adolescence that it is possible to achieve this inner, apparently singular, sense of individuality only when one sees oneself in terms of a larger social context. Or, as Erikson says, one gradually becomes capable of developing into a well-organized ego within a social reality.[15] Individuation is grounded in a world of others.

For this reason the vulnerability of young adolescents to their social milieu is great. Adolescents depend upon others to reflect to them a positive, realistic image of self that can be integrated with a personal inner image. They are dependent upon society to have a coherent sense of purpose for its young people with which, and in opposition to which, they can define themselves. We have said that adolescents are vulnerable to historical and economic phenomena. They are also deeply vulnerable to the coherence, and lack thereof, of the social reality within which they are to define themselves.

DETACHMENT AND AUTONOMY

It is a truism in the media and even in most developmental literature that adolescents must stridently assert their autonomy in order to separate their identity from that of their families. But young adolescents do not suddenly walk out the door. They have been seeking a sense of autonomy since they were toddlers. During early adolescence, the process of "desatellizing" begins, to use Ausubel's term,[16] as children look beyond parents for models, companionship, and values. Careful studies show, however, that when we break concepts like "separation" and "autonomy" into their component parts, young adolescents are beginning to form peer orientations with regard to companionship ("association"), but continue to turn to parents for models and advice ("identification" and "norms").[17] Not only are young adolescents on a con-

15. Erikson, *Identity: Youth and Crisis*, p. 23.

16. David P. Ausubel, *Theories and Problems of Adolescent Development* (New York: Grune and Stratton, 1977).

17. Charles E. Bowerman and John W. Kinch, "Changes in Family and Peer Orientation of Children between the Fourth and Tenth Grades," in *Adolescent Development*, ed. Martin Gold and Elizabeth Douvan (Boston: Allyn and Bacon, 1969), pp. 137-41. See also Denise B. Kandel and Gerald S. Lesser, *Youth in Two Worlds* (San Francisco: Jossey-Bass, 1972), p. 126.

tinuum of development where autonomy is concerned; they also are in different stages of associative, identificative, and normative autonomy. What we observe during early adolescence is the beginning of detachment from parents, with a wide range of ambivalence caused by changing loyalities, continuing emotional attachments, and strivings toward emotional and physical independence. (See chapter 3.)

ACHIEVEMENT AND COMMITMENT

Preadolescents are often strongly task-oriented. Erikson says that the stage prior to adolescence (from ages six to twelve) is characterized by industriousness. Teachers often observe how much this age group loves facts, devouring the *Book of Lists*, almanacs, and every record book available. They are good workers and good players. At some time during preadolescence, though, there is often a shift to aimlessness, a shortened attention span, moodiness, and other characteristics we mistake as being typical of adolescence in general.[18]

Early adolescence may more aptly be characterized as a period during which we seek a sense of competence and achievement in activities to which we commit ourselves for short periods of time. This view of adolescence is so radically different from our stereotypes that it bears underscoring. Konopka sees adolescence not so much in Eriksonian terms of identity-seeking, but rather as an "age of commitment," a move into "the true interdependence of men." She sees the struggle between dependency and independence in this framework as "an expression of this entrance into interdependence." Commitment, then, includes the Eriksonian search for oneself, but also "points toward the emotional, intellectual, and sometimes physical reach for other people as well as ideas, ideologies, causes, work choices."[19] In Konopka's view, to acknowledge adolescence as an age of commitment is to elevate it from a stage to be "endured and passed through as rapidly as possible to a stage of earnest and significant human development."[20]

18. Cohen and Frank, "Preadolescence," p. 13.

19. Konopka, "Requirement for Healthy Development of Adolescent Youth," p. 11.

20. Ibid., p. 12.

During early adolescence, one's self-esteem is on the line. Changing bodies, emotions, social groups, ideas, all lead to an intense self-consciousness. Young adolescents are dependent upon their peers and adults to give them opportunities to achieve a sense of competence. They are dependent upon their communities and the institutions that serve them, including schools and after-school agencies, to provide opportunities for them to make temporary commitments of their energies in meaningful, socially useful activities. The budding sense of commitment is not only toward self and friends, but also toward the social order they are just beginning to discover.

SEXUALITY AND INTIMACY

The capacity to sustain emotionally supportive relationships develops during adolescence. Theorists differ as to when adolescents move from superficial, transient friendship to stable, emotionally rewarding relationships. Researchers like Douvan and Adelson report that in early adolescence, girls engage in friendships that are not yet relational. During middle and late adolescence, sharing and responsive relationships develop.[21] Since we know so little about the nature of adolescent friendships, much of what is written is conjecture. When at its best, it is based upon long and direct experience with the age group. Cohen and Frank, for instance, report that close friendships among what they term "preadolescents" are far more demanding and complex than those of childhood and more responsive to needs and feelings. They provide support outside the family, correct unrealistic fantasies, and increase self understanding.[22] The telephone becomes a major instrument for communication, close enough for detailed and confidential sharing, but distant enough to remove the threat of intimacy while experimenting with thoughts and feelings.

It is during a review of the literature on adolescent sexuality that one is most struck by the situational nature of adolescent development. Broderick and Fowler reported in 1961 that rela-

21. Elizabeth Douvan and Joseph Adelson, *The Adolescent Experience* (New York: John Wiley and Sons, 1966).

22. Cohen and Frank, "Preadolescence," p. 13.

tionships between the sexes during preadolescence were becoming less hostile and more openly affectionate.[23] The mores of the times seemed to be changing. Likewise, mores for age-related behavior differ widely among different social classes and racial and ethnic groups. The meaning of a friendship, a sexually intimate encounter, or a pregnancy during early adolescence cannot be assigned outside a social context. In addition, age and gender norms vary so widely that one is constantly struck by the biases among researchers, theorists, and social observers whose observations become the truths of social science.

Whenever it is that adolescents become capable of sustained personal relationships, it is not a suddenly acquired ability. The testing of friendships during early adolescence, the reliance on the peer group for behavioral standards, the confidences shared with one special best friend—all are crucial precursors of the continuous, rewarding relationships that help enrich and fulfill our adult lives.

THE SHIFT TO FORMAL OPERATIONS

When we read the literature on cognition, it is easy to mistake a human potentiality for a universal phenomenon. The shift to formal operations is unlikely to occur before early adolescence; it is most likely to occur, if at all, during adolescence; it does not necessarily occur. If there is any task of early adolescent development that should but does not adequately engage the excited interest of professionals, especially educators, it is this potential shift toward thinking abstractly, generalizing, thinking about thinking, being capable of appreciating the elegance of a theorem, the wit of a metaphor, the power of an ideology. (See chapter 11.)

Young adolescents become able to observe themselves thinking. In fact, much of the self-consciousness of the age group is predicated on the newly found ability to observe oneself growing, feeling, thinking. This capacity accounts for forms of egocentrism peculiar to adolescence, just as it accounts for the ability to break out of that egocentrism.

23. Carlfred F. Broderick and Stanley E. Fowler, "New Patterns of Relationships between the Sexes among Preadolescents," *Marriage and Family Living* 23 (February 1961): 27-30.

Elkind says that the egocentrism of adolescence is characterized by two mental constructions, "the imaginary audience" and "the personal fable." The adolescent, assuming that the whole world is a stage and she or he is the only player on it, is inordinately concerned with what the "audience" thinks, feels constantly observed, admired, criticized, stage center. This form of egocentrism is caused by a failure to differentiate personal concerns from those of others.[24]

At the same time, there is a tendency to overdifferentiate, to construct a "personal fable" of uniqueness. This behavior can have its sometimes humorous side: the insistence that I am always alone, no one can understand me, I am unlike everyone else. It can also have a disturbing side: the assumption that I am unique, I am unlike anyone else, I am immortal, I cannot die.

This form of egocentrism so characteristic of early adolescence, when coupled with the young adolescent's need to take risks, be adventuresome, be spontaneous, can lead to the tragic accident rates that all our driver education classes cannot lower. It also may be what frustrates our prevention programs (for example, against teen-age pregnancy). Prevention programs are based on one's ability to say, "I am *not* unique. It *can* happen to me." Only as adolescents become able to differentiate adequately between their preoccupations and those of others, and at the same time to integrate their sense of reality with that of others, can they break out of this egocentrism that is so characteristic of the early adolescent years.[25]

The cognitive shift to formal operational thought also makes possible the conscious examination of values that is characteristic of early, middle, and later adolescence. In recent years, moral development, which used to be the domain of socialization studies, has become the interest of cognitive theorists and researchers who, following Piaget's lead, recognize that a conscious examination of

24. David Elkind, "Egocentrism in Adolescence," *Child Development* 38 (December 1967): 1025-34.

25. Joan Lipsitz, "Adolescent Psychosexual Development," in *Adolescent Pregnancy—Perspectives for the Health Professional,* ed. Peggy B. Smith and David M. Mumford (Boston: G. K. Hall, forthcoming).

values is dependent upon cognitive development.[26] Rather than
seeing moralization as solely a process of internalizing culturally
given external rules, cognitive theorists like Lawrence Kohlberg
hold that internal moral standards are the outcome of transformations dependent upon cognitive growth as well as social experience. The quality of interaction with one's social environment is
dependent upon the way in which the child organizes cognitive
structures. (See chapter 9.)

Young adolescents are often noted for their authoritarianism.
This "law and order" mentality is found in blacks and whites,
among girls and boys, in suburbia and inner cities. The role of
socialization seems to be less important in political and moral idea-
tion than are levels of cognition.[27] When young adolescents become
capable of recognizing that they are part of a social order, they
leave behind the simplistic morality of childhood, in which there
is no right or wrong beyond the individual's point of view, and
can enter a level of moral reasoning that recognizes socially shared
expectations. They see, for the first time, the need for law and
order. But it can be a justice not yet tempered with mercy. In
their zeal to acknowledge societal needs, they overlook individual
rights. One of the tasks ahead is to resolve the conflict between
moral absolutism and relativism. Such a resolution is dependent on
further cognitive development.[28]

Egocentrism, authoritarianism, a sense of personal and social
destiny, and a growing ability to consider contingencies and take
preventive actions, are phenomena of early adolescence, interrelated because they are dependent in part on a cognitive shift

26. See Lawrence Kohlberg, "The Development of Children's Orientation
toward a Moral Order," *Vita Humana* 6, no. 1-2 (1963): 11-33; Carol Gilligan,
"Fostering Moral Development in Children," *EDC News* (Spring 1974): 8;
Robert Hogan, "Moral Conduct and Moral Character: A Psychological
Perspective," *Psychological Bulletin* 79 (April 1973): 217-32; Joseph Adelson,
"The Political Imagination of the Young Adolescent," in *Twelve to Sixteen:
Early Adolescence*, ed. Kagan and Coles, pp. 106-43; Jerome Kagan, "A
Conception of Early Adolescence," ibid., pp. 90-105.

27. Judith Gallatin et al., *The Development of Political Thinking in Urban
Adolescents*, Final Report, Project No. 0-0554 (Washington, D.C.: National
Center for Educational Research and Development, U.S. Department of
Health, Education and Welfare, 1972).

28. For a strongly dissenting viewpoint, see the argument of Robert Hogan
as recounted in Lipsitz, *Growing Up Forgotten*, pp. 52-53.

toward "hypothetico-deductive reasoning," or formal operations, for their onset and resolution.

Barriers to Healthy Development: Myths

In summarizing the barriers to conducting research on adolescence in the life cycle, Hill notes "the tendency to perceive the period as discontinuous from the remainder of the life cycle, . . . the tendency to view adolescents as a homogeneous or, at best, little differentiated lot, . . . the tendency to view the nature of adolescence as endogenously programmed" and the behavior of adolescents as "determined by intrapsychic forces."[29] We insist upon discontinuity, homogeneity and genetic programming as being characteristic of this age to such an extent that "where adolescents are concerned, we are sufficiently prone to stereotypy to make the phenomenon an important one for study in its own right."[30]

Misconceptions about adolescence carry sufficient weight in our society to have the force of myths, ill-founded beliefs held uncritically but applied with ostensible explanatory power.

HOMOGENEITY

Most schools sort children according to chronological age. To be thirteen means that you are probably in the eighth grade and are studying a curriculum deemed appropriate for eighth graders. From a developmental standpoint, however, to be told that someone is thirteen is to be told almost nothing about that person (except, of course, probable grade placement).

The mean age of menarche for girls is 12.9 Their adolescent growth spurt initiates at a mean age of 9.6. Peak velocity occurs at a mean age of 11.8. Comparable milestones occur two years later for boys. These averages, however, are computed from such a broad distribution that researchers stress continually the different ages for, and variations of, pubertal patterns. As Tanner says, "To speak, therefore, of a 'boy aged fourteen' is to be vague to

29. John P. Hill, "Some Perspectives on Adolescence in American Society," Position paper prepared for the Office of Child Development (Washington, D.C.: U.S. Department of Health, Education, and Welfare, May 1973), p. 2.

30. Ibid., p. 7.

the point of leaving out almost everything that is important about fourteen-year-old boys. The same is true of talking about twelve-year-old girls (or thirteen-year-old boys or girls, naturally)."[31] Given the variability of the onset of puberty and the two-year mean age difference between boys and girls, it is not unusual to find a six-year difference in biological age between slowly developing boys and rapidly developing girls in the same classroom.

And here we are considering only biological age. There is such extreme variability among individuals who are changing not only physically, but also socially, emotionally, and intellectually, that the label of chronological age, or the assumption of homogeneity, may be the most misleading social organizer that we have adopted.

In addition to interindividual variability, there is also a remarkable intraindividual variability during early adolescence. Change along the various dimensions of growth is not necessarily synchronized. As John Money says, "It is very difficult for some youngsters to be caught in that no-man's-land between their chronological age and their physique age, trying to keep up their social age, their academic age, and their psychosexual age, in uniformity with their chronological age."[32] Young adolescents also juggle the chronological age expectations of various subcultures that may not be in harmony with those of the majority culture's social institutions (especially the schools). It is little wonder that teachers of young adolescents know from their day-to-day scars what the rest of us tend to ignore: this is the most wildly heterogeneous group of students in our entire continuum of schooling. The myth of homogeneity ("they're all alike") serves as a powerful barrier to our promoting the healthy development of individual young adolescents. Even more formidable is the barrier resulting from the lip service we pay to variable growth

31. James M. Tanner, "Sequence and Tempo in the Somatic Changes in Puberty," in *The Control of the Onset of Puberty*, ed. Melvin M. Grumbach, Gilman D. Grave, and Florence S. Mayer (New York: John Wiley and Sons, 1974), p. 455.

32. John Money, in H. E. Kulin and E. O. Reiter, "Delayed Sexual Maturation, with Special Emphasis on the Occurrence of the Syndrome in the Male," in *The Control of the Onset of Puberty*, ed. Grumbach, Grave, and Mayer, pp. 264-65.

while we set policies and programs based on homogeneity. It may be that our *adult* ambivalence about adolescence is a more potent deterrent to adolescent development than is *adolescent* ambivalence about approaching adulthood.

TRANSITIONS

Why is adolescence transitional? According to our literature, we make a transition into adolescence and a transition out of it. (Note the title of James Coleman's widely read *Youth: Transition to Adulthood,* and even the title of Jerald Bachman's *Youth in Transition* study that belies its content.) In addition, the entire stage of adolescence is seen as transitional. A transition is a passage that leads from one section of a piece to another. It lacks its own purposes. Most of our literature on adolescence suggests a similar perspective. It is a time for passage to be endured not for its own sake but because of the future promise it suggests.

To see adolescence so exclusively as a transitional stage is to deny it the integrity we grant other stages in life. No large body of literature, for instance, refers to infancy or toddlerhood as transitional.

Human beings experience two periods of intense growth, early childhood and adolescence. Our social expectations are that adolescents are intractable but, since in transition, will be more malleable when they "grow out of it." To the contrary, Waber and other researchers argue that it is likely that plasticity increases at adolescence.[33] The label "transitional" is a barrier to the healthy development of young adolescents insofar as it makes us comfortable with nonintervention.

STORM AND STRESS

As part of our tendency to overemphasize adolescent problems and maladjustment, we have accepted uncritically the view of normative adolescence as being a time of turbulent storm and stress. We accept adolescence as a pathological time in life. This acceptance leads to two barriers to healthy development. First, we fail to distinguish between distressing (that is, irritating) behavior and distressed behavior that is truly disturbed and re-

33. Personal communication from Deborah Waber, Department of Psychiatry, Children's Hospital Medical Center, Boston, Mass., July 9, 1974.

quires professional attention. Second, by branding all adolescent behavior as "off-the-wall," we create a mind-set filled with inappropriate expectations among professionals, parents, and the adolescents themselves. Our inappropriate expectations may become self-fulfilling prophecies.

Offer reports that rebellion is seen mainly in the early adolescence of his subjects, who were chosen for their normalcy. Rebelliousness is a normal part of the process of detachment from parents.[34] But, as Hill cautions us, "rebelliousness" has become a catchall to describe popularly held assumptions about adolescence, and is devoid of real descriptive meaning.[35]

Offer's study of primarily middle-class suburban high school students functioning within "the middle range of adjustment" found less psychic disruption than is usually postulated for adolescents. "*Stability*, not *change*, is the overriding characteristic in the psychological patterns of reaction of these model adolescents."[36] Bachman and his associates have reported similar findings.[37] Douvan and Adelson found that turbulence is the norm only for the adolescent at the extremes, not for the middle majority of adolescents.[38] A review of intergenerational disturbances between black parents and their teen-age children makes a parallel point. Brunswick reports that, in an analysis of data from seven national surveys, a "generation gap," connoting intergenerational strife, is not widely distributed among black families.[39]

Those of us who expect a riotous escalation of the tensions experienced during early adolescence act on inappropriate expectations of storm and stress for a population that, as a rule, experiences more continuous development than turbulence.

34. Daniel Offer, *The Pychological World of the Teen-ager* (New York: Basic Books, 1969), p. 179.

35. Hill, "Some Perspectives on Adolescence in American Society," p. 32.

36. Offer, *The Psychological World of the Teen-ager*, p. 222.

37. Jerald G. Bachman, *Youth in Transition*, vol. 2, *The Impact of Family Background and Intelligence on Tenth-Grade Boys* (Ann Arbor, Mich., Survey Research Center, Institute for Social Research, 1970), p. 194.

38. Douvan and Adelson, *The Adolescent Experience*.

39. Ann F. Brunswick, "What Generation Gap? A Comparison of Some Generational Differences among Blacks and Whites," *Social Problems* 17, no. 3 (1970): 358-71.

THE TYRANNY OF THE PEER GROUP

When and how was it that "the peer group" became a pejorative term? It would be instructive to trace the history of this term that is used only in reference to adolescents. After stressing the importance of social relations in preschools and in elementary schools, we suddenly label friends "the peer group" and do our best to fight it.

The young adolescent needs peer support and companionship in developing new beliefs and values. Konopka argues that friends are the lifeline of adolescents during these years. Because they lack a repertoire of experience, they may feel a deep sense of loneliness and a high degree of vulnerability. These feelings may be both overwhelming and qualitatively different because of cognitive and socio-emotional maturity.[40]

The preceding section on attachment and autonomy emphasized the importance of attachment to parents during the process of desatellization. Given the importance of parents to young adolescents, we may overemphasize the power of the peer group to determine more than surface behaviors. Also, just as some parents use their authority tyrannically, so do some peer groups. We cannot say that the term "tyranny" is more or less appropriate to one than to the other, given our present state of knowledge about parenting and about peer relations. The "effect of a peer group on the child depends on the attitudes and activities which prevail in that peer group," says Bronfenbrenner.[41] In addition, peer groups function in a larger social context that helps determine their attitudes and activities.

A FURTHER COMMENT

A quotation from Earl Wilson is found on many office desk calendars: "Snow and adolescence are the only problems that

40. Konopka, "Requirements for Healthy Development of Adolescent Youth," pp. 10-11.

41. Urie Bronfenbrenner, *Two Worlds of Childhood: U.S. and U.S.S.R.* (New York: Russell Sage Foundation, 1970; New York: Pocket Books, 1973), p. 113. Citation is from the Pocket Books edition.

disappear if you ignore them long enough." It is this simultaneously bleak yet optimistic picture of adolescence that informs our social consciousness. But the seriously troubled symptoms of adolescence do not melt away,[42] and the normative crises of adolescence are neither necessarily trivial nor problematic. Adolescence is a normal time in the life span that would be easier to negotiate were there fewer quips on desk calendars and greater social wisdom.

Barriers to Healthy Development: Social Contexts

Social ills afflict all ages. What is presented here is not a litany of wrongs but rather an encouragement to consider the special impact that pervasive problems have on young adolescents.

LACK OF COHERENT PURPOSES

In 1933, John Dewey said, "The most utopian thing about utopia is that there are no schools at all." Cremin comments, "Education in utopia, Dewey went on to say, is carried out without benefit of schools, since children learn what they have to know in informal association with the adults who direct their activities." Such learning would demand a society, says Cremin, "whose values were so pervasive and whose institutions so cohesive as to form the young through the very process of living."[43] Our values are not so pervasive, and our institutions not so cohesive; rather, they are tentative at best. Young adolescents are noted for questioning who they are supposed to *be*. One of the hardest questions for adults to answer is what it is they want adolescents to be able to *do*.

Lacking a meaningful ideology about what adolescence should mean in our society, we may fail to provide a sense of purpose and structure for growth at the very time in their lives when young people are seeking definition of their personal and social status. Muuss points out that some difficulties of adolescents in western society are caused by their inability to gain a clear understanding of what is expected from them as they stand on the

42. See James F. Masterson, Jr., "The Symptomatic Adolescent Five Years Later: He Didn't Grow Out of It," *American Journal of Psychiatry* 123 (May 1967): 1343.

43. Lawrence A. Cremin, *Public Education* (New York: Basic Books, 1976), pp. 7-8.

margin of society.[44] Deeply confused about social values and the functions of institutions, we cannot provide for our young adolescents the opportunities for self-definition Dewey hoped for from informal association with adults in utopia, or from schools in the real world.

PLURALISM AND RACISM

The discordance between subcultural norms and the expectations of the dominant cultures creates stress for minority youth who are seeking both personal and racial or ethnic identity. It is difficult for them to distinguish between identity issues that every adolescent must cope with and identity issues specific to their subculture. Early adolescence is a time for conscious confrontation with race and ethnicity. Greater demands, sometimes contradictory, are placed on young adolescents by societal and subgroup expectations. As Gay points out, the subgroup demands that young adolescents make a conscious commitment by conforming to its norms. Simultaneously, society demands that they rise above ethnicity and become active members of the common culture. Criteria for being mature, responsible, physically attractive, masculine or feminine may be discordant.[45] In a pluralistic society, the twofold identity struggle places special demands on these young adolescents.

Racism adds yet another dimension. In their new consciousness, young adolescents must distinguish between legitimate and unacceptable expectations of the majority culture (that is, by its institutions, especially schools). Adult underrepresentation in the job market, or the lack of "decent adult futures," denies minority students a major motivating force for school achievement.[46] The "ghettoization" of American communities, especially in urban areas, contributes to class- and race-bound bases for friendships, so

44. Muuss, *Theories of Adolescence*, p. 84.

45. Geneva Gay, "Ethnic Identity in Early Adolescence: Some Implications for Instructional Reform," *Educational Leadership* 35 (May 1978): 649-55.

46. John U. Ogbu, *Minority Education and Caste: The American System in Cross Cultural Perspective*, Carnegie Council on Children Monograph (New York: Academic Press, 1978).

that "young people interact inside the classroom mainly with similarly socialized young people with similar sociodemographic characteristics who engage in similar activities,"[47] thereby making the demands of the dominant culture even more alien.

It is impossible at this point to determine from current research findings the extent of the impact of early adolescent developmental characteristics, as against racial problems, on adolescents and institutions. Perhaps because of the importance of the peer group during early adolescence, the literature on desegregation reflects little positive change in attitudes and friendships for blacks or whites. Pascal reports that the most positive changes are found in elementary schools, the least positive in junior high schools. In a study of New York City fifth graders, investigators found a positive correlation between racial tolerance and classroom exposure to children of other races. However, both black and white eighth graders in an open enrollment school were more prejudiced than similar students in virtually one-race schools.[48]

The special vulnerability of students of junior high age emerges in a study sponsored by the Philadelphia Reserve Bank on the effects of school resources on students' learning. For black and nonblack students, there is a slight positive effect on learning reported from attending schools that are up to 50 percent black. After 50 percent, and in contradiction to findings for elementary and senior high school students, "blacks experience significant learning growth as the proportion of blacks in the school increases (all other factors remaining the same)."[49]

THE JOB MARKET

The President's annual economic report of 1977 compares teenage unemployment rates of whites and blacks in 1954 and

47. John P. Hill, "Secondary School, Socialization, and Social Development During Adolescence," position paper prepared for the National Institute of Education (Washington, D.C.: Department of Health, Education, and Welfare, NIE, June 1978), p. 3.

48. Anthony Pascal, *What Do We Know about School Desegregation?* Report No. P-5777 (Santa Monica, Calif.: Rand Corp., 1977), p. 5.

49. Anita A. Summers and Barbara L. Wolfe, "Which School Resources Help Learning? Efficiency and Equity in Philadelphia Public Schools," Federal Reserve Bank of Philadelphia *Business Review* (February 1975): 16.

1977. In 1954, 13.4 percent of white and 14.4 percent of black teenagers were listed as unemployed. In 1977, the figures rose to 15 percent and 37 percent respectively. Youth experience unemployment rates far exceeding the rate for all workers taken as a group.[50] The issue is not just, as Ogbu points out, that adolescents need to anticipate *adult* employment. Young adolescents who are beginning to ask themselves what they want to do need to anticipate *youth* employment. Instead, they hear daily the discouragement or bitterness of older siblings and friends.

A report on unemployment among young Californians, published in 1977, cites the following findings: approximately 420,000 Californians aged sixteen to twenty-four are unemployed; the unemployment rate for youth is more than double the rate of adult unemployment; the hardest hit are nonwhite urban youths; 43 percent of nonwhite Californians and 24 percent of white Californians aged sixteen to nineteen are unemployed; unemployment among the white youth in urban areas in California is at the highest level since the Depression.[51] We know that unemployment has a profound effect on youth who are deprived, at the critical point of entry into the labor market, of opportunities to develop personal, economic, and social skills. Since they remain unrecognized and not studied, we can only conjecture what the effects are on young adolescents of anticipating nonexistent or unsatisfactory entry-level jobs.

SEXISM

A major developmental task of adolescence is the establishment of gender identity. During early adolescence, girls in America begin making decisions not to continue taking courses like mathematics and science that are considered "masculine." Top career choices listed by boys in a May 1977 Gallup Youth Survey include, in order of preference: skilled worker (mechanic), engineer, lawyer, teacher, professional athlete, musician, architect, farmer, doctor, military. For girls, the choices are: secretary, teacher, nurse,

50. "The Dynamics of Youth Unemployment," *Brookings Bulletin* 15 (Summer 1978): 16.

51. *The Quiet Crisis: A Report on Unemployment among Young Californians* (Santa Barbara, Calif.: Open Roads Program of the Citizens Policy Center, 1977).

other medical, veterinarian, fashion design/modeling, doctor, social worker, business, cosmetologist/hair-dresser. While girls are starting to aspire toward formerly male professions (note the comparative listings for "doctor"), there are still considerable sex-related limitations in their choices. The same can be said for boys, but we tend to worry less about them because they aspire toward higher paying professions.

Despite a growing body of literature about the effects of sexism on adolescent development, and especially on cognition, we have little data. As Jacklin points out, the data on which we base our conclusions about cognitive sex-related differences have been collected primarily on white, middle-class Americans. "There are many reasons to believe cross-cultural data will be illuminating. For example, many girls precocious in mathematics in America are from first generation European immigrant families." Jacklin suggests that "something is different (and helpful to the girls' mathematical ability) in the immigrant families' behavior toward their daughters."[52] What we can say at this point is that young adolescents, at a critical stage of self-definition, take their signals from society at large and from their subculture. They are dependent upon social institutions, like the schools, for the limitations or the boundlessness of their aspirations.

AGE SEGREGATION

We hold out many promises to children. A ubiquitous, teasing sexuality in the media invites them to enter adolescence and eat of the fruits thereof; but then they are told to be onlookers, to wait, to bypass the spermicidal creams on supermarket shelves and the demurely wrapped "adult" magazines in airports. They are told to prepare for the responsibilities and independence of secondary education; but then they enter, in junior high schools, the most control-oriented, sedentary years of their schooling. They are told they must begin to contribute to their society, but all avenues toward participation seem blocked. Even though we preach otherwise, even believe otherwise, we have segregated young adolescents from adult and older youth activities. We make no room

52. Carol Nagy Jacklin, "Explaining Sex-Related Differences in Cognitive Functioning" (unpublished paper, 1978), p. 2.

for them. "At the core of the modern effort to reassess adolescence is . . . the extent to which we permit entry into the institutions of society for young people for purposes of their socialization."[53] This concern is usually expressed about older adolescents, especially in critiques of secondary (that is, high school) education. There has been little concern about the diversity of environments young adolescents are exposed to and allowed to participate in.

The United States is not alone in the need to define areas for youth participation. The Council of Europe of the United Nations has discussed the need for youth centers to deal with the "marginalization of youth"—advice, recreational and cultural centers that can become broader meeting places for the community. Pitfalls to be avoided, they report, include the creation of youth ghettos, and "a standard approach to young people as a homogeneous category or specific market. . . . Special attention should be paid to the current lack of policies for young people in the thirteen to sixteen age group."[54] This lack of policy, which is a problem in the United States as well, reflects the fallout from the first barrier discussed: we lack a coherent sense of purpose about and for young adolescents.

Requirements for Healthy Development

The heading of this section summarizes the thrust of a position paper that Konopka wrote in 1973 for the Office of Child Development. She argued for conditions that provide young people with opportunities to participate as responsible members of households, the work place, and society; to gain experience in decision making; to interact with peers and acquire a sense of belonging; to discover self by looking outward and inward; to formulate their own value system; to try out roles; to develop a sense of accountability among equals; to cultivate a capacity to enjoy life.[55] Konopka was talking about all adolescents.

53. John P. Hill and Franz J. Mönks, eds., *Adolescence and Youth in Prospect* (Guilford, Surrey, England: IPC Science and Technology Press, 1977), p. 2.

54. "Council of Europe Report CCC/DC/77-80-E," United Nations *Youth Information Bulletin*, no. 30 (1978): 6.

55. Konopka, "Requirements for Healthy Development of Adolescent Youth," pp. 14-15.

One prerequisite for providing these opportunities is an awareness of *early* adolescence as a critical developmental stage in the life span. Another is an examination of the responsiveness or lack thereof, the "fit" or "lack of fit" between social institutions, especially schools, and the developmental needs of young adolescents. It is one of the purposes of this yearbook to stimulate such an examination.

CHAPTER III

The Family

JOHN P. HILL

CHAPTER III

The Family

JOHN P. HILL

Transformations in Family Relations

Transformations in family relations that occur in early adolescense are only beginning to be apprehended and understood by social and behavioral scientists. The transformations come about in early adolescence owing both to changes in children and their social circumstances and to changes in parents and their social circumstances. Early adolescence is characterized by somatic changes that presage mature physical and sexual status. These are universal biological changes for which onset, timing, and duration differ[1] but which demand some degree of recognition and accommodation by those social systems in which the young person participates. At the same time, early adolescence may bring new definitions of socially appropriate behavior. In our society, such definitions often are associated with changes in schooling arrangements—for example, transitions to middle or junior high schools.[2] Basic capacities for processing information show signs of change as well. As described by Piagetian theory, it is during early adolescence that concrete operational cognitive structures become integrated and stabilized and formal operational structures emerge.[3] (See chapter 11.)

1. James M. Tanner, *Growth at Adolescence*, 2d ed. (Oxford: Blackwell Science Publishers, 1961).

2. Dale A. Blyth, Roberta G. Simmons, and Diane Bush, "The Transition into Early Adolescence: A Longitudinal Comparison of Youth in Two Educational Contexts," *Sociology of Education* 51 (July 1978): 149-62.

3. Bärbel Inhelder and Jean Piaget, *The Growth of Logical Thinking from Childhood to Adolescence: An Essay on the Construction of Formal Operational Structure* (New York: Basic Books, 1968).

In the social realm, research inspired by Piagetian and other views suggests that early adolescents do better than children in differentiating among the qualities and attributes of significant others and their relationships with them. Early adolescents perform better than children in drawing inferences about others' internal psychological dynamics and about the operation of multiple and contingent intentions and norms in social situations. Increasingly, they are able to construe social situations in the manner of which adults are capable. They can process more information about a given social situation and focus multiple perspectives upon it at the same time. Adolescents' concepts of family, of their own family, and of themselves in the family probably change, too. While the area is relatively unstudied, it seems probable that adolescents come to reason about family life in relation to ideals, principles, and possibilities and that they negotiate intrafamilial relations in ways that display their new capacities for impression management and persuasion.[4]

While we know little about the typical developmental issues faced by parents while they are coping with pubertal change in their children, it is probable that transformations in parent-child relations during the period are influenced by the life circumstances that parents of this age themselves must face. During their children's early adolescence, most parents will be between thirty and forty-five years of age. Toward the end of that age bracket, current research (to be viewed in light of its limitation to middle-class samples) at least suggests an important, if ironic, complementarity between the concerns of early adolescents and their parents.[5] The approach of mid-life brings with it increased concern about body integrity, a change in time perspective such that time is considered in terms of what remains instead of how much has passed by, and worrisome concerns about gaps between

4. John P. Hill and Wendy J. Palmquist, "Social Cognition and Social Relations in Adolescence," *International Journal of Behavioral Development* 1, no. 1 (1978): 1-36.

5. Laurence D. Steinberg, "Changes in Family Relationships at Adolescence: A Developmental Perspective" (unpublished manuscript, University of California, Irvine, 1978).

parents' occupational aspirations and their actual achievements.[6] There is evidence as well of greater marital dissatisfaction during mid-life than in earlier or later periods.[7] Unfortunately, we have little information about the issues that are salient to relatively younger parents of early adolescents, and no empirical information about the impact on young people of the coincidence of adolescence with incipient mid-life crises of parents. Nevertheless, it is likely that transformations in familial relations at adolescence are influenced by social and intraindividual changes in parents who are approaching, or are experiencing, important changes in their own life trajectories.

In what follows it should be noted that our knowing little about the intersection of parental and early adolescent development is part of a larger context of ignorance. Research on any aspect of early adolescence is rare. Research on the family and the early adolescent is even more so. And, with the possible exception of social stratification studies, the research that does exist is not sensitive to variations in family composition or context. The word "family" as used in this chapter necessarily reflects the existing literature and can be taken to refer to biologically related, intact mother-father-child triads living in the same household. We have no scientific knowledge about how the transition from childhood to adolescence varies as the result of single-parenting, divorce, stepchild status, and the like.

Two Perspectives on Parent Behavior

The research of Baumrind and of Kohn has yielded two sets of perspectives on parent behavior that are useful in summarizing and interpreting much of the literature on family relations during early adolescence. Baumrind has argued that "authoritative parenting" produces instrumentally competent children. The authoritative parent is supportive but not suffocating, is not afraid of making standards known, values disciplined behavior that is moni-

6. Roger L. Gould, "The Phases of Adult Life: A Study in Developmental Psychology," *American Journal of Psychiatry* 129 (November 1972): 521-31.

7. Boyd Rollins and Harold Feldman, "Marital Satisfaction over the Family Life Cycle," *Journal of Marriage and the Family* 32 (February 1970): 20-28.

tored by self-control, and engenders such behavior by reasoning and explaining in verbal give-and-take with the child.

In contrast, the "authoritarian parent" is more obedience-centered and dogmatic, offers orders rather than engaging in verbal give-and-take, and is less likely to reason with or explain to the child. The authoritarian parent may be either protective or neglecting. The "permissive parent" responds in a benignant, accepting, and affirmative manner toward the child. The parent is a resource that the child may or may not use but is not an active agent in shaping behavior. The permissive parent may be either affectionate or emotionally uninvolved. In the latter case, granting freedom is a means of avoiding responsibility for the child.[8]

There is plenty of evidence for the importance of the dimensions of parenting behavior reflected in these clusters and for the utility of clusters like these in interpreting parent behavior, especially in relation to the dimension of power and its exercise in the family.[9] As we shall see, aspects of authoritative parenting are implicated in those developmental outcomes that have been widely considered to characterize "normal" or "healthy" behavior in adolescence.

Kohn's research has been concerned with relations between parental participation in the world of work and its impact upon parenting behavior. Occupations lower in the stratification system are more likely than those high in it to involve tasks that are simple and repetitive, tasks that require working with one's hands and things more than with other people and ideas, and tasks whose execution is more often supervised. And working-class people, Kohn's research demonstrates, are more likely to value conformity to authority (obedience) than self-control in their children. Middle-class parents are more likely to value the develop-

8. Diana Baumrind, "Authoritarian vs. Authoritative Parental Control," *Adolescence* 3 (Fall 1968): 255-72.

9. For reviews, see Martin Hoffman, "Moral Development," in *Carmichael's Manual of Child Psychology*, vol. 2, ed. Paul H. Mussen (New York: John Wiley and Sons, 1970), pp. 261-360; Earl S. Schaefer, "A Circumplex Model for Maternal Behavior," *Journal of Abnormal and Social Psychology* 59 (1959): 226-35; Barclay Martin, "Parent-Child Relations," in *Review of Child Development Research*, vol. 4, ed. Frances D. Horowitz (Chicago: University of Chicago Press, 1974), pp. 463-540.

ment of self-control than conformity to external authority. In accord with this value are parenting practices in the middle class that emphasize intent and in the working class that emphasize consequences. The middle-class child is likely to be punished on the basis of intent and the lower-class child on the basis of the consequences of a transgression, for example.[10]

Variations in parenting by social class consistent with the Kohn formulation are found regularly in the literature.[11] As we turn to considering the impacts of family relations upon psychosocial development in early adolescence, it is well to bear in mind that theories of adolescent development, the constructs they generate, and the developmental outcomes they portray as desirable —in autonomy, in intimacy, in achievement, and in identity—are much more oriented to self-control than to conformity to external authority.

The Family and Psychosocial Development

TRANSFORMATIONS IN ATTACHMENTS TO PARENTS

The issue of changes in emotional attachments to parents during adolescence has its most influential intellectual origins in the work of Sigmund and Anna Freud. From their psychoanalytic perspective, the physiological changes of puberty mean an increase in libido, or sexual drive. This libidinal increase reactivates the person's previously repressed object ties of the earlier oedipal (phallic) stage of development. Attachments to both parents are said to involve strongly ambivalent feelings of love and hostility. The important developmental task of adolescence from this point of view is the redirection of (sexual) object ties such that attachments to parents come to be replaced by attachments to peers. The required psychic reorganization and the redirection of the

10. Melvin L. Kohn, *Class and Conformity*, 2d ed. (Chicago: University of Chicago Press, 1977).

11. For reviews, see Kohn, *Class and Conformity*; Joseph A. Kahl, *The American Class Structure* (New York: Holt, Rinehart and Winston, 1961); Robert P. Coleman and Bernice L. Neugarten, *Social Status in the City* (San Francisco: Jossey-Bass, 1971); and Robert D. Hess, "Social Class and Ethnic Influence on Socialization," in *Carmichael's Manual of Child Psychology*, vol. 2, ed. Mussen, pp. 457-557.

libido entail stormy and stressful intrafamilial encounters ("rebelliousness") that from this theoretical perspective are considered
to be a normal aspect of adolescence.[12]

Unfortunately, changes in emotional bonds to parents have
not been much studied in early adolescence. Available information
does support the conclusion, however, that positive ties between
children and their parents, in general, remain strong in early (and
late) adolescence.[13] At the same time, every day observation suggests that changes are taking place in expressions of affection as
a result of changes in appearance; the same parental caresses and
hugs that seemed all right before puberty now do not. Perhaps
this is so because of the emerging reproductive maturity of the
young person and the new sexual meaning that intimate affectional
behaviors may imply.

Given the establishment of positive parent-child ties during
early childhood, parental rejection in middle childhood and adolescence tends to be associated with increased dependency toward
peers and adults other than parents (and with antisocial behavior
in adolescence).[14] Peer-dependent boys in one study had a higher
proportion of parents who were emotionally uninvolved with
them, while the adult-dependent boys could be characterized by
their parents' authoritarian rearing.[15] A combination of warmth
and high control in childhood and adolescence proved, in one
longitudinal study, to forecast rebelliousness in adolescence.[16]

12. Peter Blos, *On Adolescence: A Psychoanalytic Interpretation* (New
York: Free Press, 1962); Anna Freud, "Adolescence," in *The Psychoanalytic
Study of the Child*, vol. 13 (New York: International Universities Press,
1958), pp. 255-78.

13. Albert Bandura and Richard H. Walters, *Adolescent Aggression* (New
York: Ronald Press, 1959); Elizabeth Douvan and Joseph Adelson, *The Adolescent Experience* (New York: John Wiley and Sons, 1966); Robert C. Sorenson, *Adolescent Sexuality in Contemporary America: Personal Values and
Sexual Behavior Ages Thirteen to Nineteen* (New York: World Book Co.,
1973).

14. Bandura and Walters, *Adolescent Aggression*.

15. William McCord, Joan McCord, and Paul Verden, "Familial and Behavioral Correlates of Dependency in Male Children," *Child Development* 33
(1962): 313-26.

16. Earl S. Schaefer and Nancy Bayley, *Maternal Behavior, Child Behavior, and Their Intercorrelations from Infancy through Adolescence*, in
Monographs of the Society for Research in Child Development 28, no. 3
(1963). Serial No. 87.

The psychoanalytic position that rebelliousness is normal during adolescence enjoys considerable support from those who work with troubled and troublesome young people. Studies of more representative samples of the population, however, do not support this position. Adolescence is not, in general, a period of overt rebelliousness and familial conflict in industrialized societies, at least if one attends to the self-reports of representative samples of parents and their adolescent offspring.[17]

TRANSFORMATIONS IN AUTONOMY

Changes in family interaction. Late adolescence is characterized by increased self-reliance and increased influence in social interactions with parents. There is a decrease in conformity to both parents and peers although both also continue to be important sources of social influence.[18] Subjective feelings of autonomy (for example, agreement with the statement "both parents give me enough freedom") increase over the high school years and, furthermore, are positively associated with feelings of closeness to parents, with enjoying activities with parents, with asking parents for advice, with wanting to be like parents, and with infrequent conflict with parents.[19]

The information presented thus far suggests that the road to behavioral antonomy and to feelings of behavioral autonomy in late adolescence is neither through the severing of affectional ties nor through the rejection of parents as sources of influence during early adolescence. Present information about parenting behavior and the development of autonomy suggests that we should attend less to notions of inevitable conflict and more to notions of orderly

17. Daniel Offer, *The Psychological World of the Teenager* (New York: Basic Books, 1969); Douvan and Adelson, *The Adolescent Experience;* Bandura and Walters, *Adolescent Aggression;* Denise Kandel and Gerald S. Lesser, *Youth in Two Worlds* (San Francisco: Jossey-Bass, 1972).

18. Bengt-Erik Andersson, "Developmental Trends in Reaction to Social Pressure from Adults vs. Peers" (unpublished manuscript, University of Stockholm, 1977); Thomas J. Berndt, "Developmental Changes in Conformity to Peers and Parents," *Development Psychology*, in press; Theodore Jacob, "Patterns of Family Conflict and Dominance as a Function of Child Age and Social Class," *Developmental Psychology* 10 (January 1974): 1-12.

19. Kandel and Lesser, *Youth in Two Worlds.*

changes in the family as a system and to the direct observation of family interaction.

Jacob studied families with eleven- and sixteen-year-old sons. Family members were first asked independently to choose between alternative responses to emotionally charged situations families face. After making their independent choices, the family triads were asked to discuss each of the situations and to come up with a family decision. Several differences in family interaction were found. In general, sons were more assertive (interrupted more often) than were their parents (particularly mothers), but the sons were less assertive at age sixteen than at age eleven, while parents tended to interrupt more when the sons were sixteen. Fathers and mothers, however, were more influential in the presence of an eleven-year-old than a sixteen-year-old, as shown in the extent to which family consensus reflected initial preferences. The greater influence of sixteen-year-olds in family decision making occurs at the expense of the mother in middle-class families and at that of the father in working-class families. A father=mother>son influence structure seems to characterize middle-class families with an early adolescent male child as contrasted with a father> mother><son structure with an adolescent age child. The shift in lower-class families is from a father=mother>son structure to a (rather unstable) father=mother=son structure.[20]

In a similar study, Alexander compared the family interactions of nondelinquent and delinquent (runaway or "ungovernable") thirteen- to sixteen-year-olds. Communication was analyzed in terms of the possible pairs of communicators. The families of delinquents demonstrated higher rates of defensive communications than did families of nondelinquents. Only the communications from child to mother and child to father were less supportive for the delinquent group than the normal group, however. In the normal families there was no reciprocity in parent and child defensive communications; while there were instances of defensiveness in the normal families, they were not systematically correlated with one another. In the delinquent families, on the other hand, there tended to be reciprocity in defensive communications. Normal families were characterized by reciprocity in supportive com-

20. Jacob, "Patterns of Family Conflict and Dominance."

munications; delinquents did not exhibit such reciprocity: ". . . normal families appear to facilitate more of the independent, 'parentlike' styles of communication (supportiveness) in their adolescent offspring, while deviant families do not."[21] Similar differences were found in a related study: nondelinquent sons were more assertive than delinquent sons.[22]

Alexander hypothesizes that the onset of adolescence generates family stress to which problematic families respond with disintegration and normal families with adaptation. He cites unpublished data showing that, in normal families with eight- to ten-year-old children, parents emit high rates of dominant and supportive communications while their children show high rates of submissive but not supportive behaviors.[23] At thirteen to sixteen, however, normal children are like their parents in emitting higher rates of dominance and support. Families of delinquents do not recalibrate. Alexander argues that for adolescents to develop adaptively a shift must occur in dominance and submission patterns that moves children more toward symmetry with parents. In delinquent families parents and children do not manage this shift and instead develop hostility around the old patterns.[24] It remains to be seen whether longitudinal studies support these conclusions and whether there are families whose interactions shift at puberty from being reciprocally supportive to being reciprocally defensive as the result of an inability to adapt to pubertal change.

A third study—this one longitudinal—further illuminates changes in parent-child interaction but this time as a function of changing pubertal status. Increases in assertiveness of the son toward the mother were found at the onset of puberty. At the same time, indications of maternal assertiveness toward the son increased over prepubertal levels. At the time of puberty, deference of

21. James F. Alexander, "Defensive and Supportive Communications in Normal and Deviant Families," *Journal of Consulting and Clinical Psychology* 40 (October 1973): 223-31.

22. E. Mavis Hetherington, Roger J. Stouwie, and Eugene H. Ridberg, "Patterns of Family Interaction and Child-rearing Attitudes Related to Three Dimensions of Delinquency," *Journal of Abnormal Psychology* 78 (October 1971): 160-76.

23. Alexander, "Defensive and Supportive Communications."

24. James F. Alexander, personal communication, 1978.

mother and son to each other was about equal, whereas before puberty sons deferred to mothers more often than mothers to sons. Fathers responded to these changes with increases in their own assertive behavior and, after the peak of pubertal change, adolescent assertiveness began to decline somewhat and family tension to decrease.[25]

These observational studies of family interaction are beginning to clarify the kinds of transformations that take place in the family as a system during early adolescence. They show that there may well be perturbations in the interaction of normal families during this period. Through the comparative perspective offered by studies of families with troubled children, the studies demonstrate, however, that *ordinary families, even with their bickering and squabbling, continue to display organized, supportive, and mutual communications during early adolescence.* Outside the laboratory, day-to-day family bickering is likely to be associated with the early adolescent's increased orientation to peer-group norms, values, and standards as well as with increased attempts to influence decision making in the family. Family squabbles are most likely to involve matters such as homework, money, and hair styles[26] rather than basic values, where differences in degree of belief are far more common than differences in quality or direction.[27]

Variations in autonomy. Even if the general picture is not one of universal and stormy conflict over the child's autonomy, it is legitimate to inquire what the determinants of individual variations in autonomous behavior are and of more serious familial conflict when it does occur. Middle-class parents are likely to begin independence training early and to continue it through adolescence. Their valuing of autonomy is consistent both with relative auton-

25. Laurence D. Steinberg and John P. Hill, "Patterns of Family Interaction as a Function of Age, the Onset of Puberty, and Formal Thinking," *Developmental Psychology* 14 (November 1978): 683-84; Laurence D. Steinberg, "A Longitudinal Study of Physical Growth, Intellectual Growth, and Family Interaction in Early Adolescence" (Ph.D. diss., Cornell University, 1977).

26. Leonard A. Lo Sciuto and Robert M. Karlin, "Correlates of the Generation Gap," *Journal of Psychology* 81 (July 1972): 253-62.

27. Richard M. Lerner et al., "Attitudes of High School Students and Their Parents toward Contemporary Issues," *Psychological Reports* 31 (August 1972): 255-58.

omy of their own work lives and with their more authoritative child-rearing patterns.²⁸ It remains to be said that authoritative as opposed to authoritarian practices actually do lead to greater autonomy in the child. This *is* the case whether one considers self-perceptions of independence, self-confidence, ratings of responsible behavior, moral judgment, or an active versus passive response to frustrating events.²⁹

Frequent use of explanations seems to be particularly important. Explanations of rules and decisions that are not understood may increase the perceived legitimacy of parental restraints whereas unexplained coercion is likely to produce resentment, especially among adolescents cognitively mature enough to reflect upon their parents' intentions and motivations and to compare their conduct to what it might be. Parenting behaviors that combine explanation with autocratic practices foster dependent and submissive behavior.³⁰

Parent versus peer relations and autonomy. Traditional perspectives on adolescent social relations assume that increasing peer attachments and increasing conformity to peer influence occur *at the expense of* the quality of parent-child relationships and of the child's overall socialization for adulthood. This does not seem to be the case, despite the fact that conformity to parents decreases during this period and conformity to peers increases, at

28. Kohn, *Class and Conformity.*

29. Urie Bronfenbrenner, "Social Familial Antecedents of Responsibility and Leadership in Adolescents," in *Leadership and Interpersonal Behavior,* ed. Luigi Petrullo and Bernard M. Bass (New York: Holt, Rinehart and Winston, 1961) pp. 239-71; Glen H. Elder, Jr., "Parental Power Legitimation and its Effect on the Adolescent," *Sociometry* 26 (March 1963): 50-65; Jerome Kagan and Howard A. Moss, *From Birth to Maturity: The Fels Study of Psychological Development* (New York: John Wiley and Sons, 1962); Kandel and Lesser, *Youth in Two Worlds;* Morris Rosenberg, *Society and the Adolescent Self-image* (Princeton, N.J.: Princeton University Press, 1965); Constance Holstein, "The Relation of Children's Moral Judgment Level to That of Their Parents and to Communication Patterns in the Family," in *Readings in Child Development and Relationships,* ed. Russell C. Smart and Mollie S. Smart (New York: MacMillan Co., 1972), pp. 3-18.

30. Glen H. Elder, Jr., "Structural Variations in the Child Rearing Relationship," *Sociometry* 25 (September 1962): 241-62; Kandel and Lesser, *Youth in Two Worlds.*

least up to about age fourteen, when it begins to decrease.[31] In general, over the adolescent period "interactions with peers support, express, and specify for the peer context the values of parents and other adults; and the adolescent subculture is coordinated with, and in fact is a particular expression of, the culture of the larger society."[32]

This conclusion follows from the fact that most families at all stratification levels tend to live in neighborhood ghettoes and that young people's neighborhood and school friends therefore tend to come from families with similar values. Such similarities are a major basis for friendship choices among young adolescents.[33] Therefore, the basic norms and values (for example, those having to do with achievement, education, and occupation) are unlikely, in general, to differ very much from those of immediate peers. Studies of parent-peer cross-pressures suggest that parents more often influence matters of educational and occupational choice, while peers more often influence matters of dress, appearance, and custom that determine peer acceptance.[34] Thus, while the potential for conflict is diminished by forces associated with social stratification, and by removal of much of peer interaction from parental purview, when conflict does occur its content is more often the minutiae of adolescent life-styles than fundamental values. And the most slavish peer conformity appears to occur when parents are either extremely permissive or authoritarian.[35] In contrast, authoritative parenting increases the probability that adolescents will associate with parent-approved peers. Apparently, authoritative—more than authoritarian or permissive—parents have a greater

31. Berndt, "Developmental Changes in Conformity to Peers and Parents"; Willard W. Hartup, "Peer Interaction and Social Organization," in *Carmichael's Manual of Child Psychology*, vol. 2, ed. Mussen, pp. 361-456.

32. Kandel and Lesser, *Youth in Two Worlds*, p. 168.

33. Hartup, "Peer Interaction and Social Organization"; Denise Kandel, "Similarity in Real-life Adolescent Friendship Pairs," *Journal of Personality and Social Psychology* 36 (March 1978): 306-12.

34. Clay V. Brittain, "Adolescent Choices and Parent-Peer Cross-pressures," *American Sociological Review* 28 (June 1963): 385-91.

35. Edward C. Devereux, "The Role of Peer Group Experience in Moral Development," in *Minnesota Symposia on Child Psychology*, vol. 4, ed. John P. Hill (Minneapolis: University of Minnesota Press, 1970), pp. 94-140.

chance of influencing the composition of peer groups that support striving for autonomy.[36]

Ultimately autonomy implies relative freedom from the immediate pressures of *both* parents and peers. Indeed, in an experimental situation requiring "baseline" responses to some moral dilemmas followed by responses under varying promises of disclosure of answers to parents and peers, those who varied least from their baseline responses (those who were autonomous by this operational definition) "tended to come from homes characterized by moderate to high levels of support and moderate levels of discipline and control." [37]

At present, we lack good descriptions of how interrelated changes in the family and peer systems work themselves out over time. Some clues are found in two studies with some convergent data. Emmerich, Goldman, and Shore show that it is not until early adolescence that the person conceives of two parallel social worlds and differentiates between their norm systems. It is only then that peers come to be seen as normative models for self-conduct. Prior to this time, the child lives in a world of adults whose standards he adopts for his behavior "and seeks adult affection, support, and approval for meeting adult standards. . . . This orientation affords a vicarious sense of being 'grown up' and sharing valued adult qualities." [38] In adolescence, however, social experience becomes assimilated to two distinct normative structures and the person can adopt the highest standards of both worlds. Other data consonant with this view are provided in a recent study by Berndt, who found that peer influence among sixth graders was greater than among third graders but that parent and peer influences were not opposed (the "two different worlds" phenomenon). By ninth grade, however, opposition between parent and peer norms was greater than at any other age. As with conformity studied in other situations, however, this opposition was not present at the end of high school, when there was a decline in reliance

---

36. Elder, "Adolescent Variations in the Child Rearing Relationship."

37. Ibid.

38. Walter Emmerich, Karla S. Goldman, and Roy E. Shore, "Differentiation and Development of Social Norms," *Journal of Personality and Social Psychology* 18 (June 1971): 323-53.

on *either* parents' or peers' advice, and a relation between rejection of parents' *and* peers' advice on prosocial decisions.[39]

Taken together, recent findings suggest, then, that authoritative parenting with its blend of nonsuffocating affection and moderate control provides a secure familial base for developing social competence in relation to peers and a degree of independence prior to adolescence. Participation in the society of peers and cognitive growth during early adolescence permit differentiation of parent and peer norms and, ultimately, in later adolescence, their integration. The developmental issue then is "not so much one of relinquishing internalized parental norms and controls as it is one of integrating parent and peer norms." [40] The most often modest opposition between parent and peer norms may actually contribute to the development of autonomy of decision making and judgment when differences in norms can be cognitively appreciated as variations in a larger scheme of what might be and when the family continues to provide a secure base for this kind of growing up.[41]

TRANSFORMATIONS IN INTIMACY AND SEXUALITY

Intimacy may be defined in behavioral terms "as mutual self-disclosure and other kinds of verbal sharing, as declarations of liking or loving the other, and as demonstrations of affection such as hugging and nongenital caressing." [42] The development of intimacy in adolescents has been studied by examining the nature and growth of friendships. From this research, it seems clear that, through differential socialization, girls' capacities for intimacy change more dramatically in early adolescence than do those of boys, particularly in relation to self-disclosure. Even by the end of high school, boys' friendships are like those found among pre-

39. Berndt, "Developmental Changes in Conformity to Peers and Parents."

40. Emmerich et al., "Differentiation and Development of Social Norms," p. 350.

41. James Garbarino and Urie Bronfenbrenner, "The Socialization of Moral Judgment and Behavior in Cross-cultural Perspective," in *Morality: A Handbook of Moral Development and Behavior*, ed. Thomas Lickona (New York: Holt, Rinehart and Winston, 1976), pp. 70-83; Devereux, "The Role of Peer Group Experience in Moral Development."

42. Robert A. Lewis, "Emotional Intimacy among Men," *Journal of Social Issues* 34 (Winter 1978): 108-21.

adolescent girls in that they involve the sharing of activities with a congenial companion rather than the sharing of feelings and ideas.[43] There seems little doubt that parental modeling and reinforcement of traditional gender-role behavior could influence such outcomes, although these matters do not appear to have been studied directly. It may be presumed that the likelihood of self-disclosure is increased when the individual trusts significant others, and it has been found that authoritative parenting is positively correlated with degree of interpersonal trust.[44]

Many, but not all, studies of self-disclosure to parents have found that girls disclose more than do boys, and this difference may increase during early (and late) adolescence. When averaged over males and females, reported self-disclosure is greater to mothers than to fathers. Disclosure to peers is greater than that to parents and greater to same than to opposite-sex peers and parents. The preference of disclosure to same-sex parents holds for both sexual and nonsexual matters, although the effect is stronger for the former.[45]

Differential socialization for intimacy and sexuality ("the double standard") means that females bring a "person-centered" orientation to early dating, while the orientation of boys is likely to be more "body-centered": "thus dating and courtship may well be considered processes in which persons train members of the opposite sex in the meaning and context of their respective commitments." [46] While the conventionality of socialization prior to

43. Douvan and Adelson, *The Adolescent Experience.*

44. Kenneth B. Stein, William F. Soskin, and Sheldon J. Korchin, "Interpersonal Trust and Disaffected High School Youth," *Journal of Youth and Adolescence* 3 (December 1974): 281-92.

45. Jack O. Balswick and James W. Balkwell, "Self-disclosure to Same- and Opposite-Sex Parents: An Empirical Test of Insights from Role Theory," *Sociometry* 40 (September 1977): 282-86; Gloria A. Mulcahy, "Sex Difference in Patterns of Self-disclosure among Adolescents: A Developmental Perspective," *Journal of Youth and Adolescence* 2 (December 1973): 343-56; Wilburn H. Rivenbark, "Self-disclosure Patterns among Adolescents," *Psychological Reports* 28 (February 1971): 35-42; Lloyd W. West, "Sex Differences in the Exercise of Circumspection in Self-disclosure among Adolescents," *Psychological Reports* 26 (February 1970): 226.

46. William Simon and John H. Gagnon, "On Psychosexual Development," in *Handbook of Socialization Theory and Research*, ed. David Goslin (Chicago: Rand McNally, 1969), pp. 733-52.

early adolescence probably exercises important if not well-understood influences, the process of integrating intimacy and sexuality obviously is centered in the peer group and not in the family.[47] Indeed the role of the family in dealing specifically with emergent adolescent sexuality is a more modest one than adolescents themselves may want.

Sorenson reports the responses of thirteen- to fifteen-year-old boys and girls to questions asked in a national survey about how they and their parents deal with sexual matters. Conversations with parents about personal sexual matters are apparently not frequent, often not productive of specific information related to the child's growth, and they are guarded. More youngsters say they would like to talk to their parents about sex then presently say they have free conversation about it. Yet three-fourths of the boys believe both that their parents trust their sexual behavior and that they think it is the child's own business. The corresponding percentages for girls, 68 and 44, suggest that the double standard is still with us. Nearly two-thirds believe that their attitudes toward sex differ from those of their parents, and yet 53 percent of the boys and 62 percent of the girls believe that their sexual behavior "is pretty much the way my parents would want it to be." [48]

Attitudes toward sexuality have changed since the 1920s and sexual activity (primarily in girls) during adolescence has increased markedly since the 1960s. Neither change appears to have resulted in open discussion or exchange of information about sex in most families. There may well be a tacit conspiracy not to raise the issue, as it was unlikely to have been raised in the parents' own childhood.[49] There are data suggesting that parents become more conservative as their children reach reproductive age.[50] In any

47. Willard W. Hartup, "Adolescent Peer Relations: A Look at the Future," in *Adolescence and Youth in Prospect*, ed. John P. Hill and Franz J. Mönks (Atlantic Highlands, N.J.: Humanities Press, 1977), pp. 171-85.

48. Sorenson, *Adolescent Sexuality in Contemporary America*.

49. Ibid.

50. Ira L. Reiss, "How and Why America's Sex Standards are Changing," in *The Sexual Scene*, ed. William Simon and John H. Gagnon (Chicago: Trans-action Books, 1970), pp. 43-57.

case, most information about sex, correct and incorrect, still comes
from peers. In the midst of increasingly greater societal openness
about sexuality, many young people remain appallingly ignorant
of the most basic information. The great majority of young people
favor sex education not only about "plumbing" but about relationships and values.[51]

TRANSFORMATIONS IN ACHIEVEMENT AND IDENTITY

In 1966, Douvan and Adelson, reporting on their national survey of adolescents, concluded that identity formation in adolescence was a more active issue for boys than girls and that, for
boys, it centered on the interrelated themes of autonomy, achievement, and vocational choice. For girls, identity was likely to be
synthesized around interpersonal relationships and the development
of intimacy.[52] Yet, girls' self-conceptions were diffuse, undecided,
and unformed. Seemingly, definition of self for girls was deferred
to, and defined in terms of, future successful experience in courtship and marriage. These findings reflect traditional gender-role socialization.

The literature continues to reflect substantial support for the
conclusion that "the child-rearing practices that are conducive to
feminine sex-typing are often antagonistic to those that lead to
achievement-oriented behavior."[53] There is evidence that, for both
boys and girls, authoritative parenting, when combined with direct
encouragement of and standards for achievement, is conducive to
achievement-oriented behavior of a variety of kinds. Attribution of
successes and failures to the self; intrinsic gratification from improving performance; approach to rather than avoidance of
achievement situations; repeated attempts at task mastery following frustration, temporary setback, or failure; high educational and
occupational aspirations all are positively correlated with aspects of

51. John J. Conger, *Adolescence and Youth*, 2d ed. (New York: Harper
and Row, 1977).

52. Douvan and Adelson, *The Adolescent Experience*.

53. Aletha H. Stein and Margaret M. Bailey, "The Socialization of Achievement Orientation in Females," *Psychological Bulletin* 80 (November 1973):
362.

authoritative parenting.[54] In the conventional gender-differential socialization of girls, however, authoritative practices often are combined with encouragement of and support for competence in interpersonal rather than (or in addition to) achievement orientations. Thus girls more often come to be motivated in achievement situations by variables extrinsic to task attainment than do boys. For many girls, expending effort and persisting at a task may more often serve to avoid social disapproval than to gain intrinsic satisfaction from succeeding at a given task.[55]

Bardwick and Douvan have argued that pressures toward conventional gender-typed behavior are likely to increase for girls during early adolescence: "some time in adolescence the message becomes clear that one had better not do too well, that competition is aggressive and unfeminine, that deviation threatens the hetero-

54. Ben Ferguson and Kevin Kennelly, "Internal-External Locus of Control and Perception of Authority Figures," *Psychological Reports* 34 (June 1974): 1119-23; Walter Katkovsky, Virginia C. Crandall, and Suzanne Good, "Parental Antecedents of Children's Beliefs in Internal-External Control of Reinforcements in Intellectual Achievement Situations," *Child Development* 38 (1967): 765-76; Bernard C. Rosen and Roy D'Andrade, "The Psychosocial Origins of Achievement Motivation," *Sociometry* 22 (September 1959): 185-218; Fred L. Strodtbeck, "Family Interaction, Values, and Achievement," in *Talent and Society*, ed. D. C. McClelland (Princeton, N.J.: Van Nostrand, 1958); Elder, "Structural Variations in the Child Rearing Relationship"; Joseph A. Kahl, "Educational and Occupational Aspirations of 'Common Man' Boys," *Harvard Educational Review* 23, no. 3 (1953): 186-203; William R. Morrow and Robert C. Wilson, "Family Relations of Bright High-achieving and Under-achieving High School Boys," *Child Development* 32 (September 1961): 501-10; Paul McGhee and Richard Teevan, *The Childhood Development of Fear of Failure and Motivation*, Technical Report No. 15, Contract Nohr 3591 (01) NR171-803, Group Psychology Branch, Office of Naval Research (Lewisburg, Pa.: Bucknell University, 1965); Zena B. Blau, "Maternal Aspirations, Socialization, and Achievement of Boys and Girls in the White Working Class," *Journal of Youth and Adolescence* 1 (March 1972): 35-38; Nancy W. Perry and C. Raymond Millimet, "Child-rearing Antecedents of Low and High Anxiety Eighth-grade Children," in *Stress and Anxiety*, vol. 4, ed. Charles D. Spielberger and Irwin G. Sarason (Washington: Hemisphere Publishing Corp., 1977), pp. 189-204; Sheila C. Field, "Longitudinal Study of the Origins of Achievement Striving," *Journal of Personality and Social Psychology* 7 (December 1967): 408-14; Kagan and Moss, *From Birth to Maturity*.

55. Virginia C. Crandall and Esther S. Battle, "The Antecedents and Adult Correlates of Academic and Intellectual Achievement Effort," in *Minnesota Symposia on Child Psychology*, ed. John P. Hill (Minneapolis: University of Minnesota Press, 1970), pp. 36-93; Kagan and Moss, *From Birth to Maturity*.

sexual relationship." [56] And there is information that girls in early adolescence differentiate skills on a gender-role basis more than in childhood and begin to opt out of and to do less well in "male subjects" in school.[57] They even may begin to underachieve in relation to their ability, apparently in response to the paired norms that "good girls get good grades" but "not too good." [58] Indeed the aversive social consequences for girls of expending effort, persisting in the face of obstacles, competing and actually succeeding, may lead to an internalized avoidance of and withdrawal from achievement situations—the so-called "fear of success." [59]

Despite these apparent transformations in achievement-oriented behaviors among girls in adolescence, we do not know empirically what role changing parental expectations (in the form of increased pressure to conform to conventional "feminine" behavior, for example) at or around puberty play in the process. It seems to be the case, however, that departures from traditional feminine roles and a career orientation in girls during adolescence are positively associated with maternal employment, maternal career commitment, and the perceived competence of the mother in nonfamilial

56. Judith M. Bardwick and Elizabeth Douvan, "Ambivalence: The Socialization of Women," in *Woman in Sexist Society: Studies in Power and Powerlessness,* ed. Vivian Gornick and Barbara K. Moran (New York: Basic Books, 1971), pp. 147-60.

57. David Elkind, "Cognitive Development in Adolescence," in *Understanding Adolescence: Current Developments in Adolescent Psychology,* ed. James F. Adams (Boston, Mass.: Allyn and Bacon, 1968), pp. 128-58; Aletha H. Stein, "The Effects of Sex-role Standards for Achievement and Sex-role Preference on Three Determinants of Achievement Motivation," *Developmental Psychology* 4 (March 1971): 219-31; Aletha H. Stein and Jancis Smithells, "Age and Sex Differences in Children's Sex-role Standards about Achievement," *Developmental Psychology* 1 (May 1969): 252-59.

58. James S. Coleman, *The Adolescent Society* (New York: Free Press of Glencoe, 1961); Carol J. Ireson, "Effects of Sex-role Socialization on the Academic Achievement, Educational Expectations, and Interpersonal Competence of Adolescent Girls," (Ph.D. diss., Cornell University, 1975); Merville C. Shaw, 2d, and J. T. McCuen, "The Onset of Academic Underachievement in Bright Children," *Journal of Educational Psychology* 51 (June 1960): 103-8.

59. Matina S. Horner, "Feminity and Success Achievement: A Basic Inconsistency," in *Feminine Personality and Conflict,* ed. Judith M. Bardwick et al. (Monterey, Calif.: Brooks/Cole, 1970), pp. 45-73.

roles.[60] Other studies suggest an alternative, more reactive socialization route to an achievement orientation for girls—through low levels of parent acceptance, even hostility from the father, and the early adoption of masculine interests.[61] Unfortunately, the complementary studies—those examining parents who expect and sanction the development of intimacy in males—have not been begun.

According to Erik Erikson, earlier phases in the life cycle contribute to the formation of identity, but identity becomes a paramount issue during adolescence because somatic changes and their implications for conduct virtually demand new images of self. Cognitive change introduces the possibility for seeing oneself and one's relationship to others in a more differentiated and integrated way (and in light of ideals and principles and of the way one and others *might* be). Increased social responsibility makes new demands on one's competencies and may lead to new assessments of self.[62] The identity crisis of adolescence can be "solved only in new identifications with age-mates and with leader figures outside the family." [63] The person "tests, selects, integrates self-images from the crises of childhood in light of the ideological climate of youth." [64]

Erikson has not provided a systematic definition of identity. He

60. Elizabeth Douvan, "Employment and the Adolescent," in *The Employed Mother in America*, ed. F. Ivan Nye and Lois W. Hoffman (Chicago: Rand McNally, 1963), pp. 142-64; Barbara R. Francis, "Effect of Maternal Employment on the Socialization of Sex Role and Achievement in New Zealand," (Ph.D. diss., Cornell University, 1975); Douvan and Adelson, *The Adolescent Experience;* Aletha Huston-Stein and Anne Higgins-Trenk, "Development of Females from Childhood through Adulthood: Career and Feminine Role Orientations," in *Life-span Development and Behavior*, vol. 1, ed. P. B. Baltes (New York: Academic Press, 1978), pp. 258-97.

61. Jack Block, Anna von der Lippe, and Jeanne Block, "Sex-role and Socialization Patterns: Some Personality Concomitants and Environmental Antecedents," *Journal of Consulting and Clinical Psychology* 41 (December 1973): 321-41; Crandall and Battle, "Antecedents and Adult Correlates of Academic and Intellectual Achievement Effort"; Kagan and Moss, *From Birth to Maturity;* Leona E. Tyler, "The Antecedents of Two Varieties of Vocational Interests," *Genetic Psychology Monographs* 70 (August 1964): 177-277.

62. Erik H. Erikson, *Identity: Youth and Crisis* (New York: W. W. Norton, 1968).

63. Ibid., p. 87.

64. Ibid., p. 210.

says that it includes a conscious sense of uniqueness, an unconscious striving for a continuity of experience, and solidarity with a group's ideals. The continuity is at least twofold in nature: that between what one has come to be through part-identifications, mainly with parents, in childhood and what one promises to be in adulthood; and that between what one conceives the self to be and perceives that others see and expect. Identity formation, then, does not involve the casting away of all childhood things nor can it be disentangled from the roles that the young person currently plays in social systems.[65]

Changes in self-conceptions and in their integration have not been much studied in early adolescence, and there is little information about developmental change during this period. Consequently, empirical knowledge of the contributions that changes in parenting behavior during this period do contribute to identity formation is slight. However, the existing literature on the development of autonomy and achievement reviewed above encourages speculation. Erikson argues that the social systems in which adolescents participate influence the process of identity formation through "confirming" manifestations of their new somatic and social statuses and their attempts to try out new ways of behaving. Such trying-on of new identities, according to Erikson, occurs primarily in the peer group.

It may be hypothesized that parents who, through authoritative parenting, provide a secure home base for the development of social competence in peer groups, and who provide increased support for independence during this period, are likely to promote the kind of exploration hypothesized to be necessary to the achievement of an individual identity. Those parents who are restrictive and foster dependence on adults are likely to retard the process. Those who provide conflictful environments may provide the conditions for the development of what Erikson calls "negative identity"—one tied up in defining oneself in terms of what parents *are not* and value least. Those who "confirm" conventional gender-role performance during early adolescence are likely to preclude exploration and to contribute to what Erikson has called "identity foreclosure." Early maturing boys may be particularly subject to

65. Ibid., p. 19.

such foreclosure. Their competitive advantages in the peer social system and the consequent approval they receive—demonstrably from peers and probably from parents as well—may forestall exploration of potentialities they may have beyond those that qualify them for super-jock roles.[66]

Erikson claims that identity, at its optimum, is experienced as a sense of well-being. "Its most obvious concomitants are a feeling of being at home in one's body, a sense of 'knowing where one is going,' and an inner assuredness of anticipated recognition from those who count." [67] These are not easy qualities to measure and the closest we have come is in the study of self-esteem and self-confidence. It should not be too surprising that a number of studies have shown self-esteem and self-confidence to be positively associated with authoritative parenting and warm attachments to parents.[68] The adolescent cannot be assured of the recognition of parents for some new, more mature trial identity if they are habitually ignoring or overcontrolling. There is some evidence, too, that parental warmth and control are associated with self-esteem only when "adult frames of reference" are used: the relation holds for felt self-esteem in adult contexts, such as the family, the classroom, and with other adults. Parenting behaviors are not correlates of self-esteem where perceived competence in dealing with peers is concerned.[69]

66. Mary C. Jones, "Psychological Correlates of Somatic Development," *Child Development* 36 (1965): 899-911; Harvey Peskin, "Pubertal Onset and Ego Functioning," *Journal of Abnormal Psychology* 72 (February 1967): 1-15.

67. Erikson, *Identity: Youth and Crisis*, p. 165.

68. Stanley Coopersmith, *The Antecedents of Self-esteem* (San Francisco: Miller Freeman Publications, 1967); Viktor Gecas, "Parental Behavior and Contextual Variations in Adolescent Self-esteem," *Sociometry* 35 (June 1972): 332-45; William J. O'Donnell, "Adolescent Self-esteem Related to Feelings toward Parents and Friends," *Journal of Youth and Adolescence* 5 (June 1976) 179-85; Jerald G. Bachman, *Youth in Transition*, vol. 2, *The Impact of Family Background and Intelligence on Tenth-grade Boys* (Ann Arbor, Mich.: Institute for Social Research, University of Michigan, 1970); Alfred B. Heilbrun and Betty J. Gillard, "Perceived Maternal Childrearing Behavior and Motivational Effects of Social Reinforcement in Females," *Perceptual and Motor Skills* 23 (October 1966) 439-46; Morris Rosenberg, *Society and the Adolescent Self-image* (Princeton, N.J.: Princeton University Press, 1965); Kandel and Lesser, *Youth in Two Worlds*.

69. Gecas, "Parental Behavior and Contextual Variations."

Existing studies demonstrate that the emotional upheaval and
neurotic symptomatology that are considered by some to characterize "the normal adolescent identity crisis" do not occur for
the majority of adolescents.[70] This expectation appears to be an
overgeneralization to all adolescents from the problems of a neurotic, privileged, upper-middle-class few. In this case, as well as
in those of rebelliousness, parent-peer conflict, and the generation
gap, prospective parents and teachers of early adolescents should
take some comfort from the substantial accumulation of information suggesting that these events are *not* typical. We could all do
with a dedramatization of adolescence.[71]

A Concluding Note

We have frequently used Baumrind's term, "authoritative parenting," to summarize what is known about the parental correlates
and antecedents of a variety of adolescent behaviors. It should be
noted that the present literature does not permit us to assess the
independent contributions of the variables included in this complex of parenting behaviors. And, in the absence of appropriate
studies, we are not in a position to specify the mechanisms of
familial socialization that influence the classical outcomes of socialization in early adolescence. Given the literature on mechanisms
of socialization, we can suggest that authoritative parenting, as
opposed to authoritarian or permissive parenting in early adolescence, "works" because authoritative parents more often are appropriate models for the kinds of psychosocial outcomes in question and because their acceptance of the child invites emulation.
Owing to their greater warmth, they also may have greater reward
value, thus making approval and its withdrawal more potent sanctions. Because authoritative parents may be less frustrating, they
may less often induce emotional responses that could interfere with
use of the more complex social-reasoning processes of which
adolescents, more than children, are capable. Authoritative parents

70. Conger, *Adolescence and Youth*; Douvan and Adelson, *The Adolescent Experience*; Offer, *The Psychological World of the Teenager*.

71. John P. Hill and Franz J. Mönks, "Some Perspectives on Adolescence
in Modern Societies," in *Adolescence and Youth in Prospect*, ed. Hill and
Mönks, pp. 28-78.

also may be more responsive to intraindividual change in their children at early adolescence than are authoritarian parents. They do seem to provide a secure base in the family for learning to deal with peers. Given that the transition to adulthood from late adolescence requires joining the ranks of adults—*with one's peer cohort*—the examination of early adolescence in terms of the reciprocal influences of parents and peers should have high priority for practitioners and scientists in their efforts to understand the years from ten to fifteen.

CHAPTER IV

The School

DONALD H. EICHHORN

Historical Background

The concept of a specialized school program serving students between the elementary and secondary years has its roots in the latter decades of the nineteenth century and the early years of the twentieth century. Prior to that time, most districts maintained eight-year elementary schools, which had their beginnings about 1810 to 1830, and four-year high schools, which originated in 1821. The "8-4 plan," as it came to be known, was the predominant pattern of organization by 1900.

Educators expressed concern about the 8-4 plan in the late 1800s. President Eliot of Harvard, troubled by the relatively late age of entering college freshmen, expressed this concern in addresses before the National Education Association. In 1892, the Association formed a series of national committees whose reports became the basis for ultimate reform of the 8-4 plan. The report of the Committee of Ten, one of the most influential committees in the history of American education, was instrumental in the reorganization of secondary education. The committee's report stated:

[Members of] the committee were perfectly aware that it is impossible to make a satisfactory secondary-school program limited to a period of four years and founded on the present elementary school subjects and methods.[1]

It is important to note that the reorganization movement, which developed out of the findings of the various committees, was clearly an attempt to restructure secondary education, although

1. National Education Association, *Report of the Committee of Ten on Secondary Studies* (New York: American Book Co., 1894), p. 3.

there was no apparent intention to establish a separate and unique level of education for the middle years. In 1899, however, the Committee on College Entrance Requirements proposed a plan for a six-year high school based upon pupils' needs. The report stated:

The seventh grade rather than the ninth, is the natural turning point in the pupil's life, as the age of adolescence demands new methods and wiser direction. . . . The transition from the elementary to the secondary period may be made natural and easy by changing gradually from the one-teacher regimen to the system of special teachers, thus avoiding the vital shock now commonly felt on entering high school.[2]

Although a number of school systems, including Richmond (Indiana), Lawrence (Kansas), and New York City had initiated modified grade organizations between 1896 and 1905, the school year 1909-10 is considered to be the real beginning of transitional schools, with the systems in Columbus (Ohio) and Berkeley (California) leading the way.

Two fundamental aspects of the early junior high school became the pillars of the movement. These were (a) the concept of the junior high school as an integral part of secondary education, and (b) the concept that the unique needs of early adolescents create a need for a transitional level. Both of these ideas have sustained and nurtured the growth of transitional schools, but each of these principles has also sparked controversy. Some educators have contended that considering this level a junior division of secondary education has resulted in a lack of necessary recognition and identity for the transitional school, inadequate preparation of teachers, and a high-school type of instructional program incompatible with the characteristics of the students. The insistence by other educators that a unique level of education existed apart from either elementary or secondary programs led to the middle-school movement of the 1960s.

The middle-school movement erupted as a protest against the program, not against the concept, of the junior high school. Middle-school advocates believed that the junior high school had lost its individuality and had reverted to programs that were too

2. National Education Association, *Journal of Proceedings and Addresses* (Los Angeles, Calif.: National Education Association, 1899), p. 659.

high-school oriented. Sensing that ninth-grade students, by virtue
of earlier maturation, had more in common socially and instruc-
tionally with high school students, and that sixth-grade students
were more compatible with seventh-grade students, middle-school
proponents argued for a reorganization that would establish a unit
composed of grades six through eight.[3] The middle-school concept
rapidly gained acceptance. Whereas Cuff identified 499 middle
schools in 1965,[4] Brooks was able to identify 4060 such schools in
1976.[5] There seems little doubt that the reorganized transitional
school has wide appeal.

The emergence of the junior high school in the early 1900s and
of the middle school in the 1960s may be attributed to a variety of
propitious cultural factors that are remarkably parallel. In the early
1900s, the desire of society to keep students in school created a
climate of acceptance for the junior high school. In the 1960s, a
population explosion, increasing geographic mobility, technological
advances, and the legal and moral demands of racial integration had
a comparable effect on the growth of the middle school. The desire of Eliot and others to have high school academic subjects
taught in earlier grades sparked the progress of the junior high
school in the earlier period. Similarly, in the post-Sputnik era a
demand for a return to the "essentials" was ignited, causing a
downward extension of high school subjects and aiding the con-
version to middle schools. The concern for adolescence initiated
by the work of G. Stanley Hall provided a student-oriented di-

3. A letter from Carl R. Streams, Supervising Principal of the Upper
St. Clair (Pennsylvania) School System to the Pennsylvania Department of
Instruction in 1959 outlined why a school composed of grades six, seven,
and eight was thought to be desirable and educationally sound. See Donald
H. Eichhorn, *The Middle School* (New York: Center for Applied Research
in Education, 1966), pp. 2-3.

4. William A. Cuff, "Middle Schools on the March," *Bulletin of the
National Association of Secondary School Principals* 51 (February 1967):
82-86.

5. Kenneth Brooks, "The Middle School: A National Survey," *Middle
School Journal* 8 (February 1978): 6-7. In 1967-68, Alexander had identified
1101 middle schools, and Compton reported 3723 in 1974. See William M.
Alexander, *A Survey of Organizational Patterns of Reorganized Middle
Schools*, Final Report No. 7-D-026 (Gainesville, Fla.: University of Florida
Press, 1968), p. 16, and Mary F. Compton, "The Middle School: A Status
Report," *Middle School Journal* 6 (June 1976): 3-5.

mension to the junior high school movement. Similarly, the work of J. M. Tanner, citing trends toward earlier biological maturation, was instrumental in the movement to reorganize the middle school. It is apparent that the transitional school still holds a strategic position in the organizational pattern of school districts. It is possible that the present "back to basics" movement, coupled with the economic impact of a declining student population, may well affect, once again, the organizational structure of the middle school.

The Learner's Relationships with the School

The interrelationships between learner and school are fundamental to the question of effectiveness. As Havighurst and Neugarten have pointed out, the school, like the family and the peer group, may be viewed as a social system with a subculture of its own—"a complex set of beliefs, values and traditions, ways of thinking and behaving that differentiate it from other institutions." [6] Historically, there has been considerable disagreement among professionals regarding the most appropriate school program for learners in the middle school. Secondary education programs have been developed under the assumption that students in the middle school are adolescents, while elementary-type programs in transitional schools reflect the belief that students are prepubescent. In either case, the programs do not accurately reflect the developmental stages of students in the middle school.

Students in the transitional school are markedly different with respect to a wide range of characteristics that develop in the stages of prepubescence, pubescence, and early adolescence. I have used the term "transescence" to refer to the stage of development that begins prior to the onset of puberty and extends through the early stages of adolescence. Since puberty does not occur for all precisely at the same chronological age, the transescent designation is based on the many physical, social, emotional, and intellectual changes that occur throughout these developmental stages.

Because of the diverse range of developmental characteristics of learners in the middle school and the interrelationship of these

6. Robert J. Havighurst and Bernice L. Neugarten, *Society and Education* (Boston: Allyn and Bacon, 1957), p. 181.

elements in the school setting, schools for young people at this level need to be considered in a transitional context. While a comprehensive treatment of the characteristics of these learners is not the purpose of this chapter, it is necessary to mention at least some aspects of those characteristics that involve internal forces created by biological and cognitive changes and others that involve external forces impinging on the learner's culture.

BIOLOGICAL CONSIDERATIONS

Pubertal change is a striking development of this period, including a marked spurt in growth and the development of reproductive capability. The impact of pubertal change is extensive, both physically and socially. The age of onset of pubertal change varies markedly, as shown in table 1. The divergence of biological maturity of middle-school students in relation to chronological age is impressive. In the study for which data are reported in table 1, there were fourteen-year-old boys who were found to be in Tan-

TABLE 1

NUMBER, PERCENT, AND AGE OF BOYS AND GIRLS CLASSIFIED IN VARIOUS LEVELS OF DEVELOPMENT OF SECONDARY SEXUAL CHARACTERISTICS (TANNER UNITS)

	LEVELS				
	I	II	III	IV	V
Boys					
Number	37	108	55	24	8
Percent	16	46	24	10	4
Age in years					
Mean	11.98	12.07	12.78	13.07	13.49
Range	10.8–14.1	10.7–13.8	11.1–14.2	11.8–14.9	13.2–13.8
Girls					
Number	22	88	74	55	18
Percent	9	34	29	21	7
Age in years					
Mean	11.2	11.8	12.4	12.11	12.5
Range	10.1–12.1	10.1–13.7	10.8–13.7	11.5–13.9	11.1–14.0

SOURCE: Donald H. Eichhorn, "The Boyce Medical Study," in *Educational Dimensions of the Emerging Adolescent Learner*, ed. Neil Atkins and Philip Pumerantz (Washington, D.C.: Association of Supervision and Curriculum Development and Educational Leadership Institute, 1973), p. 24.

ner Classification Level I (no secondary sexual characteristics present), while there were eleven-year-old girls in Tanner Classification Level V (complete development of secondary sexual characteristics). In a study of black children by Nankin and associates, a similar pattern was discerned. That study, however, reported that black adolescents were more sexually advanced by a mean of approximately 0.3 Tanner units. Of the eleven- and twelve-year-old males, approximately 5 percent were sexually advanced, that is, they were at Tanner Classification Levels IV and V. Of the eleven- and twelve-year-old girls, 10 percent of the white girls and 30 percent of the black girls were at those levels.[7]

This pubertal variance has social and emotional ramifications in our culture. Mussen and Jones reported that early maturing boys present a much more favorable psychological picture than do late maturing boys. The latter are likely to have negative self-concepts, feelings of inadequacy, strong feelings of being rejected and dominated, prolonged dependency needs, and rebellious attitudes toward parents.[8] Similar findings regarding early and late maturing girls have been reported by More.[9]

Pubertal change has far-reaching implications for the process of schooling. In many respects, current organizational practices, such as the classification of students by chronological age, deny rather than accommodate the realities of biological diversity. Assigning students to grades on the basis of chronological age has led to the establishment of graded standards of achievement and to graded textbooks as well as other graded instructional materials.

A more logical organizational concept is that of developmental or maturational age, which takes into account variations among students in physical, mental, and emotional development. Physical characteristics, normally not considered in traditional grouping

7. Howard R. Nankin et al., "Correlation between Sexual Maturation and Serum Gonadotropins: Comparison of Black and White Youngsters," *American Journal of Medical Science* 268 (September 1974): 139-47.

8. Paul H. Mussen and Mary C. Jones, "Self-conceptions, Motivation, and Interpersonal Attitudes of Late and Early Maturing Boys," *Child Development* 28 (June 1957): 255.

9. Douglas M. More, *Developmental Concordance and Discordance During Puberty and Early Adolescence*, in *Monographs of the Society for Child Development* 18, no. 1 (1953), Serial No. 56, pp. 35-36.

practices, cannot be dismissed in view of the impact that changes in physical characteristics have on the lives of transescents. If young people developed in a social vacuum, physical changes would matter little. In our culture these developments create changes in interests and attitudes that have deep significance for the transescent's associations in school. The concept of maturational age also takes into account variations in mental development, so that transescents who are grouped or placed according to their current levels of cognitive growth reflect a common educational base. A third major variable to consider in grouping is the impingement of the culture on the transescent. Anxiety and emotional stress have a marked effect on the progress of learning. The transescent's adjustment to such diverse cultural forces as stability of the home, mobility, demands of peers, and the like cannot be disregarded. The changing interests and attitudes involved in transescent growth are significant for the students' associations within the school. The changes in interests of transescents in middle schools suggest, for example, that same-sex classes may be used to advantage, whereas traditional grouping practices in schools make use of heterosexual classes.[10]

Grouping by maturity has been used successfully since 1969 in the Boyce Middle School in Upper St. Clair, Pennsylvania. Sixth, seventh, and eighth-grade students are assigned to cross-graded instructional teams on the basis of a "maturation index." This index is based in part on scores on standardized tests in reading and mathematics and in part on teachers' ratings of a student's social maturity. The placement of students is reviewed each year, or oftener in the case of students rated either very immature or very advanced. The formula for grouping by developmental age employed in this school is based on research conducted by Allan Drash of Children's Hospital, Pittsburgh.[11] Although it is notoriously difficult to separate the effects of grouping practices from other educational variables, the students in this program continue

10. Eichhorn, *The Middle School*, p. 78.

11. Donald H. Eichhorn, "The Boyce Medical Study," in *Educational Dimensions of the Emerging Adolescent Learner*, ed. Neil Atkins and Philip Pumerantz (Washington, D.C. Association for Supervision and Curriculum Development and the Educational Leadership Institute, 1972), p. 24.

to do very well on both standardized achievement tests and on measures of affect, such as self-esteem.

COGNITIVE CONSIDERATIONS

The approach to learning programs for students in the middle years has been marked by differences in theory and in application. Part of the confusion is due to different ideas among educators as to the cognitive capabilities of students at this level. Students aged ten to fourteen range in cognitive ability levels from Piaget's stage of concrete operations through the stage of formal operations. Students also vary widely in achievement. It is not uncommon to find that seventh-grade students will receive scores on tests of achievement in reading ranging from scores equivalent to those of students in primary grades to scores equivalent to those of students in the upper years of high school. Transescents clearly cannot be classified as being at one or another stage of cognitive achievement, although some schools have consistently attempted to do so. Learning programs have been developed that are appropriate for the mean of each grade level rather than for the diversity in learning and achievement exhibited by students. To characterize seventh graders as "formal operations" thinkers and as seventh-grade achievers is unrealistic, yet this is precisely what is done in most schools.

Having assumed that students aged twelve to fourteen are functioning in formal operations, educators have established increasingly more abstract curricula, where students are expected to learn in a pattern reflecting discovery and conceptualization. This practice should be reexamined. Shayer and associates concluded that, even in the top 20 percent of children at age fourteen years, some 30 percent do not manifest formal operations.[12] In studying children aged six to eleven with IQs of about 160, Webb discovered that no child showed any traces of formal operations before age eleven.[13] (See chapters 11 and 12.)

Epstein's extensive research indicates a hiatus in brain growth

12. M. Shayer et al., "The Distribution of Piagetian Stages of Thinking," *British Journal of Psychology* 46, Part 2 (June 1976): 164-73.

13. Roger A. Webb, "Concrete and Formal Operations in Very Bright 6- to 11-year Olds," *Human Development* 17, no. 4 (1974): 292-300.

during the period from age twelve to fourteen.[14] As a result of this finding, Epstein and Toepfer predict that it would be relatively more difficult "to initiate novel intellectual processes in the middle grades [roughly grades seven and eight] than in periods both preceding and following." They suggest that in those years far more opportunities should be provided for maturation in cognitive skills that have already been initiated and learned than for the acquisition of new skills.[15] Furthermore, they suggest that there may be negative consequences of efforts to introduce more complex thinking processes:

With virtually no increase of brain size and mass in the large majority of twelve- to fourteen-year-olds, there is no growth in the capacity of the brain to handle more complex thinking processes usually introduced in grades seven and eight. This continued demand for the youngster's brain to handle increasingly complex input, which he or she cannot comprehend during this period, may result in rejection of these inputs and the possible development of negative neural networks to dissipate the energy of the input. Thus, it is possible that even when the subsequent growth of the brain between ages fourteen and sixteen could support the development of more complex cognitive skills, the untold numbers of individuals who have developed such negative networks have been so "turned off" that they literally can no longer develop novel cognitive skills.[16]

The question of readiness for complex skills is basic. It is possible that educators have misjudged cognitive ability at this age level. By accepting more complex curricular concepts at earlier levels, curriculum designers may inadvertently be inducing regression in students' achievement. Conversely, educators should analyze carefully students' cognitive capabilities and present instruction at the level of students' readiness. The supposition is that this approach will lead to a more effective mastery of skills, processes, and information at the mature concrete level and prepare students

14. Herman T. Epstein, "A Biologically Based Framework for Intervention Projects," *Mental Retardation* 14 (April 1976): 26-27.

15. Herman T. Epstein and Conrad F. Toepfer, Jr., "A Neuroscience Basis for Reorganizing Middle Grades Education," *Educational Leadership* 35 (May 1978): 657-58.

16. Ibid., p. 658.

for greater mastery of abstract reasoning in the high school years, when a more advanced cognitive capability exists.

CULTURAL CONSIDERATIONS

The dramatic biological change experienced by transescents is undergone in a cultural context, with a variety of societal forces, largely outside individual control, impinging upon the students' lives. For example, the relationship between home and school has altered and has become a partnership, with parents expecting that schools provide more than merely a place to learn. They are often concerned with discipline and with other forms of custodial responsibilities.

Schools for transescents must carry on their traditional educational role, and they must do so in the context of the social and emotional nurturing of students. Contradictions in this role often arise as parents and school personnel carry out their respective responsibilities. The "hidden" curriculum, that is, what the school teaches by implication, is vastly more complex than the hidden curriculum of earlier decades, when there was more likely to be substantial agreement on moral truisms to buttress the efforts of the school.

Peer relations are intense at this stage and peer influence is significant for socialization and certainly for educational processes. At a time of emotional insecurity, interaction among peers seems to be the catalyst for the development of security. Students often react negatively to practices such as regrouping if changes in schedules mean that they have no friends in their classes. Educators need to understand the impact of peer relationships on school programs, for there is little doubt that schooling arrangements may aid or deter socialization.

It has been noted earlier in this chapter that peer relations are affected by early or late biological maturation. It would seem that schools should consider the impact of peer relations in the quest for enhancing the effectiveness of the learning process. For example, would "open-school" programs, in which students choose those with whom they work without regard to grade level, result in more effective learning?[17]

17. Bernard Schein and Martha Pierce Schein, *Open Classrooms in the Middle School* (West Nyack, N.Y.: Parker Publishing Co., 1975).

Improving learning involves many elements. Drawing attention to social and emotional factors that affect learning by no means implies that learning programs are of lesser importance. Learning is crucial for middle-school students and it behooves educators to give much thought to instructional processes.

In what context should students be educated? Should it be group-based, individualized, or a combination of group and individual approaches? Certainly it is axiomatic, given the diverse levels of achievement in transescence, that transitional schools should provide as much individual attention as possible. For example, as Dunn and Dunn have noted, the planning of instructional programs could take into account individual differences in learning styles:

Indeed many educators still believe that the stimulating teacher or relevant instructional topics, materials, or procedures will result in learning. While it is true that a dramatic teacher, an exciting presentation, or an assignment in the "real" world may enhance learning in a given instance or for an even longer period on occasion, how much more successful that teacher and those materials or assignments would be if individual learning styles are consciously used.[18]

As essential as individual attention is, it must be tempered with the awareness that transescence is an age in which groups are important. Therefore, any process that neglects group considerations runs the risk of being self-defeating. Group processes are emphasized in core programs and in much of the team teaching practiced in middle schools.

The School's Relationship with the Learner

There are two aspects of the relationship of the school with the learners that deserve particular attention here: the school environment and the educational program.

ENVIRONMENT

While it is clear that the character of the learning environment can aid or deter the learning process, there is also disagreement as

18. Rita Dunn and Kenneth Dunn, *Educator's Self-teaching Guide to Individualizing Instructional Programs* (West Nyack, N.Y.: Parker Publishing Co., 1975), p. 75.

to the nature of an appropriate environment. For example, Hudson expressed the view that progressive schools make most children happier than the authoritarian ones, but that they also "withdraw from children the cutting edge that insecurity, competition, and resentment supply. If we can adjust children to themselves and each other, we may remove from them the springs of their intellectual and artistic productivity." [19] Silberman, on the other hand, characterized most American schools as grim and joyless places that are governed by oppressive and petty rules, are conducted in an intellectually sterile and esthetically barren atmosphere by teachers and principals who unconsciously display contempt for children.[20]

An effective transitional school environment avoids both of these extremes as it reflects the student society it serves. The mercurial nature of the transescent requires a fluid but structured atmosphere. It should provide students with the security of structure, but it should be sufficiently elastic to permit students to explore learning and socialization in a manner consistent with individual needs. Since youth in the middle years are seeking greater independence, there should be provisions for activities that allow students to accept challenges and for help in meeting those challenges.

Friendliness is a needed element in the school climate. When a friendly relationship exists, the increased interaction between teachers, administrators, counselors, secretaries, and custodians enables students to develop needed competencies to meet successfully their emotional peaks and valleys. By his administrative approach, attitude, treatment of staff and students, and support of the instructional program, the principal exemplifies a model for human relations.

The learning climate should be active and dynamic. A variety of learning experiences should be provided. Experience is an indispensable element as transescents pursue their curiosity and grow intellectually. It is desirable to have a flexibility that permits students to avail themselves of learning activities at the time of

19. Liam Hudson, *Contrary Imaginations: A Psychological Study of the English Schoolboy* (Middlesex, England: Penguin Books, 1966), p. 134.

20. Charles E. Silberman, *Crisis in the Classroom* (New York: Random House, 1970), p. 10.

actual need rather than when the teacher perceives the need. Attention spans, shortened in a period of biological maturation and erratic emotional states, should be met by brief but substantive learning experiences.

An aura of learning should permeate the school. Students learn by example and a school that emphasizes learning is an effective school. This is not to suggest that other types of activities are unimportant, nor that the school climate should be a sterile one. Today's students are part of a media generation full of sound and excitement and the school climate should resonate with the "now" generation of present youth cultures.

THE EDUCATIONAL PROGRAM

There is no universally accepted prototype for an educational program for the transitional school. This situation is both a strength and a weakness. It allows educators to create a variety of approaches to learning, but it often results in confusion for those who have accepted the philosophic base for a program but who are mystified by the myriad of possible program alternatives. It seems apparent that a consensus on goals and major elements of the program must emerge if this level of schooling is to reach its potential.

Historically, instructional programs for the middle school have suffered a lack of cohesiveness. As Kindred has noted, curriculum experimentation in junior high schools "has tended at different times to focus on purpose, method, the substance of the curriculum, or organizational patterns separately rather than upon a design which sought to unite in one rationale all the essential elements of the curriculum."[21]

There appears to be some agreement regarding the dimensions of curricular organization. Alexander and associates suggest a curriculum design that includes "personal development, skills for continued learning, and organized knowledge."[22] Lounsbury and Vars propose a program involving "core, continuous progress,

21. Leslie W. Kindred, *The Intermediate School* (Englewood Cliffs, N.J.: Prentice-Hall, 1968), p. 108.

22. William M. Alexander et al., *The Emergent Middle School*, 2d ed. (New York: Holt, Rinehart and Winston, 1969).

and a variable component."[23] I have suggested elsewhere a design involving "learning processes, a knowledge component, and personal development."[24] While these models differ in degree and implementation, some common elements are discernible. In addition, each is solidly related to characteristics of the learners. The common elements merit close scrutiny.

Each model provides for acquiring essential learning skills in a sequential and individual manner. This aspect is in clear response to the diverse achievement levels, cognitive styles, and varied competencies that characterize learners at this stage. Implicit in each model is an emphasis on structure and sequential learning. There is a recognition that maturational and cultural concerns affect the pace of learning for individual students. None of the approaches suggests that students' programs should be rigidly individualized. They do, however, suggest self-pacing designs closely related to group involvement.

Another common element in the models deals with the interrelationships of knowledge. Emphasis is placed on common learnings without regard to the constraints of the various disciplines. There is a recognition that presenting skills and concepts in a practical problem-solving context will enhance learning. There is provision for "open-ended" curricula. Students are involved in learning in a peer relationship that aids socialization. This approach encourages divergent thinking at the learners' levels of cognition, yet does not expose students to abstract concepts beyond their levels of competence. Each model provides wide opportunities for students to explore content in and out of school walls.

A third dimension in each model is personal development. There are provisions for guidance and counseling through advisory programs, curriculum, and specialized help. Awareness and understanding of pubertal change and its implications for peer relationships are emphasized. Elective and activity programs permit students to explore their interests.

23. John H. Lounsbury and Gordon F. Vars, *A Curriculum for the Middle School Years* (New York: Harper and Row, 1978), p. 45.

24. Donald H. Eichhorn, "The Emerging Adolescent School of the Future —Now," in *The School of the Future—Now*, ed. J. Galen Saylor (Washington, D.C.: Association for Supervision and Curriculum Development, 1972), pp. 35-52.

These models point out the importance of multidimensional instructional programs. Despite much research on how learning occurs, there are still very few definitive conclusions. Much of what is proposed as fact is conjecture, resulting in trial and error approaches to teaching. Actually very little is known about styles of learning. It is widely assumed that mastery learning techniques will improve achievement in content subjects such as reading. But do they improve some of the skills and processes involved in reading at the expense of the total array of skills and processes required by the effective reader?

Presently, there is considerable research activity related to brain function. It is now well established that the left and right hemispheres of the brain perform quite different functions and in quite different ways.

Now both the left and right hemispheres of the brain have been found to have their own specialized forms of intellect. The left is highly verbal and mathematical, performing with analytic, symbolic, computerlike, sequential logic. The right, by contrast, is spatial and mute, performing with a synthetic spatio-perceptual and mechanical kind of information processing that cannot yet be simulated by computers.[25]

Furthermore, as noted by Samples, the right and left hemispheres can function autonomously.[26] Present educational practices emphasize the development of the capabilities of the left hemisphere, often to the exclusion of learning activities involving the right hemisphere. As Sperry has indicated:

A message that emerges from the findings on hemispheric specialization is that an educational system and modern society generally (with its very heavy emphasis on communication and on early training in the three Rs) discriminates against one whole half of the brain. I refer, of course, to the nonverbal, nonmathematical minor hemisphere, which, we find, has its own perceptual, mechanical, and spatial mode of apprehension and reasoning. In our present school system, the attention given to the minor hemisphere of the brain is minimal compared with the training lavished on the left, or major hemisphere.[27]

25. Roger Sperry, "Left Brain, Right Brain," *Saturday Review*, 9 August 1975, p. 31.
26. Robert Samples, *The Metaphoric Mind* (Reading, Mass.: Addison-Wesley Publishing Co., 1976), p. 87.

27. Sperry, "Left Brain, Right Brain," p. 33.

The research on brain function would appear to add yet another cogent reason for insisting on the use of an eclectic learning model for the education of transescents. The current "back to basics" and "competency standard" programs, while important for left-hemispheric development, have little to offer for comprehensive development of the brain. Until more definite knowledge is available, it would seem that a balanced learning model should be preserved.

Effective Implementation of Programs

Effective implementation of programs in the transitional school requires successful interpersonal relationships. While undergoing the marked personal changes we have noted, the transescents become inconsistent in their relations with peers and adults. Their relations with others become increasingly more fragile. The adult-child relationship is now replaced by an adult-transescent relationship that is a considerably more complex involvement.

Transescents are essentially happy, friendly, affectionate human beings who desire to relate to adults and peers. With maturation occurring, however, they find it difficult to maintain an even nature consistently and they often react emotionally in a variety of ways to everyday situations. Adults find their emotional outbursts difficult to understand. Under such circumstances, the real test of middle-school teachers, as Lounsbury and Vars point out, is their ability "to maintain their own integrity, to strive continuously for wholesome relations with associates of all ages, and not to take personally the testing, confrontation, and rejection directed at them by transescents as a natural, normal, and indeed necessary part of their growing up." [28]

Effort has been made during the past two decades to implement change in transitional schools. Much of this work has involved innovative ideas and practices. In these attempts to change, considerable emphasis has been placed on theory, organizational patterns, curriculum content, and instructional materials. Certainly, successful change involves all of these, but the catalyst for effective innovative change appears to be the effectiveness of the

28. Lounsbury and Vars, *A Curriculum for the Middle School Years*, p. 6.

interpersonal relations of teachers. Fullan and Pomfret believe that difficulties arise in attempts to implement curricular innovations chiefly because curricular change usually necessitates certain organizational changes, particularly changes in the roles and role relationships of those organizational members most directly involved in putting the innovation into practice.[29]

The interpersonal relations of teachers are crucial to successful implementation of programs, as is the manner in which teachers relate to students and other adults. Sweeney has summarized the qualities he believes to be important for adult models for the emerging adolescent learner.

The effective adult will be a person who sincerely values and cares about other people. He will be a good listener, a person who can understand both the verbal and nonverbal communication of the other person. In addition to being a good listener, he is able to communicate that he has understood. This person could be described as open to new or different ideas while still possessing a philosophy of life that guides his behavior without imposing it on others. He is a trustworthy person, one who is aware that others may not be trustworthy at times, but who is willing to be mistaken until proven otherwise. He has a capacity for helping other persons to honestly confront matters of relevance to them which are otherwise too threatening or anxiety producing for them to cope with rationally.[30]

A response to the need for change in roles and role relationships is the team teaching organization found in reorganized transitional schools. While this method of school organization has much potential, the inadequacy of teachers' understanding of the roles embodied in this approach often renders it less effective than its potential suggests. Team teaching provides an excellent organizational structure for coping with a variety of student needs. The insecurity of transcescents can be effectively helped by a coalition of teachers. The arrangement is ideal for providing guidance through

29. Michael Fullan and Allan Pomfret, "Review of Curriculum and Instructional Implementation," *Review of Educational Research* 47 (Spring 1977): 337.

30. Thomas J. Sweeney, "Adult Models for the Emerging Adolescent" (Paper prepared for the Council on the Emerging Adolescent Learner of the Association for Supervision and Curriculum Development, Washington, D.C., 1971).

instruction and continuous pupil-teacher contact and for strengthening the curriculum by the correlation of instructional processes and content made possible by the concerted effort of faculty members from the different disciplines, the arts, and physical education.

Concluding Statement

The transitional school has been a dynamic movement in American education. From its early beginning, it has been, in many respects, an innovation. The idea of a transitional school has had its proponents and detractors. Yet throughout a turbulent existence, it has remained a worthy and viable concept. Unlike the elementary and secondary education phases of schooling, the transitional school has not developed a set role in the total scheme of school organization. Rather, it continues to be a catalyst serving a unique group of students. By analyzing the character of this unique institution and the nature of the learners it serves, educators can assure its ultimate effectiveness. The groundwork for a successful school program has been developed over the decades. It is now clearly the responsibility of educators to capitalize on this foundation and develop programs that will insure effective realization of the great potential of the transitional school.

CHAPTER V

The Mass Media and Popular Culture

H. GORDON STEVENSON

A singular characteristic of life in the United States today is the extent to which people of all ages have access to systems of communication that deliver massive quantities of information. At least this is the case if we define information as any set of meaningful symbols or symbolic actions. The symbols are objects as diverse as the flag, Barbie Dolls, printed words, and the clothes we wear. They are also people who are real or imaginary. Heroes and martyrs, television stars, and comic strip characters all have symbolic significance. Transescents live in a world of symbols.

A World of Symbols

Symbolic actions include group activities, such as half-time shows at athletic events, religious services, and protest marches. Some obvious examples of individual symbolic actions are such activities as saluting the flag, genuflecting, and shaking hands. If one accepts sociological theories of role playing and takes a dramaturgical view of social life, other individual actions may be analyzed symbolically: feigning innocence, showing righteous indignation, and other ploys and put-ons.[1] Transescents are, among other things, learning to "act," which may be thought of as the symbolic use of the self. They rehearse and perform, trying out different roles in front of different audiences.[2]

1. A classic work based on the dramaturgical perspective is Erving Goffman, *The Presentation of Self in Everday Life* (Garden City, N.Y.: Doubleday, 1959). See also *Drama in Life*, ed. James E. Combs and Michael W. Mansfield (New York: Hastings House, 1976).

2. Comments on the numerous and complex "stages" on which transescents must act and their relationship to behavior are found in Roger C. Barker, *Ecological Psychology* (Stanford, Calif.: Stanford University Press, 1968).

Symbols and symbolic actions may be experienced as real events with real people, or they may be experienced as fantasy, as when one watches television or reads a novel. It is widely held that the diffusion of such symbols through the mass media has caused many social and psychological malfunctions. This may or may not be true, but there is no question that changes in the technologies of communication result in cultural changes. A new medium of communication provides a new way of perceiving reality. It follows that the media shape, to some extent, our perceptions of social reality. Meyer, who defines social reality by the concept "cultural ideology," put it nicely as "the unconscious premises, the basic categories, which channel and direct our perceptions, our responses, our cognitions—in short, our understanding of ourselves and the world." [3]

The transescent is very much involved in constructing both an identity and a social reality to which that identity can be related. Sometimes the processes by which this is done are so trivial and banal that we fail to see what is going on. For example, a good case has been made for the idea that the ubiquitous Barbie Doll presents the child with a new version of the American Dream, a version that could alter "basic attitudes toward sex, marriage, or a career."[4] And the popular musical culture of transescent girls may serve as a transition from dolls to boys—sort of a rite of passage.[5]

Thus, the most basic sets of meanings are imbedded in everyday activities that would seem to have little to do with the larger course of events. In the realm of action, for example, a football game may properly be identified as an athletic event, but of course it is much more than that.

A football game is a dramatic event for those who watch. It is rich in symbols, with its cheerleaders, marching bands, and, as often as not, prayers and the national anthem. For those who

3. Leonard B. Meyer, *Music, the Arts, and Ideas* (Chicago: University of Chicago Press, 1967), p. 129.

4. Don R. Cox, "Barbie and Her Playmates," *Journal of Popular Culture* 11 (Fall 1977): 307.

5. R. Serge Denisoff, *Solid Gold: The Popular Record Industry* (New Brunswick, N.J.: Transaction Books, 1975), p. 427.

participate, it is a public test of skill and strength; it is identity, selfhood, loyalty, teamwork, and pride. Whether they win or lose, it is a place where boys become men, or so we like to believe, and girls learn to sit on the sidelines and watch. It is a learning experience for everyone involved and its cultural functions have something important to do with values that many American parents hold dear. It is not surprising that these values are celebrated nationally in televised rituals that bring together symbols of God, country, and, more recently, sex, in the arena of competitive physical contact. According to Cady, the football game is a form of popular art.[6]

In the case of mechanical systems of communication, it is quite clear that such objects as cookbooks, history textbooks, and news broadcasts contain information. But so, too, do horror movies, the superhero comic books, the words and pictures printed on boxes of breakfast cereals, advertisements of all types, recordings of rock music, celebrity magazines, harlequin romances, and television broadcasts as diverse as quiz shows, situation comedies, and soap operas. If we were to assume that the aesthetic value of all such artifacts is negligible or spurious, then we would have to account for their existence exclusively in terms of their psychological or sociocultural functions. On the other hand, Gowans argues that some of these forms of communication are the only significant art of our times,[7] and Arnstine has suggested, in all seriousness, that television advertisements may one day be recognized as "the most characteristic art form in America in the twentieth century."[8]

Whether they do indeed have anything to do with art depends on our definition of art, but it is not debatable that transescents spend enormous amounts of time attending to these artifacts and experiences. In their complex totality, they are the physical evi-

6. Edwin H. Cady, *The Big Game: College Sports in American Life* (Knoxville, Tenn.: University of Tennessee Press, 1978), pp. 75-119.

7. Alan Gowans, *The Unchanging Arts* (Philadelphia: J. B. Lippincott, 1971).

8. Donald Arnstine, "Learning, Aesthetics, and Schooling: The Popular Arts as Textbook on America," *Educational Theory* 27 (Fall 1977): 266, footnote 10.

dence of the nature of our society, its hopes and dreams, its past and its future, its anomalies and contradictions.

MASS MEDIA AS CULTURE

By and large, traditional systems of classifying information are not very helpful in conceptualizing this media environment, and the whole milieu is such that it is best subsumed under the term "popular culture." As Nye has pointed out, "popular culture represents the greatest single *shared* experience of society (other than home and church), the broadest common experience in which an individual participates."[9] Phelan, McLuhan, and others believe that this milieu not only creates public opinion, but also influences our cognitive styles—the way we think about the world as well as what we think. Phelan believes that the artifacts and experiences of popular culture are the means "through which the vast majority of Americans develop most of their sensibilities and through which every American, without exception, acquires some of his sensibilities."[10] Thus, the mass media, rather than the traditional cultural institutions, are now the primary source of commonly accepted values and beliefs.

Arnstine got to the nub of the matter when he wrote that popular culture is a "textbook on America."[11] Who compiles and edits this textbook? Schiller is convinced, as are many others, that control lies with the managers of the mass media, "who create, process, refine, and preside over the circulation of images and information which determine our beliefs and attitudes and, ultimately, our behavior."[12] But to attribute such enormous powers to the media is to ignore the essential role of interpersonal communications in sustaining social systems and in mediating the impact of the mechanical media. It is clear that to understand the

9. Russel Nye, "Popular Culture as a Genre," in *Popular Culture and the Library*, Current Issues Symposium II (Lexington, Ky. College of Library Science, University of Kentucky, 1977), p. 7.

10. John N. Phelan, *Mediaworld: Programming the Public* (New York: Continuum Books, Seabury Press, 1977), p. 7.

11. Arnstine, "Learning, Aesthetics, and Schooling," p. 261.

12. Herbert I. Schiller, *The Mind Managers* (Boston: Beacon Press, 1973), p. 1.

impact of the media we have to take into account the individual as a complex and developing psychological organism that is constantly interacting with both human and mechanical information systems.

THE TRANSESCENT AND THE MEDIA

The transescent's use of this textbook on America has the manifest function of entertainment, and its perusal is a self-selected, leisure-time activity similar to play. The latent functions are certainly not the same for all people all of the time, but seem to include education, a release from pressures of family and school, socialization, and acculturation. In terms of any purposeful social or educational goals, the bulk of the content delivered through this system and the access to it are arbitrary. The transescent selects from what is at hand. What is at hand is largely determined by forces beyond the direct control of transescents, their parents, and their teachers, for virtually all of the mass media are production and distribution systems that are capital-intensive. Culture, in other words, is business, and transescents constitute a potential market. The size of this market is around nineteen million people between the ages of ten and fourteen—all of whom must be clothed, fed, and entertained. The aim of the entrepreneurs serving this potential market is to control the economic environment. This means that, in many cases, they must bypass the influence of parents and teachers.

Characteristics of Channels

The symbolic world of transescents is defined by two factors: (a) the channels to which they have access and (b) the content of those channels.

ACCESS

By the age of twelve, children are on the verge of having almost complete physical access to the full range of communications systems available in the communities in which they live. One suspects that if they have the money, there is little that transescents cannot get if they want it badly enough. Thus, physical access is largely limited—and these may be serious limitations—by what is stocked in neighborhood commercial outlets, the quality of library collections and services, and what is available in the home.

Intellectual access, however, is something else. Limitation in reading ability is the greatest barrier to the largest source of information. Such is not the case with the electronic media. One can listen to a sound recording without "understanding" anything. In the case of television, if one watches, one sees something even though thinking in the ordinary meaning of the word does not necessarily take place.

Each medium has its own unique commercial structure that affects its potential accessibility. The technology for the production of printed words and pictures and sound recordings is such that these media are amenable to serving the interests of relatively small audiences. The audience of from fifteen to twenty million viewers needed to sustain a prime-time television show is in sharp contrast to the audience of from three to four thousand readers, which can make the manufacture of a paperback book economically feasible. Magazines for nonspecialists require somewhat larger audiences, but not so large as to discourage the publication of several dozen titles for transescents.

This sort of economic system could be, but is not, associated with the sound-recording industry. The star system dominates record sales and distribution patterns. Because of merchandising policies, a sound recording produced by a major company must sell fifty to a hundred thousand copies in order to cover production and advertising costs. The result is that young people have easy access to those songs broadcast over top-forty radio stations, but access to the vast repertory of the world's music produced by around 800 record manufacturers in the United States is difficult or impossible for most transescents. These materials are distributed through channels that serve special interests not served by systems of mass marketing. In any case, the preferred sound package of the transescent is the 45-rpm disc recording. In fact, if it were not for the transescent audience, this type of disc would probably not be manufactured. One of the special attractions of sound recordings (as is the case with books) is that they can be used at virtually any time and place of the listener's choice.

CONTENT

It has been estimated that around 85 percent of the television watched by children is "adult" programming, which is to say that it consists of material not specifically designed for children. For all practical purposes, there is no programming for transescents. This is because the content of television is determined by the purpose of television. The purpose of television is to assemble an audience that, it is assumed, will watch television commercials. Since adults make most family purchasing decisions, the programs must attract adults.

Despite the importance of media managers in making decisions about what is to be broadcast, the material must first be written and produced. Stein's recent study of television content includes evidence that the bulk of prime-time comedy, adventure, and drama is created by several hundred Los Angeles writers. The image of America that they perpetuate, Stein believes, is one in harmony with their subjective images, which are remarkably circumscribed and even distorted. For example, "one of the clearest messages of television is that businessmen are bad, evil people, and that big businessmen are the worst of all."[13] This is one of the messages delivered to transescents as they abandon cartoon shows for prime-time television.

The magazine industry has responded to the specific interests of adolescents for many years with periodicals such as *Seventeen* and *Hit Parader*. We are now seeing a trend to reach younger adolescents, with periodicals such as *Sixteen, Fifteen*, and *Fourteen*. Most of these, and others (such as the very popular *Tiger Beat* and *Circus*) are closely related to the teen idols of the music industry. Their contents are hardly ever related to what an adult would think of as the real world. They deal with hopes, dreams, and fantasies. They appeal mostly to transescent girls. Boys are more likely to prefer the more raucous *Creem, Crawdaddy*, and even *Rolling Stone*. In their homes and in libraries, however, transescents use an astonishingly large number of adult periodicals.

13. Ben Stein, *The View from Sunset Boulevard: America as Brought to You by the People Who Make Television* (New York: Basic Books, 1979), p. 15.

It has been reported that some nine-year-olds read *Playboy*.[14] The zany world of *Mad* magazine is especially attractive to transescent boys. At this age, many of them are beginning to abandon comic books, and they like the *Mad* style of journalism with its hodge-podge of short comic strips, cartoons, short articles, jokes, and games. Some of this material is bizarre, cynical, and satirically critical of adult culture. Another recent example is Marvel Comic's new periodical, *Pizzazz*.

More so than any other medium, sound recordings have become the special province of the young adolescent. The artists performing on the records they purchase are those whose exploits, real and imagined, provide the bulk of the copy for the teen magazines, and their bright, smiling faces are everywhere. The central theme of this music is romantic love. One writer recently characterized this genre as "pube" rock (pubescent rock), and noted that when these artists perform at public concerts, the audiences include not only transescent girls, but also their mothers. The music is a throwback to themes produced originally fifteen to twenty years ago when the parents were in their teens.[15] Transescent boys do not admit to listening to this music.

In sharp contrast to pube rock is punk rock. If the images of pube rock are, for the most part, socially acceptable, those of punk rock, which is antisocial, gross, and bizarre, are not. The current supergroup in this genre is the group called "Kiss." Kiss is a complex phenomenon that seems to have its origins in the sick, maniacal concerts of Alice Cooper.[16] Their appeal to transescent boys is enormous. Wearing Kabuki-like costumes and masks, they perform outlandish acts in their public performances.

14. In an unpublished paper prepared for a course in popular culture at the State University of New York at Albany, J. Ells reported on her survey (made in the fall of 1978) of the magazine reading habits of 249 students in grades three through five in an upstate New York elementary school. The total number of different magazines mentioned by all of the students came to 117. *Playboy* was read by twenty-three students. The most widely read magazine was *Hot Rod* (ninety-nine students). Somewhat similar results emerged from a study in a suburban junior high school in 1970. In this study, *Playboy* was ninth on a list of the fifty-one most widely read magazines. See Nancy Jacobson, "The Junior High Years: A Profile" (1974). ED 101 665.

15. Rick Cohen, "Pube Rock: Kiddie Music is Big Business," *New York* 11, no. 47 (20 November 1978): pp. 67-77.

16. Bob Green, *Billion Dollar Baby* (New York: Atheneum, 1974).

Whereas the lyrics of pube rock deal with romantic love and have only overtones of sexuality, punk rock deals with sex and other topics normally thought taboo for any but adults. This trend was noticed by Peterson and Berger some five years ago when they examined top-forty songs. They found "songs about sexual intercourse, homosexuality, interracial dating, drugs, filicide, abortion, and the folly of being a war hero."[17] Dowling sees Kiss as being outside the pale of respectability with songs about hookers, boozing, and sexual acts.[18]

However, the aberrant aspects of popular music claim our attention much too much, for in fact there are many other themes presented to transescent and adolescent audiences in the approximately 5,000 songs issued each year. The selective and subjective perception of adults who hear this music filter out its diversity and much of its meaning. Transescents conform to group norms by identifying with current rock music, but show individuality by having their favorite performers. At any given time, there are as many as 150 performers whose names are currently known in the transescent and adolescent subcultures. The lyrical content of the songs is much more varied than the casual listener would expect. Cooper has shown how popular songs present, among other things, images of American society, social change, religion, and the future.[19]

During the past decade, we have seen changes in the reading material available to transescents. These changes are tied to larger media trends. Note the popularity of books based on the more spectacular movies. For example, "Star Wars" spins off into paperback books, comic books, teen journalism, a television series, toys, and soundtrack recordings. Science fiction, which until recently was read largely by college students, is extremely popular with

17. Richard A. Peterson and David G. Berger, "Cycles in Symbol Production: The Case of Popular Music," *American Sociological Review* 40 (April 1975): 169.

18. Colette Dowling, "An Outrage Called Kiss," *New York Times Magazine*, 19 June 1977, pp. 18, 66-71.

19. B. Lee Cooper, "Examining Social Change through Contemporary History: An Audio Media Proposal," *History Teacher* 6 (August 1973): 523-34; ibid., "The Image of American Society in Popular Music: A Search for Identity and Values," *Social Studies* 66 (December 1973): 319-21.

transescents. And we now have novels that deal realistically (too realistically for many parents) with the physical, emotional, and sexual problems of early adolescence. Six million copies of books by Judy Blume are in print because she writes about things that trouble pubescent girls.[20] Such topics have not heretofore been dealt with in adolescent or transescent literature, and there is no way they could be dealt with on television. For transescents who use them, books, sound recordings, and magazines seem to serve needs that are not met by other media.

The Effects of Media Use

One of the central problems of mass media research is to find out how the images delivered by the media are transformed into personal and social knowledge: How do people interact with media? How does this interaction change people? How are these mechanical stimuli internalized? What does it all have to do with the cognitive and affective development of transescents?

RESEARCH PROBLEMS

In exploring the recent research literature, two problems emerge. In the first instance, age-specific research generally deals with discrete categories of children, adolescents, and adults. Data relevant to a consideration of transescents are often averaged out and lost in the larger categories. The second problem is the great extent to which television has dominated mass communications research as the major communications variable. The type of research recently proposed by Adler indicates the serious shortcomings that now exist in this research. He wrote that we need research "to determine, for the first time, the importance of television as an influence on children—in comparison with other major socializing factors, such as parents, relatives, peers, school, church, and other media."[21]

20. Joyce Maynard, "Coming of the Age with Judy Blume," *New York Times Magazine*, 3 December 1978, pp. 80-94.

21. *Research on the Effects of Television Advertising on Children: A Review of the Literature and Recommendations for Future Research*, Report prepared for the National Science Foundation, Richard P. Adler, principal investigator (Washington, D.C.: U.S. Government Printing Office, 1977), p. 152.

PRESUMED DYSFUNCTIONS

Popular myths about the effects of various media, although supported by little if any empirical evidence, continue to have considerable credibility with the general public. The atmosphere today is only slightly more enlightened than it was thirty years ago, when unwarranted assumptions about the causes of juvenile crime led to a wave of censorship. It was assumed that there was a direct causal relationship between sex and violence in comic books and sex and violence among young people. Thus, the Code of the Comics Magazine Association was created by the comics industry as a self-regulating standard. This Code, like the code governing commercial films, assumed that large segments of the public were "highly susceptible to corruption of morals" and that the medium was "capable of suspending the readers' critical faculties."[22]

While many parents continue to place much emphasis on the need for governmental controls because of these presumed dysfunctional effects, researchers are becoming ever more cautious in their statements about cause and effect relationships. Today, one seldom hears such statements as "All mass media in the end alienate people from personal experience and . . . intensify their moral isolation from each other, from reality, and from themselves,"[23] or that the heavy consumption of sensational periodicals is "likely to help render its consumers less capable of responding openly and responsibly to life" and "is likely to induce an underlying sense of purposelessness in existence outside the limited range of a few immediate appetites."[24]

THE EFFECTS OF TELEVISION

The most recent summary of what is known about the effects of television on human behavior illustrates the problems of re-

22. William L. Rivers and Wilbur Schramm, *Responsibility in Mass Communication*, rev. ed. (New York: Harper and Row, 1969), p. 217.

23. Ernest van den Haag, "Of Happiness and Despair We Have No Measure," in *Mass Media and Mass Man*, ed. Alan Casty (New York: Holt, Rinehart and Winston, 1968), p. 5.

24. Richard Hoggart, *The Uses of Literacy* (London: Chatto and Winston, 1957), p. 202.

search in effects generally. This massive volume is largely a guide
to probable effects and unanswered questions. Even in the case
of violence, the most studied aspect of television, few definitive
conclusions have been reached. For example, we read: "Television
viewing itself *appears* to be unrelated to either aggression or
antisocial behavior. The viewing of television violence *appears* to
increase the likelihood of subsequent aggressiveness."[25] Here are
other limited propositions: "Commercials *appear* to inspire appeals to parents to purchase products."[26] "Television is *probably* an
important factor in the image and expectations young persons hold
in regard to politics and government."[27] "Television should *probably* be considered a major agent of socialization."[28] One of the
more definitive statements in the report is not much comfort:
"Any medium and any content may serve for a given individual
almost any purpose and may provide almost any conceivable
gratification."[29]

Uses and Gratifications

We turn now to a discussion of the uses of television and the
gratifications received from using that medium.[30]

MOTIVATIONS TO ATTEND TO THE MEDIA

If we consider information from the point of view of its uses,
we can identify three categories: (a) information sought for the
purpose of making decisions, (b) information sought for its intrinsic value, and (c) information sought for use in social inter-

25. George A. Comstock et al., *Television and Human Behavior* (New
York: Columbia University Press, 1978), p. 13 (emphasis added).

26. Ibid., p. 12 (emphasis added).

27. Ibid., p. 13.

28. Ibid., p. 14 (emphasis added).

29. Ibid., p. 11.

30. For a recent review of the state and prospects of uses and gratifications research, see *The Uses of Mass Communications*, ed. Jay G. Blumler
and Elihu Katz, Sage Annual Reviews of Communication Research, vol. 3
(Beverly Hills, Calif.: Sage Publications, 1974).

actions.[31] The use of the media may be content-specific or media-specific. For example, the novels of Judy Blume are probably read as content-specific sources; if the information could be found elsewhere, these other sources would be used. Television, for many people, offers a type of relaxation that cannot be replaced by another medium. For these people, this is a media-specific source.[32]

When children and adolescents are asked why they watch television, they place varying degrees of emphasis on these reasons: (a) to learn about things and oneself; (b) to pass time, because it is a habit; (c) for companionship; (d) to forget or escape; (e) for arousal or excitement; and (f) for relaxation.[33] Rubin found that across the age groups of nine, thirteen, and seventeen there is a "motivation to watch for the sake of filling time rather than to fulfill personal information-seeking social needs." [34] Also, as the child moves into transescence, each of the six reasons decreases in importance. This is consistent with the ample evidence that the peak years for television viewing coincide with the end of childhood and begin to decline between the ages of ten and thirteen. Part of this change in media use can be related to the rising interest in music.

What is the special attraction of music? There are a number of needs, some very personal and some social, that seem to be met by music. When they are lonely, many transescents turn to it:

> While television was still an important relief from loneliness for the tenth graders, it had fallen behind music. One of the most signif-

31. The second category is based on Downs's categories, in which "all such information procured solely for the edification it provides we call *entertainment information*, no matter how serious its content." A distinction is not made between high culture and popular culture. See Anthony Downs, *An Economic Theory of Democracy* (New York: Harper and Row, 1975), p. 215.

32. One study of the functions of different media concluded that "television does not displace books," because "some of the functions they serve, although limited, are still salient to children." See J. R. Brown, J. K. Cramond, and R. J. Wilde, "Displacement Effects of Television and the Child's Functional Orientation to Media," in *The Uses of Mass Communications*, ed. Blumler and Katz, p. 105.

33. Alan M. Rubin, "Television Usage, Attitudes and Viewing Behavior of Children and Adolescents," *Journal of Broadcasting* 21 (Summer 1977): 358-60.

34. Ibid., p. 367.

icant points . . . is the testimony of the overwhelming importance of music in the life of teenagers. Listening to music outscored television even for entertainment and had an overwhelming lead for relaxation and a relief from loneliness. Music had become important for these purposes for the sixth graders—particularly the girls, but among tenth graders it reigned supreme. The sole exception was that talking to somebody rated slightly higher among older girls.[35]

Other studies have shown that some people use music as a respite from anxiety and tension.[36] How this works, we do not know. More than likely it is a neurophysiological function and music provides an altered state of consciousness. The same may be true of some television watching that takes place regardless of what is being broadcast. Television may provide a release from tension, but at the same time the transescent's views of morality, concepts of sex roles, and political beliefs may be challenged or reinforced.

The motivation to read has decreased as print has lost its former autonomy as the major information source serving a large range of uses. The most recent surveys do not provide unequivocal evidence, but it is generally accepted that during the past two decades there has been a long-range decline across generational lines in the amount of time spent reading. Lyle and Hoffman found that the amount of time spent in reading begins to drop off in the sixth grade and this decline continues through the tenth grade.[37] Jacobson's study, however, showed an increase in reading as the transescent moved through grades seven through nine.[38] The amount of time spent in reading shows many more variations across socioeconomic, class, and intelligence variables than does the use of television and sound recordings.

35. Jack Lyle and Heidi R. Hoffman, "Children's Use of Television and Other Media," in Television and Social Behavior, vol. 4, Television in Day-to-Day Life: Patterns of Use, ed. Eli A. Rubinstein, George A. Comstock, and John P. Murray (Washington, D.C.: U.S. Department of Health, Education, and Welfare, 1972), p. 185.

36. Peter O. Peretti, "Changes in Galvanic Skin Response as Affected by Musical Selection, Sex, and Academic Discipline," Journal of Psychology 89 (March 1975): 183-87.

37. Lyle and Hoffman, "Children's Use of Television and Other Media," p. 158.

38. Jacobson, "The Junior High Years: A Profile."

INTERPERSONAL FUNCTIONS

Changes in the use of media have been related to social-psychological maturation. "When significant others change," Johnstone writes, "patterns of mass media exposure are also likely to change so they fit better within the milieu in which one interacts with significant others." [39] The significant others in the lives of transescents, more often than not, do not present a favorable image of reading. If the stars of television and the teen-age music idols have anything more than the most basic functional literacy, it is never apparent in their public activities. Reading does not appear to offer a big payoff in the construction of images, roles, or high status in peer groups. Gentile and McMillan say that "reading may be considered an 'antisocial' activity," and may even be rejected because it is associated with the world of adults. [40] Landy found that "students of either sex who read when they don't have to are apt to be regarded as rather peculiar individuals." [41] She concluded that "in the final analysis, each individual [in her research population] presents his own unique and dynamic pattern in reading which remains ostensibly unknown to the researcher." [42]

It seems a reasonable premise that what the transescent professes to like and dislike becomes a symbol of the self. More than likely, it is the symbol rather than the substance of the symbol that becomes important. Many transescents, for example, seem to be incapable of judging music in any other terms than group norms. [43] Be that as it may, participation in popular culture permits the transescent to become part of a group, and the use of the media

39. John W. C. Johnstone, "Social Integration and Mass Media Use among Adolescents: A Case Study," in *The Uses of Mass Communication*, ed. Blumler and Katz, p. 39.

40. Lance M. Gentile and Merna M. McMillan, "Why Won't Teenagers Read?" *Journal of Reading* 20 (May 1977): 652.

41. Sarah Landy, "An Investigation of the Relationship between Voluntary Reading and Certain Psychological, Environmental, and Socioeconomic Factors in Early Adolescence" (1977), p. 13. ED 145 409.

42. Ibid., p. ii.

43. Why transescents dislike certain types of music has not been the subject of research. It is the author's contention that the sounds of the music as such are only marginally related to transescent musical tastes and preferences.

is related to the extent that the transescent is integrated into a group.

In studying how popular periodicals are used to seek information about music, Clarke found that the type of music a child admits to liking provides others with information about that child.[44] He concluded that those who are the heaviest users of this medium constitute an information elite, and are so recognized by their peers. The concept of an information elite has been used in the study of adult systems of communication and has been related to the concept of a "two-step" flow of information, which assumes that certain key individuals draw ideas from the media that they pass on to others who have not used the media sources.

SOCIALIZATION

General functions. It is assumed, and probably rightly, that the mass medium that has the greatest impact on socialization is television. This socialization is not only direct but also indirect through the impact of television and other media on the family and other social institutions. For example, how does one learn to be a parent? Lipsitz writes that "parenting education is by and large left to the mass media, and in particular is shaped by the stereotypes and distortions on television." [45]

Socialization is clearly a latent function of television. For example, its manifest purpose is not to display a variety of social and occupational roles to the transescent audience, but it does do this. Noble takes a positive attitude towards this socialization function, arguing that the individual has become increasingly isolated as a result of urbanization and industrialization. In nonindustrial societies, role models are learned within the network of kinship relationships. This is not possible in highly complex societies. Thus, Noble writes, "television's important function is to show viewers how to behave in a variety of different situations . . . [because] not all the social roles to be occupied in the future are clearly

44. Peter Clarke, "Teenagers' Coorientation and Information-seeking about Pop Music," *American Behavioral Scientist* 16 (April 1973): 553.

45. Joan Lipsitz, *Growing Up Forgotten: A Review of Research and Programs Concerning Early Adolescence*, A Report to the Ford Foundation (Lexington, Mass.: Lexington Books, 1977), p. 171.

visible in the real-life family group." [46] But these role models are seen and interpreted by individual transescents, each of whom has a very personal point of view that is conditioned by social and psychological variables.

Personal filtering systems. Communications research has shown that meaning is as much in the individual as it is in the content of a message. The same content does not necessarily mean the same thing to each member of an audience. Little research has been directed to finding out why this is so. However, research models that should supply information on the impact of psychological filters are available in empirical studies of individual responses to literature.[47] When we are told that readers of a short story relate that story to their personal experiences by reenacting it in such a way as to fit it into personal characteristics, it is reasonable to entertain the possibility that transescents also use television and perhaps even sound recordings the same way. In the case of literature, Farrell points out the educational implications of this research when he writes that literature is "a form of role playing, or dramatic enactment, which enlarges the universe of choices, of possible selves, available to . . . the person who empathically responds." [48] But most transescent responses outside of school hours are unguided, and thus responses to any medium—one would assume—could be equally capable of supporting dysfunctional and self-destructive roles, and circumscribe the universe of choices and possible selves.

Media and cognitive development. Ordinarily, we would assume that people of any age do not attend to messages they do not understand. In the case of the printed word, this seems to be unassailable, but this is not the case with other media. A young child may watch television commercials, but it is by no means clear what the child understands during and after this experience. For

46. Grant Noble, *Children in Front of the Small Screen* (London: Constable, 1975; Beverly Hills, Calif.: Sage Publications, 1975), p. 218.

47. Charles R. Cooper, "Empirical Studies of Responses to Literature: Review and Suggestions," *Journal of Aesthetic Education* 10 (July 1976): 88.

48. Edmund J. Farrell, "Literature for a Time of Change," in *English for the Junior High Years*, ed. Stephen Dunning (Champaign, Ill.: National Council of Teachers of English, 1969), p. 126.

this reason, it is unfortunate that considerations of media use in terms of cognitive development have only recently been undertaken.[49]

In studying the information-processing skills of second and eighth graders as they deal with social information delivered by television, Collins and Westby found that young children "make alarmingly little sense" of what is seen. Fragments of scenes and discrete bits of behavior are retained, but few causal connections are recognized. All but a few of the eighth graders "appeared to be organizing, integrating, and actually inferring relationship." [50] As more sophisticated cognitive structures develop, the child places less credibility in the social reality of what is seen on the screen. Rubin found this growing skepticism begins as early as the sixth grade and continues through the tenth grade.[51] Obviously, in many cases the opportunity to test the media's reality within the framework of the child's social environment is frequently circumscribed. In the case of advertising, this is less likely to be the case.

Apparently there is a developmental process in consumer-advertising socialization. One study found that children between the ages of seven and nine are frustrated in their attempts to integrate advertising into their lives. Frustration and contradictions lead to cynicism, so the ten-year-olds resolve ambiguity by deciding that all advertising is deceptive. Finally, the eleven- and twelve-year-old is able to temper this completely negative view by recognizing both good and bad features of advertisements. On rather scant empirical data the researchers involved in this study concluded that advertising is socially dysfunctional and leads to increased tolerance of social hypocrisy.[52]

49. The most recent studies of the relationship between the media and the development of thought, speech, and understanding may be found in *Children Communicating*, ed. Ellen Wartella, Sage Annual Reviews of Communication Research, vol. 6 (Beverly Hills, Calif.: Sage Publications 1979).

50. W. Andrew Collins and Sally D. Westby, "Children's Processing of Social Information from Televised Dramatic Programs" (1975), p. 5. ED 113 024.

51. Rubin, "Television Usage, Attitudes and Viewing Behavior of Children and Adolescents," p. 356.

52. T. G. Bever et al., "Young Viewers' Troubling Response to TV Ads," *Harvard Business Review* 53 (November-December 1975): 119-21.

If one accepts Piagetian theories of cognitive development, then the transition from concrete to formal operations around the ages of eleven or twelve surely must be accompanied by a crucial change in the transescent's potential ability to make moral judgments about media content. As Wackman and Wartella wrote, transescents "can transcend the here and now to think abstractly about ideas." [53]

Conclusion

Transescents need guidance in their use of media. Those who have the responsibility for providing that guidance must understand the age group, but they must also understand the place of the media in the economic system.

A CONSUMER MARKET

Media directed to transescents are part of the economic system and are designed to deliver consumer products at a price or to assemble an audience for the purpose of advertising products. The purpose of advertising is to change or direct behavior. Two aspects of this system have implications for formal public education. First, the fundamental principles of the democratic ideology insist on a free market in both manufactured products and ideas. It is not likely that federal laws will regulate television content except in the case of gross violations of decency and false advertising. The second aspect of the system is best understood in terms of cultural externalities. The transaction or interface between the transescent television viewer and the advertisement is intended to sell a product. But to do this, the advertiser must supply images of human life. These images are presented within the framework of social settings and cultural institutions that, however distorted they may be, have their counterparts in real life. For almost everyone involved in the production of the mass media, the transescent is nothing more than a potential consumer. Thus, at a time of great curiosity, uncertainty, and intellectual growth, transescents are left largely

53. Daniel B. Wackman and Ellen Wartella, "A Review of Cognitive Development Theory and Research and the Implication for Research on Children's Responses to Television," *Communication Research* 4 (April 1977): p. 217.

to their own resources in dealing with a symbolic world that they have neither the ability nor the inclination to deal with rationally.

THE SCHOOL AND THE MEDIA

Parents and teachers have the joint responsibility of guiding transescents in the use of media. But as is the case in many other areas of education, a heavy burden falls upon the teacher. For the most part, parents limit their guidance to attempts to control the amount of time spent with the media and the choice of programs, books, sound recordings, and periodicals. Parents are not likely to analyze the more subtle implications of content based on stereotypes of various classes of people and social institutions; they are not likely to understand the extent to which advertisers exploit human needs; nor are they likely to supply the sort of in-depth background necessary to place television news in a critical perspective.

Educators can provide transescents with guidance in their use of the media by structuring curricula that include critical studies of all media, the messages they deliver, and their influences on individuals and on society. If one may judge by current textbooks on the media and material in the educational literature, many educators have been doing this for some time.[54] The resources are at hand, and by drawing on their own resources and those of related disciplines, educators will surely discover new ways of teaching that will help transescents make constructive use of all media. In the long run, the development of critical and analytical skills in the young is bound to improve the quality of all media and, indeed, the quality of life.

54. An early instance of this concern with the relationships between the media and education was evident in the Educational Policies Commission's *Mass Communication and Education* (Washington, D.C.: National Education Association, 1958).

CHAPTER VI

Youth Groups and Agencies

EDITH BLAKESLEE PHELPS

Early adolescence has always been a period of concern and challenge for youth-serving organizations.[1] Most youth groups have long had special programs, activities, and responsibilities designed specifically for this age group. And indeed, it is the challenge of adolescence as a whole that has been a major impetus for the broad and important changes that most voluntary youth organizations have undertaken in recent years.

Overview of Present Situation

Youth agencies are in a special position to offer the kinds of services and supports needed by young adolescents. At a time when young people are spending more time with their peers and away from home, many organizations can provide them with a place of their own where they can be with friends and obtain support from adults other than parents. This is especially true of building-based organizations like YWCA, YMCA, Girls Clubs, and Boys Clubs. Whether building-based or not, youth organizations traditionally provide recreational facilities needed for fast-growing young bodies and activities and programs that will expand young persons' abilities and help them explore the wide and complex worlds of work and interpersonal relations outside the home and school.

Ironically, however, most organizations that serve youth throughout the school years have experienced a notable drop in membership as the young people approach the early teen years. In

1. The organizations identified in this chapter are members of the National Collaboration for Youth. It is beyond the scope of the chapter to refer to all programs and organizations that serve youth today.

the process of moving away from the things of childhood, many young adolescents also move away from the clubs and organizations that were part of their early years, rejecting them as "kid stuff." This is a traditional problem, and many organizations have developed special programs specifically to attract and hold young people during these years—programs long in existence such as the Webelos division of the Boy Scouts of America, the Adventure and Discovery programs of Camp Fire Girls, Inc., and the Junior Scout and Cadette positions in the Girl Scouts of the U.S.A.[2]

Part of the problem stems from the fact that adolescence is a difficult age, not only for the young but for adults as well. Since many adults never fully resolve for themselves the conflicts and questions raised during adolescence, they often find it difficult and threatening to work with young people. It is not easy to find flexible, creative adults who feel comfortable helping young adolescents develop their independence and a secure sense of self. The recruiting and training of such volunteers and staff represents a perpetual challenge.

Nonetheless, until the late 1960s, the leadership of most youth organizations believed they were doing an adequate job of meeting the needs of most young people, and they felt satisfied with their efforts to integrate adolescents of all ages into their program structure. Few efforts were made to reach out to the large numbers of young people whose needs these programs did not meet. Then, as the tides of broad social and economic changes surged around us over the last decade, these organizations, like most other institutions, had difficulty understanding and responding to those events. They stood accused, and with some justice, of being rigid, authoritarian, and irrelevant to the needs of youth today. The critics ranged from the youth themselves to sociologists to government programmers and to private funding sources.

During this period, from the late 1960s to the mid-1970s, many youth organizations experienced a substantial drop in membership, first among the older teens, later among adolescents as young as

2. The programs cited in this chapter are intended to offer concrete examples of concepts mentioned here and in no way indicate the complete range of programs within each organization.

twelve or thirteen.[3] At the same time, the numbers of youth involved in juvenile delinquency and drug and alcohol abuse rose
sharply. For example, in 1970, arrests of juveniles for all infractions
were double the figures for 1960. Moreover, throughout the 1970s
the age at which these behaviors begin and peak has steadily
dropped. By the middle of the 1970s, the mean age of onset of
delinquency was 14.2 years for whites and 13.3 years for non-
whites, while chronic juvenile offenders were starting two years
younger (ages 12 and 11.6 respectively).[4] Between 1972 and 1977
the number of runaways doubled and girl runaways out-numbered
the boys; the average age for running away dropped to 14.5.[5]
In New York City 43 percent of all runaways are between ages
eleven and fourteen.[6] In the 1970s, young adolescents were the
only age group for whom the rate of admissions to mental institutions increased,[7] and girls fifteen years old and younger were the
only age group experiencing a rise in birthrate.[8]

For youth organizations, which have always held a major part
of their mission to be the provision of positive alternatives to delinquency and trouble, these facts weigh especially heavily. By
the early 1970s, most organizations were deeply involved in tough
reevaluations of their programs, their organizational structures, and
even their fundamental stated purposes. As the decade draws to

3. For her study *Young Girls: A Portrait of Adolescence* (Englewood
Cliffs, N.J.: Prentice-Hall, 1976), Gisela Konopka interviewed hundreds of
girls ages twelve to eighteen; 83 percent had once belonged to a youth
organization and were no longer affiliated. "They had withdrawn from them
earlier than we had expected, most of them at ages twelve and thirteen, during the critical period of early adolescence." (p. 129)

4. Joan Lipsitz, *Growing Up Forgotten: A Review of Research and Programs Concerning Adolescence* (Lexington, Mass.: Lexington Books, D.C.
Heath and Co., 1977), p. 185.

5. Joan Lipsitz, "National Institute on Early Adolescence" (unpublished
paper), p. 2.

6. Birch Bayh, opening statement in *Runaway Youth*, Hearings before the
Subcommittee to Investigate Juvenile Delinquency, Committee on the Judiciary, U.S. Senate, 92d Congress, 1st Session, January 13, 1972, p. 6.

7. Joan Lipsitz, "National Institute on Early Adolescence," p. 2.

8. Alan Guttmacher Institute, *11 Million Teenagers: What Can Be Done
about the Epidemic of Adolescent Pregnancies in the United States* (New
York: Planned Parenthood Federation of America, 1976).

an end, many groups feel they have achieved major reorientations designed not only to meet the challenges of the near future, but to help them maintain their creativity and influence in a world of continuing change and uncertainty.

Historical Background of Youth Organizations

Voluntary youth organizations have their origins in the late nineteenth and early twentieth centuries, an era of growing social awareness and philanthropic concern, an era also concerned with the "temptations" of idleness and the potential waywardness of youth. As the Industrial Revolution brought thousands of young boys and girls from the countryside to the mills and factories of the big cities, concern grew to provide these young people with some kind of healthful recreational facilities and social activities, in contrast to their only alternative, the life of the streets.

The first Girls Clubs and Boys' Clubs started in the latter half of the nineteenth century when groups of individuals in various New England towns opened rooms to give these young people a place where they could be safe and feel cared for. Individual clubs sprang up in most cities up and down the east coast, but they were not brought together as coherent national organizations until the twentieth century. The YMCA and the YWCA were the first organizations to take up concern for young men and young women on a national scale, with the purpose of meeting social and educational as well as recreational needs. Settlement houses also took an active role in seeking to improve the social conditions of the burgeoning nineteenth century cities, by providing health aid, child care, recreational areas, and instruction in music and crafts for an otherwise dispossessed population.

The early twentieth century saw another kind of youth organization forming, directed toward the needs of middle-class children, with the main purpose of building character, training for leadership and developing "sturdy bodies, alert minds, self-reliance, and resourcefulness." The prototype for this, of course, was the Boy Scouts of America, founded in 1910, followed quickly by Camp Fire Girls and Girl Scouts of the U.S.A., founded in 1911 and 1912 respectively. It is interesting that the origins of all three of these organizations lay in the efforts of a small group of professional educators and youth workers, several of whom were colleagues of G. Stanley Hall, whose book entitled *The Psychology of Adolescence* (1905) shaped the thinking about this age group for four decades. They were all movers in the progressive education movement, which urged, among other things, learning-by-doing through supervised extracurricular activities.

This philosophy and concern for youth had broad ramifications in the first two decades of the century. During World War I, for example, the American Red Cross, whose mission embraced a vast range of concerns, established a Youth Services division to give young people the opportunity to take an active role in serving the nation's needs. As early as 1914, the federal government created the 4-H program for youth education when it established the Co-operative Extension Service of the state and land-grant colleges. In 1917, President Wilson signed the first National Vocational Education Act into law, providing the basis for vocational clubs for high school students, including the Future Homemakers of America.

Altogether, the turn of the century was a period of rapidly expanding concern for youth as a separate group distinct from adults and children. Despite the mix of philosophies and social goals of the major youth organizations, the men and women who brought these institutions into being shared basic assumptions and attitudes. The late nineteenth and early twentieth centuries were a period of great social flux and change, but there remained a fundamental social consensus about the goals of society; about what constituted "progress"; about the roles of the family, the church, and the school; and about what were the acceptable modes of youthful behavior. In the 1950s and throughout the 1960s, this consensus began to disintegrate and no clear replacement is yet in sight.

Looking back from the perspective of three quarters of a century, we can see today that many of the attitudes underlying institutions serving youth (including the schools and the courts) were founded on certain Victorian assumptions that are changing rapidly in the late twentieth century but are not wholly abandoned. Some of the assumptions were articulated by G. Stanley Hall: that adolescence is invariably a time of tumult and stress requiring special attention, often meaning special control; that the sexes must be rigidly segregated and centralized adult authority imposed to regulate the spare-time activities of youth. Behind these beliefs lay a certain mistrust, even hostility, toward the desires of young people to engage in adult society and concerns.[9] (Hall himself wrote of "the lust to know" and held that the precocity of youth who inquired too actively into the adult world could lead to such problems as truancy and running away from home.)[10] Among the objectives of youth work in the early decades of this century was the intent, whether conscious or unconscious, to keep the young from confronting too soon the contradictions and conflicts of the real world, to maintain as long as possible the illusion of childhood innocence. This tendency to control and segregate youth has meant, right up to today, that young people on the whole must learn about such fundamental matters as sex and work without the sanctions or guidance of adults. For youth agencies, it frequently meant a gradual abandonment, over the decades, of their broader social purposes of improving the social conditions in which young people must live, and a concentration on sports and recreation intended to instill discipline and prevent juvenile delinquency.[11]

The Impact of the 1960s

By mid-century, sociologists noted signs among youth of boredom with the institutional rituals of adolescence. In the late 1960s this restiveness burst forth into full rebellion, and youth began to take it upon themselves to define what they need and want. It seems now, a decade later, that the fundamental, long-term need of these young people was to reestablish their role as important active members of human society. The demands were for respect

9. David Bakan, "Adolescence in America: From Idea to Social Fact," in *Studies in Adolescence,* ed. Robert E. Grinder (New York: Macmillan Co., 1975), p. 13.

10. Robert E. Grinder, "The Concept of Adolescence in the Genetic Psychology of G. Stanley Hall," in *Studies of Adolescence,* ed. Grinder, p. 25.

11. For many of the ideas in this section, I am grateful to Joseph Kett, professor of history, University of Virginia, whose speech, "Understanding, Interacting, and Communicating with Youth in the Seventies," was the keynote address at the first Youth Institute, sponsored by Rutgers University, November 17, 1975.

as individuals, for the right to participate in decisions affecting their own lives, for opportunities to expand their independence and take on new responsibilities, for the right to engage with adults in serious examination of values and to formulate their own value system. The anger and fear that accompanies such rebellion also led growing numbers of young people into serious problems with drugs and alcohol, with family breakdown, and with the juvenile justice system.

Initially, of course, most of these young people were older adolescents of college or high school age, and the research and data gathering on youth of the 1960s focused on this age group. What has not been documented is the impact of the events of the 1960s on the younger adolescents. But the trend of the past decade toward social pathology at ever younger ages indicates that the turmoil left a serious mark on the process of coming of age from the earliest years onward.

Certainly the turmoil left its mark on society's institutions. Their inability to respond quickly and constructively to the needs of youth in the 1960s is old history by now. Youth agencies were no different. On the whole, their professional and voluntary staffs, as well as their boards of directors, were unprepared to relinquish adult control, to permit young people significant decision-making roles, to confront the changes in values and mores, or to address the needs of an urban society vastly more complex and pluralistic than the world their organizations had been created to serve. As a result, teen membership in most of these organizations dropped sharply in the late 1960s and the broad social action seemed to be taking place elsewhere.

As the demands of the 1960s outran the ability of the traditional voluntary organizations to respond, a host of new agencies sprang up to address a variety of conditions. These included drug centers, runaway houses, hotlines, counseling services, and community action agencies. All were intended to reach out to different populations of young people with a wide range of concerns or problems. Federal agencies and other sources funding these new efforts tended to bypass and ignore the extensive service capacity and delivery systems of the traditional youth groups on the assumption that they were largely divorced from the vital social issues of poverty, racism, and social change.

Yet the evidence shows that voluntary agencies were doing more in these areas than they were given credit for. When the Office of Economic Opportunity ordered a study of nonfederal antipoverty programs in the United States, for example, they found that thirty-one national voluntary organizations were expending nearly $2.5 billion—25 percent of their total annual expenditures—on the poor. More than $1 billion of this went for education, including literacy education, remedial education, adult education, and programs for school dropouts. A total of 17.3 percent was spent for health services.[12]

Another study, done in 1964, of 2,081 families living in blighted substandard housing in Detroit disclosed that while the majority were receiving service from the public welfare department, hospitals and clinics, and the health and social service programs of the schools, a significant 10.1 percent reported contact with voluntary agencies, including youth agencies.[13]

Efforts of Youth Agencies to Meet the Challenge

In the 1970s, many youth organizations undertook explicit commitments to serve large populations of youth previously ignored—from those who were quietly alienated to those who were in active rebellion, young people who did not join teams or clubs, who were not necessarily of "good character" or who actively rejected the values and expectations imposed on them by adults. Such commitments frequently required new knowledge of the needs of youth; some important shifts in attitude on the part of the staff and board members; new kinds of programs, services, and delivery systems; and new organizational flexibility.

ORGANIZATIONAL REVISION

Many of the largest organizations, such as the YMCA and Boys' Clubs of America, undertook major corporate restructuring similar to that of large business corporations, reorganizing on modern

12. Gordon Manser and Rosemary Higgins Cass, *Voluntarism at the Crossroads* (New York: Family Service Association of America, 1976), pp. 189-90.

13. Ibid., p. 190.

management principles to permit greater flexibility and long-range planning for change and determining new goals and objectives at regular intervals. Girls Clubs of America developed an advocacy position in light of the urgent needs of girls in low-income urban environments who comprise more than 90 percent of the membership, and undertook a major organizational overhaul to heighten efficiency and capability for meeting new needs and ideas quickly and creatively. Camp Fire underwent a major philosophical examination, developing a new and more active statement of purpose, and a reorganization that stresses multiple program initiatives from the community level rather than a single-program structure imposed from the national level.

Many organizations that formerly served one sex began to open their programs to both girls and boys. The YMCA decided to address all members of the family, including women and girls. In 1971, the Boy Scouts admitted girls to full membership in their Explorer division, a specialized program for high school students, and it now permits women to hold leadership positions at all levels of the organization. In 1978, a girl was elected National Explorer President for the first time. In 1973, Future Homemakers of America elected its first male national officer. Both Future Homemakers and Camp Fire have become officially coeducational and are reaching out to involve boys in all their programs as a major effort to combat sexism and sex stereotyping. Camp Fire has informally (until legal matters are worked out) dropped the "Girls" from "Camp Fire, Inc."

Taking a very different point of view, Girls Clubs of America, The National Board of the YWCA, and Girl Scouts of the U.S.A. renewed their commitment to a primary focus on girls. They hold that in a society in which women are still far from equal, and in which women's roles are changing dramatically, special supports and programs are required to meet fully the needs of young women. Dedicated to girls and young women, Girls Clubs of America, The National Board of the YWCA, and Girl Scouts have determined to be a strong voice for girls and their equal legal and human rights. They have vigorously supported the Equal Rights Amendment, and through their programs they seek to combat sex stereotyping in the society and in the minds of the young people themselves. With the assistance of a National Task Force of individuals and organizations, Girls Clubs of America is sponsoring nationwide seminars to call attention to the changing needs of girls and to focus on three primary issues: sexuality; education/ career development; juvenile justice.

Many organizations created places for youth members on their major decision-making bodies, from the national board level, where they are mostly older youth members, to local planning and programming committees that involve young people of all ages. For some of the agencies, this represented an important philosophical shift, recognizing the need of adolescents of any age to participate in decision making and to take on new responsibilities according to individual ability rather than arbitrary age group. This is a special focus for Future Homemakers. For YWCA, the development of leadership potential and decision-making skills of youth as full partners with adults is consciously planned in the administration of services and in advocacy efforts.

Partly as a response to losing many of their older members, and partly in response to the changing needs and attitudes of younger adolescent members, many organizations began to offer the younger teens some of the programs and opportunities originally addressed to the older teen groups. These programs include leadership training, career awareness, sex education, community service, and high-risk competitive sports. Working pragmatically with day-to-day situations, many program directors at both the local and national levels recognized that their members wanted and responded to these kinds of experiences at ages three or four or five years younger than was true a decade ago. As scholarly attention turns to the early adolescent years, the research seems to corroborate the importance of providing broader opportunities at younger ages, and of facing squarely, before they become serious problems, the issues of sex, attitudes toward work, drugs and alcohol, family relationships and the like, as they affect ten- to fifteen-year-olds.

Vital to the success of such restructuring are board members and volunteer and professional staff who can understand and deal flexibly with the changing needs and desires of the young adolescent age group. It is still very difficult for many adults to face the fact that ten- and twelve-year-olds may be involved with the law, use drugs, be active sexually, or may have already developed cynical and rebellious attitudes toward society. Regular and ongoing staff and board training is a major component of most of the directions the voluntary youth organizations are undertaking today.

NEW PROGRAMS, NEW SERVICES, NEW DELIVERY SYSTEMS

The trend among the organizations toward decentralization permits program needs to be defined at the local community level, with the national level supplying technical assistance, educational materials, necessary staff training and some sources of funding. It releases building-based organizations to develop programs outside the building wherever the need demands—in housing projects, community storefronts, group homes for children in need of supervision. It encourages more small-group work and one-to-one counseling in addition to the traditional group work of the clubs.

It permits such programs as peer counseling by teen leaders in a sex education program at the Girls Clubs in Memphis, Tennessee; the operation of a Black Cultural Center by the East Orange, New Jersey, YMCA; the administration of a central city drop-in center by the Camp Fire Council in Waco, Texas; weekly rap sessions at the Cleveland Boys' Club on problems like drugs, boy-girl relationships, race, and divorce, to cite but a few examples of many new departures. The decision to reach out to all youth populations has brought the traditionally rural and small town 4-H into the central cities and led the traditionally suburban Girl Scouts to work with the children of migrant agricultural workers in seven midwestern states.

New directions require new mechanisms for linking with other institutions, including the schools, welfare departments, courts, federal programs, and among the youth organizations themselves. Most organizations have developed a variety of collaborative arrangements with public schools to provide career counseling, tutorial programs, programs for potential dropouts or potentially delinquent students, educational and counseling services for pregnant teenagers and teenage mothers, programs for handicapped youth, and information on drug and alcohol abuse.

Most youth agencies have worked with the federal government to deliver the Education for Parenthood Project of the U.S. Department of Health, Education, and Welfare. The Girl Scout migrant project was funded by the Irwin-Sweeney-Miller Foundation. Such grants and funding for special projects and services, almost unknown to private voluntary youth agencies a decade ago, now represent the means to fast-growing, increasingly sophisticated efforts in programming to meet specific social needs.

The most ambitious of these programs is the National Juvenile Justice Program Collaboration, undertaken by the major youth-serving agencies in collaboration with such membership organizations as the Association of Junior Leagues, the Urban League, and the National Council on Crime and Delinquency. (See chapter 7.)

The program was funded in 1975 by the Office of Juvenile Justice and Delinquency Prevention to develop the capacity of the national voluntary organizations and their local affiliates to serve status offenders and to develop, through collaboration, community-based services as alternatives to detention in five demonstration sites. The grant was channeled through the umbrella organization of the National Assembly of National Voluntary Health and Social Welfare Organizations, Inc.

As the program developed it was highly successful and was refunded recently for another two years to consolidate the five established projects as well as to give technical assistance to thirty additional communities, and to develop structure and funding for their perpetuation. At this time, the effort embraces twenty-three national organizations.

JUVENILE JUSTICE AND DELINQUENCY PREVENTION

During the 1970s, agencies have come to realize that if they are to affect the tough problems affecting youth, they must learn to work with delinquent or potentially delinquent youth and with the juvenile justice system. Most young adolescents, when they first become involved with the courts, have not committed serious crimes; many have not committed crimes at all, but only status offenses—offenses that are punishable only because they are committed by minors, such as truancy, running away, being disobedient to parents or other adult authorities, using obscene language in public, engaging in active sexual behavior. Often such behavior is simply a defensive response to an impossible situation, such as learning problems in school or serious difficulties in the home.

Many of the voluntary youth organizations have undertaken, individually as well as collaboratively, a wide range of approaches to helping these young people. Some are complex and include staff and volunteer training courses and require outside funding, such as the Delinquency Prevention Programs of the Boys' Clubs of America, United Neighborhood Centers of America, Salvation Army, and the Girls Clubs of America.

Other approaches include homes in individual communities to provide shelter for youngsters declared to be "in need of supervision." In Baltimore, Maryland, for example, the State had a facility for a home but no one to manage it; the Camp Fire Council of Chesapeake proposed a program and took over the management. The Girl Scouts have licensed six detention homes in different parts of the country to use their program.

Many organizations have developed programs in collaboration with public schools. In Worcester, Massachusetts, the Girls Club runs a "satellite school" for girls having a wide range of difficulties. The United Neighborhood Centers of America is seeking public school and other community support for its Juvenile Delinquency Prevention programs in major cities across the country.

YMCAs in several communities have used facilities as alternative living situations. This agency counts as one of its most successful programs the National Youth Project Using Minibikes (NYPUM), a motorbike program partially funded by Honda for delinquent teens, mostly ages eleven to fourteen.

Several organizations have grants from the National Institute on Alcoholism and Alcohol Abuse and the National Institute on Drug Abuse to develop, for nationwide replication, model prevention and intervention programs on drug and alcohol abuse, in part to combat the increased first usage among nine- to twelve-year-olds. These programs may be carried out independently or in collaboration with public schools and other youth-serving agencies. Alienation and delinquency are growing long-term problems in modern societies and many youth-serving organizations are de-

veloping capacities, in terms of skills, programs, and funds, to deal
with troubled youth on a continuing, long-term basis.

YOUTH EMPLOYMENT AND CAREER EDUCATION

Since it is widely agreed that the exclusion of youth from the
world of adults, particularly the world of meaningful work, is a
primary cause of youth alienation and delinquency at all social and
economic levels, the need to open the world of real work to
adolescents must become a top priority of society. At present, the
jobs available to young people tend to be narrowly concentrated
in low-paying, small nonunion firms that lack in-firm training and
chances for promotion. As a result, many young people see work
as inevitably demeaning, with no opportunity for personal satisfaction or pride of accomplishment. This cynicism drifts easily
down to the younger age groups that are anticipating their own
futures.

In most youth organizations, job and career education has become a major activity for all age groups, from the youngest to the
oldest. The programs range from dealing with attitudes and teaching basic work habits, to inviting young people to explore through
courses and experience a wide range of career possibilities, to placing older youth in actual paying positions. For young adolescents,
the emphasis is on helping them understand some of the physical,
mental, and educational requirements of a wide range of jobs.
Many programs involve field trips, guest speakers from local busi-
nesses and institutions, and, because of the child labor laws, in-club
work experience. Frequently these job and career awareness programs are carried out through a wide variety of cooperative arrangements with the public schools.

The Girl Scouts recently developed a new career exploration
program called "From Dreams to Reality" specifically for twelve-
to seventeen-year-olds to introduce them to a wide range of
traditional and nontraditional careers for young women. A new
program now directs the same material for use with six to twelve-
year-olds. The 4-H has a "service in leisure" program to help
young people see that self-fulfillment is possible through service
to others. Red Cross youth programs have as one of their main

thrusts the opportunity for youth to serve, rather than to be served.

In what may be a more important move over the long haul, some organizations are calling on their National Board members, some of whom are chief executives of large corporations, to use their substantial influence to change the marketplace itself and open new employment opportunities for youth.

GIRLS: A GROUP WITH SPECIAL NEEDS

As the career education programs of the youth organizations indicate, the potential opportunities for girls and women seem to be expanding dramatically. Yet as the pressures and confusions encountered by girls growing up in the 1970s have increased, the numbers of girls experiencing serious difficulties have also increased. For example, arrest rates for girls are rising twice as fast as those for boys—254 percent compared to 124 percent. More than half of the estimated one million runaways each year are girls, mostly aged eleven to fourteen. Almost 25 percent of all girls drop out of school before completing high school. Unemployment rates for minority teen-age women are unofficially believed to be 40 to 50 percent, the highest for any group in the nation.[14]

There is evidence that girls are discriminated against in the justice system, that they are more likely to be arrested for minor offenses, to be adjudicated, and to be given longer and harsher sentences for status offenses than boys receive for criminal violations. As John M. Rector, administrator of the Federal Office of Juvenile Justice and Delinquency Prevention, has said: "The brutal truth of the matter is that the young woman who has done nothing more threatening to the State than to run away from home is likely to be treated as harshly as a young man who has held up a store."[15]

In the marketplace, the official picture for girls is also grim. Unemployment for white teen-age girls is 15.2 percent[16] and for

14. Girls Clubs of America, *A Report for 1976* (New York: Girls Clubs of America, 1977).

15. John M. Rector, keynote address before the National Conference on Juvenile Justice for Young Women, Kissimmee, Florida, December 1977.

16. Women's Bureau, Employment Standards Administration, *Women Workers Today* (Washington, D.C.: U.S. Department of Labor, 1976).

minority girls, 38 percent. Yet most people think of boys, not girls, when thinking of unemployed youth. The types of jobs open to young women still tend to be largely stereotyped, despite some changes in recent years. These jobs rarely offer opportunity for career or personal development and generally are the lowest paid in the economy. A young woman with a high school diploma can expect to earn no more than a man with an eighth-grade education.[17]

Opening doors of traditionally male organizations and programs to girls, as the YMCA and the Boy Scout Explorer program have done, helps provide more opportunities; however, there is a special need for financing and programming specifically directed to girls in this age group.

Yet resources for girls, traditionally an underserved group, have not expanded to meet the need. Consider the following, for example:

1. United Way allocations in 1976 to organizations serving girls and women were approximately 7.6 percent of the total compared with 13 percent of the total to boys' and men's organizations.

2. Almost twice the amount of United Way allocations in 1978 went to boys' and men's organizations, more than $116 million compared to $65,373,596 for girls' and women's groups.

3. Foundation grants to girls' organizations in 1977 were approximately one third of the amount of grants to boys organizations—$1,429,000 for girls, $3,682,000 for boys.

4. From 1970 to 1976 foundation grants to boys' organizations totaled over $22 million; girls' organizations received only $5,500,000.[18]

For these reasons organizations like Girls Clubs of America, the YWCA, and Girl Scouts feel it imperative to continue directing their opportunities and programs primarily to girls. They have taken leading roles in programs across the country to deinstitutionalize status offenders, the majority of whom are girls. They are developing, sometimes in collaboration with public schools,

17. Women's Bureau, Employment Standards Administration, *Twenty Facts about Women* (Washington, D.C.: U.S. Department of Labor, 1975).

18. Girls Clubs of America, *A Report for 1976.*

sex education and career awareness programs for girls as young as age six, since research shows that girls accept many erroneous assumptions about their potential at a very early age.

Girls Clubs and the YWCA have taken positions as frank advocates of the needs for girls and young women in the society at large. Other directions for the agencies devoted to girls include expanding the opportunities for young people to engage in the types of adventurous and competitive sports that are frequently reserved for boys, such as basketball, hockey, team tennis, or mountain climbing, canoeing, and backpacking. Nationwide, these agencies are helping girls to explore all vocational opportunities from truck driving to engineering.

A major aim of the girl-serving organizations is to expand the horizons of young people about their abilities and their career and life opportunities. Essential to this is helping them make their life decisions based on fact (for example, nine out of ten girls will work during a substantial portion of their lives; married women work an average of twenty-five years, single women an average of forty-five years),[19] rather than on myth (for example, Prince Charming will be a protector forever.)

The need for more youth workers skilled at working with young girls, including girls with problems, is enormous. In 1976, a nationwide training program to address this need was established by the Center for Youth Development and Research at the University of Minnesota, under the direction of Gisela Konopka. The National Youth Workers Education Project, funded by the Lilly Endowment, has provided short-term intensive training sessions for selected staff of eight girl-serving organizations, as well as for probation and parole officers. One long-range aim is to foster between the private agencies and court personnel the development of coordinated programs to help improve the services available to young women in need, whatever their age. Other goals include the building of broad effective community networks and an increase of youth workers who are sensitive to the needs of girls today.

19. Women's Bureau, *Twenty Facts about Women.*

The National Collaboration for Youth

One of the most significant responses to the changing needs of youth and youth organizations was the joining together of twelve major youth organizations as a National Collaboration for Youth (NCY). Through this collaboration the agencies have been able to work together on programs addressing those urgent needs and to speak collectively on policies and legislation affecting the needs of all young people.

Twelve youth organizations make up NCY: Boys' Clubs of America, Camp Fire Girls, Inc., 4-H Program, Future Homemakers of America, Inc., Girls Clubs of America, Girls Scouts of the U.S.A., the United Neighborhood Centers of America, National Jewish Welfare Board, Red Cross Youth Service Programs, the National Board of the YMCA, and The National Board of the YWCA. These organizations serve 30 million young people with 40,000 professional staff and the services of over 6 million volunteers. In 1973, the value of such a unified voice for youth became overwhelmingly clear.

Shortly after the National Collaboration had come together, a bill on juvenile justice and delinquency prevention was before the Senate Subcommittee to Investigate Juvenile Delinquency. Many organizations working with young people recognized the urgent need for legislative remedies to the juvenile justice system, and they testified individually before the Subcommittee to this effect. That year the bill never even got out of committee.

The National Collaboration for Youth recognized this issue as one on which there could be a common position. The next year, through cooperative staff work, the members developed a joint position paper, and a delegation of six top executives testified as a panel before Congress. In addition, the local affiliates and councils of these organizations mobilized to develop pressure at the community level.

In 1974, the Juvenile Justice and Delinquency Prevention Act passed the Senate by a vote of 88 to 1 and the House of Representatives by 329 to 200. The potential of a unified voice for youth became dramatically clear. Having played a major role in the passage of the legislation, Collaboration members were committed to ensuring its implementation, and formed the basis of the National Juvenile Justice Program Collaboration. (See chapter 7.)

Simultaneously, the Collaboration has turned its attention to another issue vital to its members—youth employment. A Task Force on Youth Education/Employment was established to identify legislative areas in which the NCY members can act, and also to recommend programs to be developed, particularly addressing the difficulties of transition from school to work and the overall youth unemployment problem.

In addition to affecting specific issues, the creation of the Collaboration has had a fundamental impact on relations between public and private agencies at the federal level. In the last four years, regular liaison has been established with several federal agencies and relevant cabinet members, and NCY members regularly contribute to the development of public policy. A current example is their contribution to raising the priority of youth services in the President's Reorganization Project for the federal government.

The Future for Youth Agencies

In the work of the National Collaboration for Youth, on both the advocacy and program levels, youth agencies claim a new and vital role in affecting the conditions in which young people grow up in our society. For adolescents of all ages, these multipurpose agencies represent services and opportunities not available through other community institutions. They also have the range and flexibility to address a wide variety of needs not met by family, school, or church.

The importance of working collaboratively with these and other community organizations, however, could not be more clear. Agencies are only beginning to understand how to build bridges between the public and private sectors, how to build networks of many services and approaches to meet the needs of young people. The collaborative impact needs to be felt at the state and municipal levels as well as at the federal level.

Each agency has a long tradition of service and commitment that is unique to itself, and it is this sense of special purpose that has given each the courage and commitment to change and develop new capacities to confront vital social issues. While this individuality must be maintained, agencies must find ways to coordinate and not duplicate these special strengths. It is essential to create a comprehensive system for serving a far broader range of young people than agencies do today.

The voluntary youth organizations need to continue to expand their joint efforts to develop training programs for volunteers, staff, and board members, to enhance their abilities to work with adolescents. The lack of adults with sufficient sensitivity and skill to work with this age group is one of the most serious obstacles.

Beyond their own networks, agencies need to reach out for greater cooperation with families, school, churches, courts, employment bureaus, and other public agencies serving youth. And they need to develop, through vigorous public information programs, a far broader constituency that understands and supports the needs of young people.

Collaboration and active support for youth needs are necessary components of youth work in the future. In recent years, through profound reexamination of purpose, through restructuring organizations and programs, and sometimes through sheer will and determination, the major youth organizations have begun to reach larger numbers and more diverse groups of young people.

In fact, adolescent membership is beginning to climb; in Girls Clubs it is the fastest growing group. This in itself is witness to the effectiveness of new organizational directions and program changes chosen by many agencies. Young adolescents, in particular, need a place to go, to belong, to be with significant adults and peers in an atmosphere of respect and trust, to meet a broad range of personal needs and coping skills essential to an increasingly pluralistic and changing society.

Youth organizations must accept the responsibility to be an effective part of that process of change. As they are able to do so, they will create unlimited opportunities to make a positive difference in the lives of young people in the future.

CHAPTER VII

The Juvenile Justice System

MILTON G. RECTOR, STEFANIE M. BARTH, AND
GWEN INGRAM

Juvenile delinquency has been the focus of increasing concern for several years. Intensive research has been undertaken, new juvenile statutes and codes have been developed, large expenditures have been allocated, and three national commissions,[1] in addition to innumerable state and local commissions, have been assigned to investigate this problem. The result of all of this has not been a solution, but a greater awareness of delinquency as a complex social problem that requires a commitment from many segments of society.

It is no longer possible for the community to pass laws that define delinquency and then simply expect the police, courts, or correctional institutions to control such behavior. The problem extends well beyond the boundaries of the juvenile justice system. Much of the problem exists within the social institutions of the community—the school, the family, the church, and the local government.

The juvenile justice system is not equipped to deal with social problems at these levels. Working with potential sources of delinquent activity and preventing its occurrence are the responsibility of the community. The community can act before a crime is committed, but the juvenile justice system cannot.

In this chapter we present a broad overview of the problem

1. President's Commission on Law Enforcement and Administration of Justice, *The Challenge of Crime in a Free Society* and *Task Force Reports* (Washington, D.C.: U.S. Government Printing Office, 1967); National Advisory Commission on Criminal Justice Standards and Goals, *Reports*, 6 vols. (Washington, D.C.: U.S. Government Printing Office, 1973); National Advisory Committee on Criminal Justice Standards and Goals, *Reports*, 5 vols. (Washington, D.C.: U.S. Government Printing Office, 1976).

in terms of historical perspective, the current state of the system, and the role of the school in promoting or preventing delinquent behavior.

Historical Development of the Juvenile Justice System

As is the case with any institution of society, the juvenile justice system has developed out of surrounding social, political, and economic circumstances. Each phase in the development of this system was a response to a perceived need. As needs changed, so did the character of that part of the social structure that dealt with the behavior of children.

From the very beginning of American history, children in unusual circumstances were accorded a different status.[2] In early American settlements, children were transported from England in order to solve many of the problems of labor shortages in the process of colonization. Growing urbanization in the mother country and subsequent social decay created a large pool of labor in the form of orphans and destitute children. These children were persuaded or coerced by merchants into indentured service in America.

As the population grew, wider gaps between the rich and the poor created by industrialization were reflected in the treatment of children. Initial efforts to deal with juvenile delinquents and dependent and neglected children came from the wealthy, professional levels of society. The first juvenile institutions were founded in New York, Boston, and Philadelphia in the late 1820s by a group of philanthropic reformers. Founded to reform and instruct juveniles, these "Houses of Refuge" contained both delinquent and nondelinquent youth. The courts established their right to remove children from their parents under the concept of *parens patriae*, which gave the state the role of common guardian and

2. An in-depth historical analysis of juvenile treatment and delinquency in the United States can be found in the following sources from which this overview was developed: Barry Krisberg and James Austin, *The Children of Ishmael* (Palo Alto, Calif.: Maywood Publishing Co., 1978); Robert M. Mennel, *Thorns and Thistles: Juvenile Delinquents in the United States, 1825–1940* (Hanover, N.H.: University Press of New England, 1973); Anthony M. Platt, *The Child Savers: The Invention of Delinquency* (Chicago: University of Chicago Press, 1977).

the right to place a child in the Houses of Refuge, not as punishment, but as protection.

Under such protection, the children continued to be economically exploited. They were contracted to merchants, farmers, or for domestic service. Such labor was touted as necessary to teach the children skills with which to earn a living, but in reality it provided the institution with revenue and a tool for maintaining order. Such a practice further assured that the children would be kept from their families. According to the thinking of the day, removing and keeping the children from those people from whom they had inherited their depraved criminal nature was crucial to reforming the child.

Midway through the nineteenth century, growing urbanization fostered growing slums, and delinquent children were regarded as by-products of deprivation. Such children were seen as victims of a sick environment where crime was a contagion. Given the opportunity of a sane, disciplined environment with more acceptable social conditioning, it was reasoned that the child could be saved.

The state had begun to take over the management of the institutions, which were now called reform schools. Because they were seen as the places where children could be reformed and cured, it was in such institutions that the therapeutic model of penology developed. This model was based upon the use of treatment to rehabilitate the child. Again, children were not sent to a reformatory for punitive purposes, but to change their behavior to conform to socially acceptable norms. Officials felt that it was necessary to maintain juveniles in the reformatory until treatment produced a rehabilitated child. Because it was not possible to determine in advance how long this would take, the child was given what amounted to an open-ended sentence. Release from a reformatory was based upon a determination by the staff that the child had successfully attained strength of character and an improved value system.

The juvenile reform movement gained momentum as the country experienced even greater changes caused by rapid industrialization and urbanization. A natural outgrowth was the formalization of the Illinois Juvenile Court Act of 1899. A formal children's court had never before existed. The court was given jurisdiction over all juveniles whom society regarded as wayward—delinquent, dependent, neglected, and a new category, those juveniles who are today referred to as "status offenders" (incorrigibles, runaways, truants, and the like). Similar juvenile courts were subsequently developed throughout the country.

Basic to the philosophy underlying the juvenile court was the belief that delinquents were different from adult criminals by virtue of their status as juveniles. Therefore, it was determined that personal, individualized attention, rather than the formal, legal procedures of the adult court would assist the rehabilitative process. Thus a special language and philosophy was formed around juvenile court proceedings: juveniles had hearings rather than arraignments and trials; they were adjudicated and not convicted; and they received a disposition instead of a sentence.[3]

Although the creation of the juvenile court was hailed as a major step in the reform of juvenile treatment, little attention was paid to the fact that children were being denied legal rights. Rather than ensuring that a child would receive due process under the law, the juvenile court operated under the *parens patriae* concept, which allowed treatment of the child in terms of his protection and rehabilitation, instead of in terms of his offense.

As juvenile reform moved into the twentieth century, psychological explanations for delinquency became more evident; testing was conducted and treatment plans were developed for each child entering the juvenile justice system. Philanthropists and social reformers were replaced by professional specialists: psychologists and psychiatrists, sociologists and social workers, probation officers and criminologists. Even greater reliance was placed upon institutional placement as an acceptable means of custody and treatment of children.

As America began to feel the effects of the Great Depression, however, scholars looked more toward social and economic factors to explain delinquency. Sociological theories fostered ecological approaches to delinquency. Large-scale community-based efforts

3. President's Commission on Law Enforcement and Administration of Justice, *Task Force Report: Juvenile Delinquency and Youth Crime* (Washington, D.C.: U.S. Government Printing Office, 1967), p. 3.

were geared toward assisting residents to cope with solving their own problems and thereby preventing delinquency. The desire to reduce environmental influences supported an even greater use of commitments of youth to institutions.

By the 1950s and into the 1960s community social programs were concentrating more and more on youth and specifically on urban youth. Private foundations and the federal government financially supported efforts to study and deal with delinquency in the context of poverty, racism, and unemployment.

Greater emphasis was placed on formalized efforts at prevention, especially by means of diversion from the juvenile justice system. Informal diversion had been taking place at the police and court level for some time, but in the face of the civil unrest of the 1960s large-scale diversion efforts were emphasized in 1967 in the report of the President's Commission on Law Enforcement and Administration of Justice, which had been appointed following President Lyndon B. Johnson's declared "war on crime." Through a wide array of programs, greater efforts were made to prevent juveniles from entering the juvenile justice system.

The Commission recommended that Youth Service Bureaus be established in communities to coordinate all community services for youth and to create whatever new programs should prove to be needed.[4] However, neither Youth Service Bureaus nor diversion efforts stopped at merely preventing children from entering the system. Diversion also became the method by which juveniles were to be prevented from proceeding further into the system after having already entered it. Diversion programs were developed at levels other than the community; police and court diversion programs gained momentum in the early 1970s.

Unfortunately, as a result of such massive diversion efforts many more youths may have been brought into the system rather than being kept out of it.[5] Many youth who, in the past, may have been ignored or released by police have been referred to

4. President's Commission on Law Enforcement and Administration of Justice, *The Challenge of Crime in a Free Society*, p. 83.

5. Edwin M. Lemert, "Instead of Court: Diversion in Juvenile Justice," in *Back on the Streets: Diversion of Juvenile Offenders*, ed. Robert M. Carter and Malcolm W. Klein (Englewood Cliffs, N.J.: Prentice-Hall, 1976), p. 134.

diversion-type programs in order to benefit from the services offered. Thus, they have become involved in what are recognized as delinquency programs and have often received a delinquent label by implication.

The civil unrest of the 1960s and early 1970s witnessed major changes in attitudes toward the juvenile court and juvenile institutional care. Efforts to effect change and to correct abuses of the system were undertaken in the three branches of the federal government.

In a series of decisions, the U.S. Supreme Court established that it was no longer acceptable for juveniles to be totally without due process rights. The original efforts of the Court to protect children from the harshness of adult legal proceedings had, in effect, prevented them from receiving legal protection under the law. With *Kent v. United States* (1966), *In Re Gault* (1967), and *In Re Winship* (1970), the Court acknowledged that juveniles must be accorded some extension of due process protection.[6] Juveniles, however, have not been accorded the same due process protection that is given to adults in criminal proceedings. (See chapter 10.)

The President's Commission on Law Enforcement and Administration of Justice, after two years of study, issued a report containing two hundred recommendations. As a result of this study, Congress passed the 1968 Omnibus Crime Control and Safe Streets Act. The Law Enforcement Assistance Administration (LEAA) was established by this legislation for the purpose of administering federal grants to assist in reducing the level of crime and in improving the criminal justice system. Congress further enacted the Juvenile Justice and Delinquency Prevention Act of 1974, which placed additional emphasis upon delinquency prevention, deinstitutionalization, and the development of community diversionary alternatives.

The Current Situation

The Juvenile Justice and Delinquency Prevention (JJDP) Act of 1974 represented a federal effort to sustain the national move-

6. *Kent v. United States*, 383 U.S. 541, 86 S. Ct. 1045, 16 L. Ed. 84 (1966); *In Re Gault*, 387 U.S. 1, 87 S. Ct. 1428, 18 L. Ed. 2d 527 (1967); *In Re Winship*, 397 U.S. 358, 90 S. Ct. 1068, 25 L. Ed. 2d 368 (1970).

ment toward diversion of youth from confinement and the development of community-based alternatives to provide needed services
for youth. The act identified as inappropriate the institutionalization of young people who had not committed criminal acts and
mandated that they be removed from institutions. The act reflected congressional recognition that institutions were "schools of
crime" that were harmful to young people because, among other
things, they encouraged negative and antisocial self-images, limited
the future potential of youth, and could foster increased youth
involvement in crime.

It was anticipated that this act would stimulate what already
appeared to be a decline in the incarceration of youth. State
institutionalization of American youth was at its highest level in
1965, when it was estimated to be 40,000. The total number of
imprisoned juveniles was 37,000 in 1970; 28,298 in 1975; and
26,000 on January 1, 1978.[7]

State institutions, however, reflect only a small portion of the
young people displaced from families and communities by the
juvenile justice system. Detention is seldom included in official
statistics and the practice is widely abused and underreported.
Each year, an estimated 400,000 young people are incarcerated in
local and state detention centers and as many as 600,000 youths
are held in adult jails.[8] Detention of these juveniles occurs primarily prior to court hearings when they have not been proven
guilty of an offense, or for a status offense, which is noncriminal
if committed by an adult.

Youth held in private secure facilities are also seldom included
in public reports. The LEAA report on children in custody, however, identified 21,033 juveniles committed to 1,261 private correctional training schools, ranches, camps, and farms in 1974 and
16,754 juveniles in 1,211 private facilities in 1975.[9]

7. Rob Wilson, "Juvenile Inmates: The Long-Term Trend is Down," *Corrections Magazine* 4 (September 1978): 9.

8. Rosemary Sarri, *Under Lock and Key* (Ann Arbor, Mich.: National
Assessment of Juvenile Corrections, 1974).

9. National Criminal Justice Information and Statistics Service, U.S. Depart-
ment of Justice, *Children in Custody: Advance Report on the Detention and
Correctional Facility Census of 1975* (Washington, D.C.: U.S. Government
Printing Office, 1977).

Furthermore, the number of children incarcerated does not accurately reflect the number actually committing crimes. Self-report studies have demonstrated that approximately 80 percent of all youth have some involvement in delinquent behavior before the age of eighteen.[10] This number includes juveniles from all socioeconomic levels and races, yet those youth who are actually incarcerated are not representative of all groups. In reality, the sex, ethnicity, and social class of a juvenile are determinants of how antisocial acts are perceived and how authorities respond.

Delinquent activity (as measured by police contact and arrests) is much higher for working-class youth and those on welfare than for middle-class and wealthy youth.[11] Race is also a crucial factor with regard to the likelihood of being arrested. In 1976, blacks comprised only 14.3 percent of American youths aged eleven to seventeen, but 22.9 percent of arrests in this age group were of blacks.[12] While girls commonly receive informal treatment for delinquent behavior, they represent the majority of all juveniles detained and institutionalized for status offenses.[13]

Children of middle- and high-socioeconomic status families are involved in delinquency, but authorities tend to overlook their behavior or to handle them informally. These youth often avoid incarceration because of the greater availability of private-sector alternatives to children of the upper classes.

The JJDP Act focused national attention on the inappropriate use of institutionalization and the need to develop alternatives for all youth. The act offered financial support to those states that agreed, within two years, to stop placing status offenders in juvenile detention or correctional facilities ("deinstitutionalization"), and

10. Martin Gold, *Delinquent Behavior in an American City* (Belone, Calif.: Brooks/Cole Publishers, 1970).

11. Marvin Wolfgang, Robert Figlio, and Thorsten Sellin, *Delinquency in a Birth Cohort* (Chicago: University of Chicago Press, 1972), p. 67; Delbert S. Elliot and Harwin L. Voss, *Delinquency and Dropout* (Lexington, Mass.: Lexington Books, 1974), p. 83.

12. National Council on Crime and Delinquency, *Dealing with Delinquency* (Hackensack, N.J.: National Council on Crime and Delinquency, forthcoming), p. 74.

13. Female Offender Resource Center, *Little Sisters and the Law* (Washington, D.C.: American Bar Association), p. 12.

to stop detaining juveniles in institutions in which they would have regular contact with alleged or convicted adult criminals ("separation").

STATUS OFFENDERS AND THEIR "CRIMES"

"Juvenile status offender" is a special category for youth who have committed an act or engaged in activity that is illegal only for minors. Such acts include, but are not limited to, running away, truancy, ungovernability or incorrigibility, curfew violations, and promiscuity. Of all youth under eighteen years of age committed to correctional institutions in 1976, 50 percent of the girls and 17 percent of the boys were status offenders.[14] Although guilty only of nonviolent and victimless acts, young people held for status offenses remain incarcerated an average of four to five months longer than children convicted of criminal offenses. Furthermore, studies show that more than 200,000 status offenders were held in secure detention pending court hearings in 1975 and an estimated 18 percent were incarcerated in adult jails.[15]

Running away from home is the most common status offense for which children are confined in juvenile institutions and detention. The U.S. Public Health Service estimates that one out of every ten children between the ages of twelve and seventeen will run away from home at least once. Thus, between 500,000 and 1,000,000 youngsters run away from home each year, according to the Senate Judiciary Subcommittee on Juvenile Delinquency. Two-thirds of these runaways are over fifteen, remain away from home for no more than two days, and spend that time with a friend or relative less than ten miles from home.[16] In other words, running away from home can be considered a fairly normal behavior for young people and can often be resolved without court intervention.

The vast majority of status offenders accused of incorrigibility have been brought to the court because they have engaged in be-

14. Ibid.

15. Gwen Ingram, *The Innocent Criminal: Leader's Guide* (Hackensack, N.J.: National Council on Crime and Delinquency, 1977), p. 27.

16. Ibid.

havior that is offensive to someone for one reason or another. A closer examination of the "incorrigible" child's basic social and economic environment reveals a child who is basically neglected or unwanted. About one-third of the incorrigible children who are termed "neglected," "dependent," or "abused" by the court are later labeled as status offenders to avoid the delays and red tape involved in a neglect proceeding. Obviously, it is unfair to treat a child who is actually abused or neglected (for example, a child who has been tossed out or beaten by his parents) as the accused. This is often the case with a great number of "incorrigible" children.

These children, labeled status offenders, reflect problem situations not appropriate to the juvenile justice system. Truancy, for example, can be better handled in the schools. Although an estimated 40 percent of the juvenile court caseload involves status offenders, it is widely recognized that court personnel have neither the time nor the training to solve the complicated social, familial, and personal problems of such offenders. As a result, the juvenile justice system is robbed of the valuable time and resources needed for effective processing of violent and dangerous juveniles while the status offender is often much worse off than if he had received no treatment at all.

PROGRESS IN DEINSTITUTIONALIZATION

Status offenders have been the major focus in the implementation of the JJDP Act. Eleven states and a collaborative group of private-sector agencies were recipients of Deinstitutionalization of Status Offender (DSO) grants, which are designed to move status offenders from institutions into community-based services.

Evaluation of these efforts shows that impressive progress has been made. A study of the impact of DSO grants in ten states found that few status offenders were being institutionalized on a long-term basis. Most importantly, the study stated that "some status offenders are at least as well off alone, with no public intervention, to mature out of their problems." [17] Taxpayers will be

17. Arthur D. Little, *Responses to Angry Youth: Cost and Service Impacts of Deinstitutionalization of Status Offenders in Ten States* (Washington, D.C.: Arthur D. Little Co., 1977), p. 7.

pleased to learn that the study also found that noninstitutional services were much less expensive. With a few exceptions, the per unit (per child/per day or month) cost for providing noninstitutional services to youth was less (an average of $1,500 to $2,400 per year) than the per unit cost of maintaining children in secure detention or correctional facilities (approximately $9,580 per year per child).[18] The study concluded that, once established, a community-based service system would be less expensive than the services of the present juvenile justice system.[19]

The most comprehensive, multistate DSO Grant is the National Juvenile Justice Program Collaboration (NJJPC). Supported by sixteen national agencies, the NJJPC represents a private-sector effort to demonstrate its capacity to serve status offenders in voluntary, community-based programs.[20] Six local collaboration efforts have made possible the development of a comprehensive system of community services to status offenders and have encouraged the sharing of resources. Although great potential has been seen in these early efforts, the full power of private-sector resources joined in advocating change in the system is just being realized. (See chapter 6.)

JUVENILES IN ADULT FACILITIES AND COURTS

The second requirement of the JJDP Act focuses on the separation of juveniles from adults in both detention and institutions. However, the wording of the law is weak. It forbids only "regular contact" and has been skirted by administrators. Many felt the federal legislation should have stopped all housing of juveniles in adult facilities, especially in jails.

Again and again, national commissions and standard-setting

18. Ingram, *The Innocent Criminal*, p. 27.

19. Little, *Responses to Angry Youth*, p. 25.

20. Among the organizations comprising the National Juvenile Justice Collaboration are the following: American Red Cross; Association of Junior Leagues; Boy Scouts of America; Boys' Clubs of America; Camp Fire Girls, Inc.; Girl Scouts of the U.S.A.; Girl's Clubs of America, Inc.; Jewish Welfare Board; National Council for Homemaker-Home Health Aide Services, Inc.; National Council of Jewish Women; National Council on Crime and Delinquency; National Federation of Settlements and Neighborhood Centers; The Salvation Army; Travelers Aid Association of America; National Board, Y.W.C.A. of the U.S.A.; National Council, Y.M.C.A. of the U.S.A.

agencies have stated emphatically that adult county jails should not be used for the detention of juveniles. In 1977, the Task Force on Juvenile Justice and Delinquency Prevention of the National Advisory Committee denounced this practice by stating that "under no circumstances should these juveniles be held in the same detention facilities with adults," [21] but the practice continues nationwide.

The National Jail Census done in 1970 by LEAA found 7,800 juveniles in 4,037 adult jails. Two-thirds of those young inmates were awaiting court hearings; the rest were serving sentences or awaiting transfer. Even more alarming was the finding by a Children's Defense Fund study that "the overwhelming majority of children we found in adult jails were not detained for violent crimes and could not be considered a threat to themselves or the community." [22]

Currently, the number of juveniles in adult state prisons is relatively small. There is clear indication, however, that many states are trying to solve the problem of violent juvenile crime by transferring more and more youth to adult courts. This is not a new phenomenon. Virtually every state allows for the transfer of juvenile offenders to adult courts for serious offenses. Representing an extreme, Indiana permits ten-year-olds to be certified as adults and sentenced to the state penitentiary for murder. Due to public pressure, the juvenile justice system appears to be giving up on the handling of serious youth offenders and turning them over to the adult criminal courts.

The Schools and Delinquency

It is all too apparent that the juvenile/criminal justice system is not the answer to delinquency reduction. As a reactive system, it can only deal with delinquent behavior after it has occurred. And, because of the very nature of the system, whatever actions are taken are perceived as negative or punishing rather than positive. Something must take place prior to the involvement of the

21. National Advisory Committee on Criminal Justice Standards and Goals, *Juvenile Justice and Delinquency Prevention* (Washington, D.C.: U.S. Government Printing Office, 1976), p. 667.

22. Wilson, "Juvenile Inmates," p. 10.

justice system, something that can prevent a delinquent act and subsequent processing under the justice system.

This something can only be found in a larger social context—the community. There are many theories of delinquency causation, all of which ultimately agree that a variety of variables impact upon a juvenile and determine his behavior. These variables include the social and economic environment, the family, peers, physical and mental health, and institutions of society. All of these factors influence a child's behavior and should be the concern primarily of the community or the social system rather than the justice/legal system.

Here is where the school plays a critical role. The school, perhaps more than any community institution, brings together those forces affecting juvenile behavior. Gold has concluded that the school may have the capacity to prevent and reduce delinquency since it "may be in control of major social psychological forces that generate delinquency." [23] Because of this, he theorizes that, as an institution, the school is "a significant provoker of delinquent behavior." [24] Elliott and Voss have also determined that "the school is the critical generating milieu for delinquency." [25]

When a child first enters school, he has been primarily influenced by his development within his family and his surrounding social, economic, and political environment. Once he enters school, his world is broadened by an ever-expanding peer group, new authority figures, and the information given him as part of his educational experience. The child, new to the school environment, may bring problems with him. Unfortunately, the school can accentuate these problems, and can create new ones as well.[26]

Children do not come to school identified as failures or successes. Such conditions are created by the school's standards of achievement, which play an important part in identifying students'

23. Martin Gold, "Scholastic Experiences, Self-esteem, and Delinquent Behavior: A Theory for Alternative Schools," *Crime and Delinquency* 24, no. 3 (1978): 290.

24. Ibid., p. 307.

25. Elliott and Voss, *Delinquency and Dropout*, p. 203.

26. William Glasser, *Schools without Failure* (New York: Harper and Row, 1969).

roles and often encourage failure. Very early in the educational process, children undergo a sorting process based upon presumed abilities. Socioeconomic and racial backgrounds affect this process. Children from minority or low-income families are often placed within low-ability, noncollege tracks.[27]

This process may have nothing to do with ability. Children who have been raised in homes without books or other forms of intellectual stimuli may appear educationally backward. While their future chances of success may be the same as children raised in a more intellectual environment, they are labeled as slow or low-ability learners, which is often translated to mean failure.

The consequences of being labeled a failure are many and grave. Most importantly, the child develops a poor self-image. The label of failure can become self-fulfilling and the child becomes a low achiever scholastically. Students who do poorly in their studies are often excluded from school social activities and are not regarded as popular students. They tend to relate to other juveniles who have similarly been identified as failures. They have also been found to have a greater tendency toward misbehaving in school and toward dropping out of school.[28] Finally, "delinquent behavior, particularly disruptive behavior in school, is a defense against self-derogation (a feeling that one is not worth much and will never be)."[29]

Teaching methods can further add to the stigma felt by the child experiencing failure. Teachers often underestimate the potential of those students identified as having low ability and expect them to misbehave, thus further alienating these juveniles. Many teachers also experience negative feelings when working with low-ability groups and positive feelings when working with high-ability students. These attitudes often bring similar reactions from students, another irritant to an already bleak situation.[30]

27. Kenneth Polk and Walter E. Schafer, *Schools and Delinquency* (Englewood Cliffs, N.J.: Prentice-Hall, 1972), p. 34.

28. Ibid., p. 45.

29. Gold, "Scholastic Experiences, Self-esteem, and Delinquent Behavior," p. 293.

30. Polk and Schafer, *Schools and Delinquency*, p. 46.

Classroom frustrations and ability labeling are not the exclusive domain of low-income and minority students. While the past two decades have witnessed massive efforts to upgrade urban school systems, it has been recently recognized that schools in the more affluent areas are experiencing the same problems as those in poorer areas: vandalism, alienation, apathy, drug abuse, and truancy. This can be due to the fact that students from varying socioeconomic situations are experiencing frustrations, anxiety, and boredom within the classroom. Perhaps the key lies in the theory that while the world becomes increasingly complex, educational programs continue to be based upon concepts geared to a stable society.[31] Failure on the part of the schools to deal with growing social problems results in juveniles ill-prepared to handle those difficult social pressures impacting upon them both within and without the institution.

Some researchers have concluded that disruptive or delinquent behavior, especially when it takes place within the school environment, is a coping mechanism to deal with the pressures of school and the low self-esteem associated with failure. Gold further proposes that those students who are too controlled to engage in disruptive behavior may use other coping skills that can manifest themselves in various forms of mental illness.[32] Elliott and Voss also see delinquent behavior as a response to "social stigma and loss of self-esteem."[33] In a study of the relationships between delinquency and dropout in two high schools, they learned that dropouts had a higher rate of police contacts while in school than graduates. After dropping out of school, however, their police contacts declined to the point that ultimately the contact rate for the group that dropped out was lower than that of the group that graduated from high school.[34]

The issue of learning disabilities must also be addressed. Much research is still required in the area of learning disabilities, espe-

31. Ernst Wenk, "Schools and Youth Unrest" (Paper presented at the International Symposium on Youth Unrest, Israel, October 1971).

32. Gold, "Scholastic Experiences, Self-esteem, and Delinquent Behavior," p. 294.

33. Elliott and Voss, Delinquency and Dropout, p. 204.

34. Ibid., p. 128.

cially on the question of the relationship between those disabilities and delinquency. Some relationships have been found. For example, it has been estimated that approximately 10 percent of the general population has some form of learning disability, whereas the estimates run from 26 percent to 73 percent in a delinquent population.[35]

Identifying learning disabilities and distinguishing them from other learning problems are important and difficult tasks. Learning problems can be related to intellectual or cultural deprivation, emotional disturbance, or mental retardation. Learning disabilities include brain injury or dysfunction, perceptual handicaps, and dyslexia. That the culturally deprived child and the dyslexic child both experience learning barriers does not mean that they should both receive the clinical label associated with learning disability.[36]

It is crucial that learning problems or learning disabilities be determined at the earliest possible age so that suitable programs can be developed for these children. Failure to do so can mean the loss of a productive human being. A chain of events can take place that could be very similar to the labeling process already discussed. An acting-out child can be seen as disruptive by a teacher, who then treats the child accordingly. While this may be an indication of learning disability or of a learning problem, the child may be labeled as disruptive. This affects the child's self-esteem, which can already be affected by his inability to understand or control his behavior. Not only does he feel incompetent, but he is perceived as incompetent by others. The result can be rejection, alienation, and hostility. The end product can be delinquency. "Is it possible that children [with learning disability] are sentenced in the court not because of what they did on the streets, but because of what they could not do in the classroom?"[37]

35. Joel Zimmerman et al., *Some Observations on the Link between Learning Disabilities and Juvenile Delinquency* (Williamsburg, Va.: National Center for State Courts, 1978).

36. Charles A. Murray, *The Link between Learning Disabilities and Juvenile Delinquency*, Executive Summary (Washington, D.C.: U.S. Government Printing Office, 1976), p. 15.

37. Zimmerman et al., *Some Observations on the Link between Learning Disabilities and Juvenile Delinquency*, p. 20.

What Can Be Done?

Young adolescents need guidance and support both to avoid and to survive the juvenile justice system. The school is one of several societal institutions from which the needed help must come.

IN THE SCHOOLS

Perhaps most important of all is the need for greater sensitivity and awareness on the part of the school administration and teachers. It has already been indicated that disruptive behavior can be symptomatic of many things other than a "bad" child. Beyond learning disability and learning problems, an example from the juvenile justice system can further highlight this need for awareness.

Truancy may be a child's way of saying that he does not like school, or cannot read, or has not been placed in a program appropriate to his needs. Or, it can mean that there are problems outside the school that result in truancy—provocation from other children en route to school, embarrassment due to shabby clothing, lack of encouragement at home.

All of these possible reasons for truancy do have solutions. Yet, instead of the motive behind truancy being investigated, these youth are most often suspended or referred to juvenile court. The juvenile court can provide no substitute for provision, by the community and by the educational system, of educational atmospheres appropriate to children with special needs.

There is also a need for closer relationships between students and teachers so that sensitivity to students' needs can be fostered and a problem can be identified before an illegal act occurs. This means that the school must find more teachers who are not disheartened by having to teach slow learners. A great need exists for competent teachers who are committed to working with these particular students.

Schools and teachers must also create an environment where individual abilities are recognized and self-growth is encouraged. This can mean alternative programs or even alternative schools where programming is done in accordance with individual uniqueness in a low-competition environment. The maximum opportunity for success must be allowed. Many studies have shown that, given a supportive and individualized learning environment, children do want to learn and do want to graduate.

IN THE COMMUNITY

Yet the problem of delinquency is far greater than the schools can handle. As one of the primary community institutions, however, the school must assist in providing alternatives for those juveniles who are too often alienated from the school and/or community. Because community characteristics very much define and determine the degree of delinquency within the community, the community must ultimately accept responsibility for these youth. School, family, and community solutions are required that are obviously beyond the capacity and coercive intervention of the juvenile justice system.

We have already noted how the juvenile justice system handles the delinquency problem. Detention and institutionalization, often far from home, are not only an enormous waste of tax dollars, but of children's lives, especially when they have not committed a crime by adult standards or are nondangerous offenders. These juveniles can most effectively be helped within the community.

The Juvenile Justice and Delinquency Prevention Act of 1974 gave national attention to the inappropriate use of institutions and the dangerous abuse of children committed to them. A majority of the states have made a determined effort to refer status offenders to community services rather than to impose some form of confinement. It is now imperative that appropriate community programs be developed so that further deinstitutionalization of youth can take place and that community alternatives to incarceration be developed for the nondangerous juvenile offender.

Through the use of Deinstitutionalization of Status Offender Grants, it has been determined that status offenders can be served in voluntary, community programs without detention or institutional custody. It is hoped that the continued use of these services and the replication of these efforts on a national scale will dramatically reduce the number of children flowing into the juvenile justice system within the next few years. Such reallocation of personnel and fiscal resources may prove to be one of the largest and most effective delinquency prevention programs in the nation.

This is the positive new direction for juvenile justice in the United States. Its success will depend directly not only upon a strong commitment from the juvenile justice system, but also upon leadership and commitment from schools, churches, youth, social welfare, and mental health agencies, to keep their children in the community and out of secure detention institutions.

SOME AREAS OF INTERVENTION

CHAPTER VIII

Protecting Physical and Mental Health

DAVID BROMBERG, STEPHEN COMMINS, AND
STANFORD B. FRIEDMAN

The dramatic physical and psychological metamorphosis that occurs during adolescence places a tremendous stress on the equilibrium within the organism itself, as well as on the equilibrium existing between the organism and its environment. The physician and the educator are in a unique position to evaluate this balance and to intervene when disequilibrium occurs.

The normal changes that occur between the ages of ten and fifteen, a period covering early and middle adolescence, are staggering. The teenager will add the final 25 percent of his ultimate adult height, and as much as 50 percent of his adult weight. From the relatively immature child's body will emerge the sexually adult male and female with appropriate physique and body composition. The psychological developments that accompany these changes are equally impressive. The child must accommodate to a new body image and sense of self. He must begin to separate from his family and consider his position in the world as an independent entity.

The relatively smooth, predictable progression through this complex series of physical, biological, psychological, and social changes results in the state we call health. Any aberrations impacting on one of these processes, however, may influence functioning, growth, and development in other areas. Illness in adolescence well demonstrates these interdependent relationships.

In spite of what seems like endless opportunity for malfunction, the adolescent years generally are years of good health. The physician should, however, provide several opportunities to assess developmental progress during adolescence. "Well-health" physical exams are scheduled during this period and are, in fact, often mandated for entrance into high school or college, or for participation in sports. During these visits, assessments are made of the status of preventive measures such as immunizations. Medical screening for hypertension, tuberculosis, anemia, vision, hearing, spinal abnormalities, and cervical cancer should be made available to the adolescent patient. The physician also sees adolescent patients for acute illness. Medical services may be sought for specific counseling, especially in the areas of sex, contraception, nutrition, drug abuse, and driving or motorcycling safety.

Normal Growth and Development

PHYSICAL CHANGES

Growth and development during adolescence represent the culmination of an orderly process that has progressed throughout childhood.[1] Distinguishing it from the prior process, however, are the numerous hormonal changes that occur during this phase of life. This change in hormonal milieu and its consequent changes in growth and development is termed "puberty." The endocrinologic changes of puberty involve complex interactions of the higher cortical and limbic centers of the brain. These interactions influence hypothalamic function, which in turn regulates the reproductive system via the anterior pituitary gland and the ovaries or testes. Physical, sexual, and psychosocial development, as well as nutritional requirements, are affected by these changes.

There is wide variability in the onset and duration of puberty, with pubertal changes beginning normally as early as age eight or as late as age fourteen in females, and between ages ten and fifteen in males. Girls develop almost two years earlier than boys, although there is great variability in development among both sexes.

1. The discussion in this section draws upon the following sources: James M. Tanner, "Sequence, Tempo and Individual Variation in the Growth and Development of Boys and Girls, Aged 12-16," *Daedalus* 100 (Fall 1971): 903-30; idem, *Growth at Adolescence*, 2d ed. (Oxford: Blackwell Scientific Publication, 1962); H. Verdain Barnes, "Physical Growth and Development During Puberty," *Medical Clinics of North America* 59 (November 1975): 1305-18; Thomas E. Cone, Jr., "Secular Acceleration of Height and Biologic Maturation in Children During the Past Century," *Journal of Pediatrics* 59 (May 1961): 736-40.

Important characteristics separate the adolescent growth period from other periods of growth. First, there is the increased rate or velocity of growth. From birth until puberty the velocity of skeletal growth, in general, decreases. At puberty, however, the rate of growth begins to increase markedly and peaks at a rate that the child has not experienced since two years of age. Second, there is equally precipitous decline in growth rate following this peak, leading to the characterization of growth at adolescence as a "growth spurt." Third, there is the sexual maturation in growth and development that occurs during adolescence.

Before adolescence, males and females grow and develop in an essentially parallel fashion, both quantitatively and qualitatively (usually with the boys slightly behind the girls) at any given developmental stage. Therefore, there is a similarity between the sexes in body composition (percent muscle and fat), body shape (fat distribution and skeletal shape), muscle strength, and overall size. In fact, it is often claimed that in viewing an undressed prepubertal child from the back, observers would be unable to tell if they were looking at a boy or a girl. It is the differential growth and development occurring during adolescence that makes noting this distinction significantly easier.

Typically, the growth spurt begins at about age 12.5 years in males and 10.5 years in females, and peaks at age 14.0 and 12.0 years respectively. The magnitude of the adolescent growth spurt can be easily appreciated from the velocity curve seen in figure 1. In spite of all the variability that exists in the initiation and timing of puberty, it remains possible to examine the orderly sequence of the events that mark the physical growth of this period.

Skeletal changes start with rapid growth in the extremities. The peak increase in trunk length, by far the greatest contributor to overall height increase, may not occur until a year after the increase in leg length. The widening of the shoulders begins about six months after the peak increase in leg length. The sequencing and differential growth rate explain the problem, for example, in fitting a suit for a young male adolescent. Initially, either the pants are too short or the jacket too broad.

Weight changes closely parallel changes in height, occurring simultaneously in males and lagging six months behind height

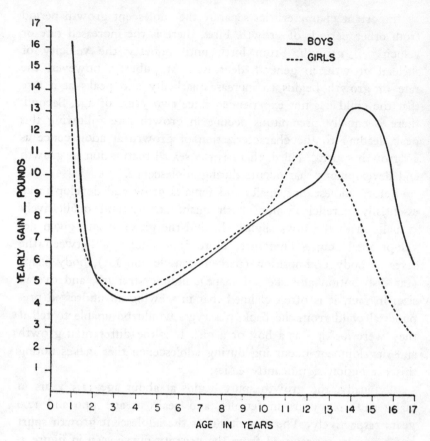

FIG. 1. Velocity of average weight growth in boys and girls from birth through adolescence

changes in females. Comparisons can also be made for changes in organ size, muscle mass (and correspondingly, muscle strength), and fat mass. By the end of adolescence the average male will have more than doubled his muscle strength, added up to 20 percent of his total linear growth, and gained approximately 50 percent of his total body weight.

Other differences in growth and development lead to a greater degree of sex differentiation. Men generally are larger than women. Skeletal shape differentiates, with men acquiring broader shoulders and longer arms and legs than women. Men have a larger increase in muscle mass than women, and a smaller increase in fat. Women develop broader hips and a wider pelvic inlet than men.

SEXUAL DEVELOPMENT

Sexual development during puberty includes gonadal and hormonal changes and the development of secondary sexual characteristics.[2] Sexual maturation begins with the gradual enlargement of the gonads, the testes in males and the ovaries in females. Clinically, however, the emergence of pubic hair in males and the beginning of breast development in females are used to date the onset of puberty.

In males, as the testes increase in size, increased levels of testosterone, the male hormone, are observed. Sperm maturation within the testes begins at puberty, resulting in mature spermatids with reproductive capability. In females, as the ovaries increase in size, there is an increase in the production of the hormones estrogen and progesterone. Females reach menarche, or the onset of menstrual periods, related to the cyclical pattern of hormonal secretion. As maturation is reached, and this pattern of secretion develops, there is an eruption of an egg from the ovary, or ovulation. In the year following menarche, many of the cycles may be anovulatory, particularly in early maturing females.

Physical changes seen during this growth period include the development of secondary sexual characteristics. In boys the enlargement of the penis and testes and changes in body hair, and in girls the development of breasts and growth of pubic hair are most significant. There are changes in body shape, musculature, skeletal growth, voice, strength, body odors, and sebaceous glands of the skin.

In boys, the genital developmental sequence begins at the stage

2. For this section we have drawn upon the following: Tanner, *Growth at Adolescence*; Paul H. Mussen, J. J. Conger, and Jerome Kagan, *Child Development and Personality* (New York: Harper and Row, 1974), pp. 542-651; P. Botstein and J. W. McArthur, "Physiology of the Normal Female," and H. N. B. Wettenhall, "Growth Problems," in *Medical Care of the Adolescent*, ed. J. Roswell Gallagher (New York: Appleton-Century-Crofts, 1976), pp. 519-28, 567-77; Edward O. Reiter and Allen W. Root, "Hormonal Changes of Adolescence," *Medical Clinics of North America* 59 (November 1975): 1289-1304; Edward O. Reiter, "Sexual Maturation in the Female," *Pediatric Clinics of North America* 19 (August 1972): 581-604.

where an increase in testicular size is first noted, generally at approximately 11.5 years. Pubic hair growth usually follows closely behind genital growth. Progression to full genital maturity takes about three years, ranging from less than two years to as long as five years. There seems to be less variation in sequencing of the various secondary sexual characteristics in boys than in girls.

The beginning of pubertal development in girls (elevation of the breast tissue, the breast buds) varies from about eight to thirteen years of age. Full, mature breast development averages four years from the time of onset. The relationship of these developmental stages of breasts and pubic hair can also be correlated to the onset of menarche, with breast and pubic hair development preceding menarche by about two years.

Over the last century, a trend toward acceleration of maturation in adolescent growth and development has been noted. Data from several sources in both the United States and in western Europe point clearly toward increasing size and toward an earlier onset of puberty.[3] For example, school children in Boston at age thirteen in the period from 1930 to 1956 were 10 cm. taller than a group in the same city in 1877. The height of the average Yale freshman increased from 5' 7.5" to 5' 10.5" between 1885 and 1957, and the weight increase in the same period was from 136 pounds to 156 pounds. As an indicator of maturation, menarche has also shown a dramatic change, with increasingly earlier onset, as shown in figure 2.

Carefully documented studies in the United States have shown a decrease in menarche from about 14.2 years of age in 1900 to 12.8 years in 1960. Many theories exist as to the etiology of this acceleration, and include nutritional, medical, and sociological explanations. It is unknown what will happen to this trend, although recent evidence suggests stabilization in ultimate growth and age of maturation.

PSYCHOSOCIAL DEVELOPMENT

Teenagers enter adolescence with a set of past experiences and

3. Cone, "Secular Acceleration of Height and Biologic Maturation in Children During the Past Century."

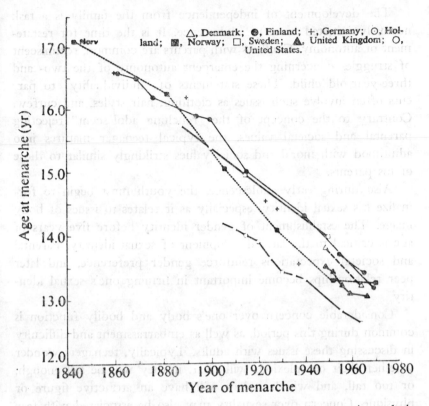

FIG. 2. Trends in menarcheal age in some European countries and the United States, 1840-1970

Source: James M. Tanner, *Growth at Adolescence*, 2d ed. (Oxford: Blackwell Scientific Publications, 1962). Reproduced with permission from J. M. Tanner.

approaches toward problem solving based on these experiences.[4] Four major tasks are generally considered necessary for the adolescent to progress from childhood to adulthood: separation from one's family and increasing independence, development of a sense of one's self or identity, establishment of a sexual identity leading to the ability to form significant interpersonal relationships, and creation of educational and vocational plans.

4. For this section we have drawn upon Mussen, Conger, and Kagan, *Child Development and Personality*, and S. R. Leichtman, "Psychosocial Development of Adolescence," in *Principles of Pediatrics: Health Care of the Young*, ed. Robert A. Hoekelman et al. (New York: McGraw-Hill, 1978), pp. 636-42.

The development of independence from the family is a task normally initiated in early adolescence. It is the time for restatement of autonomy. Conflicts with parents are common, reminiscent of struggles concerning the emergent autonomy of the two- and three-year-old child. These statements of "individuality" to parents often involve such issues as clothing, hair styles, and curfew. Contrary to the concept of the "rebelling adolescent" rejecting parental and societal values, the typical teenager matures into adulthood with moral and social values strikingly similar to those of his parents.

Also during early adolescence, the youth must begin to formalize his sexual identity, especially as it relates to issues of body image. The establishment of gender identity before five years of age is critical to the later development of sexual identity. Parental and societal expectations reinforce gender preference, and later peer relationships become important in firming one's sexual identity.

Considerable concern over one's body and bodily function is common during this period, as well as embarrassment and difficulty in discussing these issues with adults. Typically, teenagers wonder whether their complexions will clear, if they will be tall enough, or too tall, and whether they will have an attractive figure or physique. Concern over sexuality may also be associated with fear and anxiety over menstruation, masturbation, homosexuality, and nocturnal emissions.

The need to develop an identity as separate from one's parents promotes a strong peer-group alliance. Young teenagers are unsure of their place in adult culture and therefore seek support from among themselves and their own youth culture. Acceptance by peers is important, and strict adherence to group fashions, fads, ideals, and idols is the general rule. This strong relationship with peers also offers young teenagers a "mirror" for measuring their progress through adolescence. Locker rooms and slumber parties provide the opportunity for validation that changing bodies and sexual interests are also occurring among one's friends.

Concerns about gender identity and body image are usually followed by concerns about sexual behavior and interpersonal sexuality. These concerns illustrate the interaction of biologic, psychologic, and social factors impinging on the adolescent's development. Sexuality in both males and females is influenced by social and cultural factors. The acceptance of sexual behaviors such as hugging, masturbation, and nudity vary greatly among families and cultures. There appears to be an increase in sexual experimentation, including intercourse, in the teen-age years, typically with a single partner during a stable relationship. In contrast to this is promiscuous sexual behavior, usually involving several partners in a nonmeaningful relationship and indicative of psychosocial problems. Depending on the adolescent's value system, family support systems, and sexual outlets, these sexual behaviors and fantasies may be accompanied by fear and anxiety. Masturbation, for example, is often of great concern to the adolescent. Despite the commonality of the experience, there remain many religious and cultural taboos, as well as exotic myths about masturbation. Homosexual fantasies or experiences, such as mutual masturbation, a common occurrence in adolescence, also engender anxiety in this age group.

NUTRITIONAL REQUIREMENTS

Nutritional requirements of the adolescent are markedly increased over previous needs.[5] These nutritional needs are based upon stage of growth, level of activity, body size and composition, and climate and ecological factors. Consider two youngsters, age twelve. One weighs 120 pounds, is 5′4″ tall, is a jogger, is on the football team, and is on the ascending portion of his velocity curve. The other weighs 90 pounds, is 4′10″ tall, and prefers chess and music, and has not yet entered his adolescent growth spurt. These two youngsters will have quite different nutritional needs. Psychological factors, body image, food fads, and eating habits all must be considered when evaluating nutritional planning.

Recommended dietary allowances have been established by the National Research Council, but they must be considered in terms of the variables described above. Generally, the caloric needs of

5. Our discussion of nutrition draws upon Felix P. Heald, "Adolescent Nutrition," *Medical Clinics of North America* 59 (November 1975): 1329-36, and C. M. Young, "Adolescents and Their Nutrition," in *Medical Care of the Adolescent*, ed. Gallagher, pp. 15-25.

the average early adolescent male (ages eleven to fourteen) are equivalent to those of the average adult male (ages twenty-three to fifty). Protein requirements per pound of body weight, however, are almost 30 percent higher in the adolescent than in the adult. Vitamin requirements are approximately the same (despite the smaller size) and mineral requirements (calcium, phosphorus, and iron) are higher in the adolescent than the adult.

The picture for the young adolescent female is even more striking, with the teen-age girl having an absolute greater caloric need than the adult female, and increased iron is required in girls of this age group due to menstruation. In the pregnant female, all nutritional requirements are greatly increased.

To adolescents themselves, nutrition generally assumes much less importance than the more pressing concerns of body image, peer alliance, and independence. Dietary practices often suffer as a result. The relatively inactive female teenager utilizing few calories, who is attempting to achieve the "thin" look, may be sacrificing necessary nutrients. For the active adolescent beginning to loosen close family ties, mealtime may often be chosen as the time *not* to be with the family. Instead, he may snack at home and with friends with little regard for nutritional adequacy.

Mention must also be made of "food fads" and "junk foods." With strong demands for peer-group alliance and identification with "youth culture" as separate from adult culture, adolescents occasionally reject traditional diets for ones that are currently popular with their peers. Examples are Zen diets (featuring as their primary components cereal grains), various vegetarian diets, or organic foods. Dieters as well may become involved in fads such as water diets or banana diets. Some of these are, or can be, nutritionally sound, but care must be taken that they do indeed meet current growth needs. "Junk foods," the appellation often given to foods commonly available from drive-in/take-out restaurants that feature the hamburger, french fries, shakes, and pizzas, are also frequently associated with the teenager. These diets, too, may provide a good basis for meeting nutritional needs, but should be supplemented by the appropriate groups of fruits and vegetables. The controversy over the additives and preservatives frequently present in these foods continues. In spite of dietary variances from adult eating patterns, widespread gross nutritional abnormalities are not present in the adolescent age group in the United States.

Physical Growth and Development: Variations

The beginning of pubertal changes is an important landmark for teenagers, and precocious development or delay may cause embarrassment and anxiety. Common problems include deviations from average in stature, weight, and sexual development. Studies have shown significant differences between groups of early and late maturers.[6] The early maturing boys tend to be in positions of leadership throughout adolescence. Boys with late development, on the other hand, are more likely to have difficulties with social adjustments. In contrast to feelings of self-confidence and independence of the early maturers, the late maturers seem to be inadequate and rejected. These problems of growth variations are frequently brought to the attention of a physician who must separate the abnormal medical conditions from those representing normal variations, appreciate the teenager's concerns about the problem, and weigh the potential benefits against the disadvantages of therapeutic intervention.

The physician's evaluation of each of these growth variations follows a similar pattern. A history of prior growth and development, as well as a complete medical history, is obtained. The presence of nutritional deficits and chronic illness is carefully excluded. The family history of growth patterns and ages of sexual maturation (for example, menarche, facial hair) of same-sexed individuals also adds a useful perspective in separating normal from abnormal variation. School records are often invaluable in providing information on prior growth. A thorough physical examination provides the physician with an assessment of maturational age and helps identify abnormal medical conditions. The striking physical differences between teenagers of the same chronological age but with differing maturational ages are seen in figure 3. Laboratory tests often include X-rays of the skeletal growth

6. Mary C. Jones and Paul H. Mussen, "Self-conception, Motivations and Interpersonal Attitudes of Early and Late Maturing Boys," *Child Development* 28 (June 1957): 243-56; idem, "Self-conception, Motivations and Interpersonal Attitudes of Early and Late Maturing Girls," *Child Development* 29 (December 1958): 492-501.

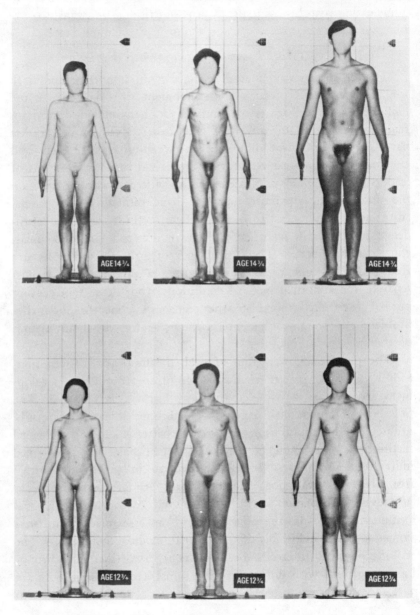

FIG. 3. Variation in size and pubertal development of three boys (upper row) aged 14.75 years and three girls (lower row) aged 12.75 years. Reproduced with permission from J. M. Tanner.

centers (usually the wrist) as an indicator of maturational age, with more sophisticated tests occasionally needed.

This evaluation is often all that is necessary to identify those growth deviations that represent normal variations. The major intervention in these cases is reassurance and counseling. From the information gathered, an estimate can often be made on the timing of future developmental changes and eventual adult height. It is critical to allow time for counseling and longitudinal follow-up, and to not dismiss these concerns casually. Late maturing teenagers need an opportunity to share their concerns with someone who will listen in a nonjudgmental manner. "Acting out" and demonstrations of "manly" behaviors such as fighting and stealing may be a compensation for short stature or delayed development. The physician must recognize this and institute appropriate counseling.

SHORT STATURE AND DELAYED PUBERTY

The "late" maturer usually presents to the physician with a combination of short stature and pubertal delay.[7] Medical consultation is usually sought as awareness increases that the teenager has grown and matured less than his peers. Evaluation should be considered in boys without initiation of their growth spurt or increasing testicular size by age fourteen and girls without beginning breast development by age thirteen and a half or pubic hair growth by fourteen.

Over 90 percent of the adolescents seeking medical attention in one adolescent clinic for delayed puberty were found to be "normal," but slow, in their maturation.[8] The remainder are the consequence of numerous medical abnormalities including chronic

---

7. For this section we have drawn upon Wettenhall, "Growth Problems"; W. A. Marshall and James M. Tanner, "Variations in the Pattern of Pubertal Changes in Girls," *Archives of Diseases of Childhood* 44 (June 1969): 291-303; idem, "Variations in the Pattern of Pubertal Changes in Boys," *Archives of Diseases of Childhood* 45 (February 1970): 13-23; J. Roswell Gallagher, "Short and Tall Stature in Otherwise Normal Adolescents: Management of Their Medical and Psychologic Problems," in *Endocrine and Genetic Diseases of Childhood and Adolescence*, ed. Lytt I. Gardner (Philadelphia: W. B. Saunders, 1975), pp. 99-105.

8. H. Verdain Barnes, "The Problem of Delayed Puberty," *Medical Clinics of North America* 59 (November 1975): 1337-48.

illness, hormonal disorders, skeletal disease, and metabolic disorders.

Specific medical drug intervention is, of course, dependent on the outcome of the evaluation. If an underlying pathologic condition is uncovered, it must be addressed therapeutically (for example, by correcting a thyroid hormone deficiency or by treating a chronic kidney infection). If no organic process is discovered, relatively little can be done to increase growth. The testosterone-like hormones do increase growth, but they simultaneously accelerate cessation of bone growth, thereby diminishing ultimate height potential.

TALL STATURE

The early maturing girl is usually the patient who presents with tall stature as a complaint.[9] Girls whose predicted adult height will be greater than six feet are included in this category. Abnormal medical conditions are only rarely uncovered. The concern and embarrassment frequently diminish as peers, especially boys, begin to "catch up" in height. The sex hormone, estrogen, may potentially be used to accelerate fusion of the bony growth centers, thereby diminishing height potential; however, there is some controversy over the efficacy as well as the safety of this treatment. To have any chance of success, therapy must begin very early in adolescence, prior to the peak height velocity and menarche, which on the average will be somewhere between eleven and twelve years of age.

OBESITY

Obesity is generally considered as a weight that is 20 percent or more above ideal body weight for age, sex, and height.[10] The vast majority of these cases are classified as exogenous obesity resulting from excessive caloric intake. Very rarely metabolic or endocrinologic abnormalities may cause obesity, and these are usually easily identifiable. Obesity has been clearly related to in-

9. Wettenhall, "Growth Problems"; Gallagher, "Short and Tall Stature in Otherwise Normal Adolescents."

10. Felix P. Heald and M. A. Khan, "Obesity," in *Medical Care of the Adolescent*, ed. Gallagher, pp. 125-38; Albert J. Stunkard, *The Pain of Obesity* (Palo Alto, Calif.: Bull Publishing Co., 1976).

creased mortality from a number of disease processes. Alterations in metabolism and hormonal functions have also been found to result from obesity and further complicate the medical picture. There is a strong tendency for obesity to run in families, with 80 percent of the children of two obese parents being obese as opposed to only 9 percent of the children of normal weight parents.[11] The contributing role of genetic versus sociocultural factors is not clear at this time. The outcome in childhood and adolescent obesity is discouraging, with a large number becoming obese adults.

Obesity may have a serious effect on psychosocial development of the adolescent. It interferes with acceptance and status within the peer group, and may severely damage the developing body image. Further, it has been shown that some obese adolescents, who later slim down to become adults of normal weight, continue to have images of themselves as "fat people." [12] There are often fears relating to one's attractiveness as a sexual partner in the obese teenager, which may hamper the development of heterosexual relationships. In terms of overall identity, obese individuals will often question their total self-worth and frequently downgrade their own attributes and abilities. Thus, obese adolescents may be depressed, although outwardly they may appear carefree.

These medical and psychological factors would certainly suggest that intervention efforts are of paramount importance. The success of these measures, however, has been disappointing. The principles of obesity management are simple and consist of increasing activity and consequently increasing caloric expenditure at the same time that one decreases caloric intake. Translating these principles into effective treatment regimens, however, has proven exceedingly difficult. During adolescence the problem is further complicated by the need to supply sufficient nutritional intake to meet growth requirements. Fad diets, for this reason, often prove to be particularly dangerous to growing adolescents. Drug therapy in the form of "appetite suppressants" (usually amphetamines) has been shown to have no long-range benefits, and may be dangerous in terms of abuse potential. Group programs

11. Heald and Khan, "Obesity."

12. Stunkard, *The Pain of Obesity*.

that offer both peer pressure and support have had some success. Surgical intervention is considered only in the most severe cases, and must be weighed against many potential complications.

UNDERWEIGHT

There are usually less serious health ramifications to being underweight than to being overweight in adolescence. The teenager who has always been thin as a child must be differentiated from the adolescent who loses weight, as the teenager who loses weight (other than appropriate dieting in an overweight youth) is following an abnormal pattern and must be thoroughly investigated. It may, for instance, mark the beginning of a chronic illness, metabolic disease, or an emotional problem. In the lower socioeconomic groups, significant undernutrition also must be considered.

Rapid severe weight loss in teenagers with no underlying medical disease is also found in the illness called "anorexia nervosa."[13] Patients with this condition, usually preadolescent or adolescent females, embark on a program of severe dietary restriction resulting in the loss of as much as 50 percent of their body weight. It is believed that there is significant psychosocial pathology in these children and in their interactions with their families. As a result of their weight loss, there are serious medical complications. Treatment involves a coordinated team approach with physicians, psychiatrists, dietitians, and family all playing significant roles.

DISORDERS IN SEXUAL DEVELOPMENT

Disorders of sexual development include delayed puberty (see above), precocious puberty, and disorders of breast development, all potentially causing problems with sexual identity and behavior.[14] Precocious puberty, unlike pubertal delay, is more commonly related to pathologic and medical conditions, including central nerv-

13. Robert A. Hoekelman and S. Munson, "Anorexia Nervosa," in *Principles of Pediatrics: Health Care of the Young*, ed. Hoekelman et al., pp. 669-77.

14. Reiter and Root, "Hormonal Changes of Adolescents"; J. H. Seashore, "Breast Enlargements in Infants and Children," *Pediatric Annals* 10 (October 1975): 542-64.

ous system diseases and metabolic abnormalities. Evaluation by a physician is therefore essential. Aberrations may include the development of female sex characteristics in the male and male sex characteristics in the female.

The growth of breast tissue at inappropriate stages of development, abnormal masses or swellings, and unusual breast size, are all of concern to teenagers and their parents. These concerns may be exaggerated by the importance our culture places on breast development. In contrast to breast lesions in the adult, disorders of the breast in children and adolescents infrequently require surgery, and extremely few cases are the result of a malignant disease.

Rapid extreme enlargement of the breasts in females is occasionally seen, with breast development out of proportion to general growth. This condition may represent an unusual sensitivity of the breast tissue to the hormonal stimuli of puberty. Although some regression may occur at the end of adolescence, the resulting pendulous breasts may require surgical reduction in size.

Development of breast tissue in the male, gynecomastia, is common in normal boys between the ages of ten and sixteen. This usually regresses spontaneously in six months to two years. Careful physical examination is indicated to eliminate the possibility of underlying medical abnormality. Because of the teenager's embarrassment, withdrawal from peer contact, especially in sports or in the gym, is sometimes observed. Extreme cases may require removal of underlying breast tissue.

Common Health Problems

At this generally healthy, though accident-prone time of life, several conditions and illnesses are a cause of concern and sometimes of serious problems. While some are rare, others are quite widespread.

DERMATOLOGIC PROBLEMS

Skin disorders among children and adolescents are common.[15]

15. Our discussion here draws upon J. S. Strauss and P. E. Pochi, "Acne and Some Other Common Skin Disorders," in *Medical Care of the Adolescent* ed. Gallagher, pp. 145-52; Ronald M. Reisner, "Acne Vulgaris," *Pediatric Clinics of North America* 20 (November 1973): 851-64.

Because of the visibility of the skin, these problems are often brought to the attention of parents and subsequently physicians for treatment. While facing the tasks of developing a positive body image and independence, adolescents may be troubled by changes in their bodies that may interrupt this development. Of geatest concern to the teenager is acne, the most common of skin disorders in adolescence. Generally it begins at puberty due, in part, to the stimulation of the sebaceous glands by the sex hormones. There is a spectrum of problems with clinical acne ranging from a few comedones (blackheads) to severe inflammatory reactions that are more destructive and may result in permanent scarring.

Acne usually increases during the mid to late adolescent period, then subsides. It is generally more severe in males than females. The primary sites of acne are the face, chest, back, and shoulders. Adolescents may have concern about the relationship of acne with sexual feelings, sexual relations, venereal disease, masturbation, diet, and general cleanliness. Attention should be paid to these concerns. The control, rather than the cure, of the disorder and the proper management of the problem are important to emphasize. Therapy for acne consists of no single treatment and must be individualized according to the severity. It has recently been found that elimination of various foods from the diet, especially chocolate, has no apparent benefit on the control of acne. The modes of therapy usually include topical agents such as cleansing agents, abrasives, and astringents, with relatively few cases justifying the use of an antibiotic.

CHRONIC ILLNESS

The more common major chronic illnesses seen among teenagers include diabetes mellitus, cystic fibrosis, asthma, and seizure disorders.[16] Chronic illness may significantly interfere with a child's physical and emotional development. In adolescence, chronic illness may directly interfere with the completion of adolescent developmental tasks and may impinge on the individual's family or peer relationships. Thus, there may be difficulty in developing

16. Martin G. Wolfish and John A. Maclean, "Chronic Illness in Adolescents," *Pediatric Clinics of North America* 21 (November 1974): 1043-50.

a positive self-image, especially in the context of feeling "different" from peers. In school, the chronically ill teenager may be unable to participate in some sports and social activities, again separating him from his peers at a time when they are most important. The physicians should inform the school as to the exact nature of the medical restrictions, and also what the teenager *can* do. Over-protectiveness, which is a common parental response to chronic illness, is liable to lead to arguments within the family.

The teenager with diabetes may experience many restrictions. He must follow diets and is usually dependent on insulin to control his disease. These changes in life style may be in conflict with peer group participation, for example, being able to eat pizza after school with friends. The teenager with diabetes may try to deny his illness, missing insulin doses and failing to test his urine, resulting in repeated hospitalizations. The well-controlled teenager with this disease should be able to participate in sports and most other normal activities.

Cystic fibrosis is a pulmonary disease that affects children and teenagers. Children with cystic fibrosis are now living through adolescence into adulthood, in contrast to a shorter life expectancy in the past. Their poor tolerance for exercise and frequent episodes of severe illness and hospitalization may exclude them from normal teen-age experiences. Male patients with cystic fibrosis have been found to be sterile, further interfering with development of sexual identity.

Asthma, a respiratory disease with reversible "wheezing" attacks, often limits school attendance and participation in sports. Allergies, infection, exertion, and emotional stress may all have a role in precipitating asthmatic attacks.

The diagnosis of a seizure disorder can alter the teenager's life. If not well controlled by drugs, seizures may also interfere with everyday functioning and schooling. Even well controlled, a seizure disorder may separate an individual from his peers. As with other illnesses, use of medications to treat seizures may cause the adolescent to perceive himself as "not normal."

PREGNANCY

Teenage pregnancy is a major health and social problem in

the United States.[17] It is estimated that approximately half of all teenagers by age nineteen, and one-fifth of all thirteen- and fourteen-year-olds, have had sexual intercourse. This sexual activity among teenagers resulted in more than a million pregnancies in 1974 among fifteen- to nineteen-year-olds. Two-thirds of those led to out-of-wedlock births. Of the one million teen-age pregnancies, approximately one-fourth were terminated by induced abortion and approximately 15 percent resulted in miscarriages. The remainder, approximately 600,000 babies born to teenagers that year, represented one fifth of all births. It is estimated that approximately 30,000 girls below age fifteen become pregnant every year. Less than 4 percent of these babies were given up for adoption, with over 90 percent being kept by their young mothers. The problems of teen-age pregnancy are not limited to the numbers of new babies born, but extend to the increased morbidity to mother and child and the multiple psychosocial effects on the families.

For pregnant teenagers under fifteen years of age there is a greater risk of having infants who are premature or of low birth weight and therefore have a higher mortality rate. Toxemia and anemia, two complications of pregnancy, are higher among young teen-age mothers. The pregnant teenager is more likely to drop out of school, for she generally does not "fit" with the normal school routine, and it may be difficult for her to go back after the baby is born. Schools for pregnant teenagers and special tutoring programs may help with these problems.

There are many reasons why teen-age women become pregnant. As noted previously, sexual maturation is occurring earlier now than seventy years ago. Many sexually active teenagers do not use contraception. There also are psychosocial factors involved; some teenagers want to express their masculinity or femininity by having a child. Some may be rebelling against parental or societal authority. In addition, a significant number of teen-age girls wish to have a child so as to feel needed and significant to another human being.

17. Stanley C. Marinoff and David H. Schonholz, "Adolescent Pregnancy," *Pediatric Clinics of North America* 19 (August 1972): 795-802; Alan Guttmacher Institute, *11 Million Teenagers: What Can Be Done about the Epidemic of Adolescent Pregnancies in the United States* (New York: Planned Parenthood Federation of America, 1976).

What can be done about this problem? An important area may be education about sexuality, contraception, and child care. In our opinion, this education should be provided in schools through classes and counseling services. During and after the pregnancy, education and services relating to health and child care should be made available. Education about abortion services and their availability should be provided so that teenagers who desire abortions have that choice.

SEXUALLY TRANSMITTED DISEASES

A major disease entity with epidemic proportions in adolescent medicine is venereal disease.[18] Gonorrhea is most prevalent, although it represents only one of approximately a dozen diseases transmitted through sexual contact. Other significant diseases, also increasing in incidence, are certain vaginal infections (yeast and trichomonal), genital warts, and genital herpes. Changes in sexual mores and removal of the fear of pregnancy are often held responsible for the rapid increase in gonorrhea. In fact, none of these tenets has been clearly demonstrated.

Gonorrhea is spread by sexual contact and causes an infection at the site of innoculation. Therefore, depending on the type of sexual activity, it is possible to acquire gonorrhea in the penis, vagina, throat, or rectum. Spread by inanimate objects (toilet seats, glasses) is thought to be virtually nonexistent. The male who contracts genital gonorrhea is usually symptomatic within three to five days, with burning pain on urination and a penile discharge. A minority of men have asymptomatic infection, whereas almost 75 percent of women will have no initial clinical symptoms. Treatment with penicillin usually results in a cure with no further complications. On occasion, the infection will spread beyond the immediate site of innoculation and a generalized systemic illness may occur. Other complications include spread to adjacent genital structures, which in the female may result in fallopian tube infection or abcess. If untreated, this condition may ultimately lead to

18. M. S. Stern and R. G. MacKenzie, "Venereal Disease in Adolescents," *Medical Clinics of North America* 59 (November 1975): 1395-1406; Iris F. Litt et al., "Gonorrhea in Children and Adolescents: A Current Review," *Journal of Pediatrics* 85 (November 1974): 595.

sterility. Unfortunately, having a gonococcal infection confers no immunity, for an individual is again susceptible on the next exposure.

Efforts to control the epidemic spread of this infection include public health measures, education, and research into new forms of medical management. Approaching teenagers in a nonjudgmental and confidential manner may increase their willingness to name contacts and encourage their seeking therapy. The use of condoms, besides providing a moderately effective means of birth control, will prevent the spread of infection. On the medical front, research into postcoital therapy and vaccine development is being conducted in the hope of arresting the spread of the disease.

SUBSTANCE ABUSE

Drug and alcohol abuse in the adolescent age group has been a significant medical and social concern over the last two decades.[19] Studies over this time period have shown changing patterns of abuse, with different drugs peaking in incidence and then disappearing from the scene. At the current time, abuse involving heroin (and other narcotics) by adolescents appears to be decreasing from its peak in the mid and late 1960s, when its use was viewed as a new "epidemic." Marijuana appears to be maintaining its popularity with continued widespread use. Concern over alcohol abuse is growing as evidence is accumulating of heavy widespread use in younger populations. Particularly disturbing is the popularity of phencyclidine (PCP, angel dust, flakes), which may cause bizarre thoughts and actions, unawareness of pain, and extreme aggressive and impulsive behaviors. The use of psychedelics (LSD, psilocybin) has decreased. Abuse of other substances (amphetamines, cocaine, glue sniffing, and barbiturates) appears to wax and wane.

A careful distinction must be made between the *use* and *abuse* of drugs during adolescence. So, for example, while a majority of high school students report having tried alcohol or having used it occasionally, only a very small minority would be considered

19. Iris F. Litt and Michael I. Cohen, "The Drug-using Adolescent as a Pediatric Patient," *Journal of Pediatrics* 77 (August 1970) 195-202; L. Wurmser, "Drug Use and Abuse in Adolescence," in *Medical Care of the Adolescent*, ed. Gallagher, pp. 708-20.

abusers. During adolescence, experimental use of drugs is common, undoubtedly being related to many of the developmental factors already discussed. The potential difficulties with occasional alcohol or marijuana usage have not been fully studied, but at present appear to involve minimal dangers. Compulsive drug use, or abuse, is a different category, with far different implications. The youth involved frequently have major psychosocial problems leading to drug abuse and may develop physical or psychiatric problems as a result of the abuse.

"Illness" related to drug and alcohol abuse should be looked at in the medical, social, and psychological realms. Medical problems depend on the type of drug used, the amount and chronicity, the combinations, and the route of administration. Commonly, users of drugs that are injected into veins are at risk for hepatitis, allergic reactions, and "blood poisoning." A prevalent problem, intrinsic to illicit drug use, is the "quality control" of street drugs, both for content and concentrations. There have been reports of death from injection of rat poison sold as heroin, or overdosage from an unusually "pure" batch of drug used in the routine fashion. Medical complications of chronic alcohol use are well known and include under-nutrition, stomach irritation, and cirrhosis of the liver. Some of the health problems arise indirectly from drug use, for example, vehicular accidents because of altered perceptual states with alcohol. Overdosage, always a concern, may result from ignorance, poly-drug use, or self-destructive intention. Depending on the drug, the situation may be life threatening. Untoward psychologic reactions, the so-called "bad trip," may also necessitate medical intervention.

Drug abuse potentially causes major social "illness." To be a participant, the teenager must go against societal law, exposing himself to possible criminal prosecution. Widespread disregard for established law may have serious social ramifications. Barring this, implicit or explicit acceptance of illegal behavior, which frequently occurs within families and even within the judicial system, offers a confusing social message. For the addictive drugs, expensive physiological habits develop, making it necessary for the teenager to obtain large sums of money, often resulting in criminal activity such as stealing, mugging, dealing drugs, and prostitution.

The psychological etiologies for drug usage and the potential dangers that exist for the abuser are complex. Some teenagers are attempting to gain peer acceptance, while others are withdrawing from reality and attempting to camouflage a severe depression. For the experimenter, drug use may represent rebellion or separation from his family and thereby serve an important developmental function. Compulsive drug use, on the other hand, rarely serves any adaptive purpose and is commonly associated with psycho-pathology.

DEPRESSION AND SUICIDE

The teenager experiences great fluctuations in mood, with high levels of confidence at times and feelings of doubt and depression at others.[20] The depressive mood swings of adolescence are normal responses to losses, disappointments, or difficulties in adaptation. They must be differentiated, however, from the more serious depressive illnesses that may lead to suicidal behavior. Depression is thought to be the most significant precursor to successful suicide. The underlying theme is the experience of a loss—loss of a personal relationship through death, separation, or a broken friendship. There may be loss of self-esteem after failure to attain a desired goal.

Recognizing the depressed adolescent is not always easy. The "normal" depressive mood swings, however, are usually short-lived. When looking at how clinically significant depression presents in adults, one notes eating disorders, psychosomatic complaints, insomnia, and withdrawal. There may be an increase in alcohol and drug use. In children and adolescents, however, delinquent behavior, school problems, drug abuse, or sexual promiscuity are more often encountered. There is often a decreased ability to concentrate and also a withdrawal from peers and family. Frequently these behaviors are dismissed by adults, and the adolescent himself may not recognize that he is depressed and may complain merely of boredom, fatigue, or restlessness.

20. A. Mattsson, "Adolescent Depression and Suicide," in *Principles of Pediatrics: Health Care of the Young*, ed. Hoekelman, pp. 665-69; Irving B. Weiner, *Psychological Disturbance in Adolescence* (New York: Wiley Interscience, 1970); Elizabeth R. McAnarney, "Suicidal Behavior in Children and Youth," *Pediatric Clinics of North America* 22 (August 1975): 595-604.

During their depressed mood swings, many adolescents will have thoughts of suicide or of being dead. However, they lack the intention of hurting themselves. After significant losses or a persistent depressive period, the teenager may become preoccupied with thoughts of suicide and see it as a "way out." It may represent an attempt to alter an intolerable living situation, to resolve an insurmountable conflict, or to punish certain significant people. Suicide is now the fourth leading cause of death during the teenage years, following accidents, malignancies, and homicide. The incidence may be higher than thought in that it is probably highly underreported. Between ages ten and fourteen, there are approximately two hundred successful suicides per year and from ages sixteen to nineteen there is an eight- to twelvefold increase, resulting in approximately 2,000 deaths per year. The ratio of attempted to completed suicides is approximately 100 to 1. Evaluating the suicidal adolescent includes recognition of the adolescent at risk, determining the significance of the suicidal act, assessing the teenager's support systems, and knowing what resources are available to help him.

ACCIDENTS

Accidents represent the leading health problem in the adolescent age group.[21] They are responsible for a majority of the deaths in adolescence (ages ten to nineteen), and are a leading cause of hospitalization and absence from school or work. The causation of accidental injuries and death has varied over the decades, depending on current recreational and vehicular fashions. The rate of death from accidents, however, has remained relatively stable over the past century. To study patterns of accidental injury, the adolescent age group is frequently divided into younger (ages ten to fourteen) and older (ages fifteen to nineteen) subgroups. The latter group is responsible for a much greater percentage of accidental injury and death, related in part to a sharp increase in driving and in behaviors related to the use of alcohol and drugs. Males die as a result of accidents approximately twice as often as females. This male preponderance is found in all classes of accidental death.

21. Felix P. Heald, "Morbidity and Mortality," in *Medical Care of the Adolescent*, ed. Gallagher, pp. 11-14.

The motor vehicle accident is the major contributor to these deaths.

Accidents have traditionally been thought of as "acts of fate." Increasingly, however, the victim's contribution to accidental injury is becoming clear. Hypotheses have related accident occurrence (including motor vehicle accidents) to suicide-like or self-destructive behavior, risk-taking behavior, and impulsivity. As these factors become better understood, it may become possible to identify accident-prone persons and to aim preventive measures directly at them. Present intervention attempts using educational methods, such as public announcements about seat belts, have been disappointing, and more sophisticated educational techniques are needed.

Intervention Efforts

Providing medical and mental health services to adolescents is a major challenge to families, physicians, counselors, and educators. Who should provide the services, where they can be received, and how to convince the adolescent he needs these services are some of the difficulties that arise. Most services are now provided by emergency rooms, emergency medical clinics, and adolescent or general out-patient clinics and private practitioners. These resources are far from adequate in many communities. Primary care physicians, including pediatricians, internists, and family practitioners, could provide much of the health care to this often neglected group. Over the past twenty-five years, subspecialty training in adolescent medicine has gradually developed to provide direct services to the adolescent. Whatever service is provided must balance the adolescent's need for confidentiality and privacy with his continuing but diminishing dependence upon his parents.

An area of great need for the adolescent is health education. Providing the developing teenager with information about nutritional needs, physical exercise, and education about smoking, alcohol, and drug abuse, could help to avoid later problems. Education in the areas of mental health and sex education is important. The adolescent should understand his developmental tasks. If we expect teenagers to have a clear understanding of themselves, we must provide the information to them.

CHAPTER IX

Fostering Moral Development

MARTIN L. HOFFMAN

For over half a century morality has been a popular topic in the child development literature. The probable reasons are twofold. First, morality is the part of personality that most clearly links the individual to society and it epitomizes the universal problem of managing the inevitable conflicts between personal need and social obligation. Second, morality has obvious social significance in an urban society characterized by increasing crime, decreasing religious involvement, and events like Watergate, Jonestown, the Kitty Genovese murder, and the activism of the 1960s, all of which are brought home by the mass media. Despite the interest, little systematic research has been done with adolescents, most of it being confined to young children. Fortunately, young adolescents are often subjects, and although the reasons for this may be practical rather than a special interest in this age group, the findings are pertinent.

Since Freud and Durkheim, there has been agreement among social scientists that most people do not go through life viewing society's moral norms (for example, honesty, justice, fair play) as external, coercively imposed pressures. Although initially external and often in conflict with one's desires, the norms eventually become part of one's motive system and guide behavior even in the absence of external authority. The challenge is to find out what experiences foster this internalization. The aim here is to pull together the relevant findings and theories.

Parental Influences on Moral Internalization

Since the parent is the most significant figure in the child's life, every facet of the parent's role—disciplinarian, affection giver, model—has been studied.

DISCIPLINE AND AFFECTION

Moral internalization implies that persons are motivated to weigh their desires against the moral requirement of a situation. Since one's earliest experience in handling this type of conflict occurs in disciplinary encounters with parents, it is reasonable to expect that the types of discipline used will affect the child's moral development. Affection is important because it may make the child more receptive to discipline, more likely to emulate the parent, and emotionally secure enough to be open to the needs of others.

A large body of research done mainly in the 1950s and 1960s dealt with correlations between types of discipline and various moral indices, such as resisting temptation and feeling guilty over violating a moral standard.[1] The findings suggest that moral internalization is fostered by (a) the mother's frequent use of inductive disciplinary techniques, which point up the harmful consequences of the child's behavior for others, and (b) the mother's frequent expression of affection outside the disciplinary encounter. A morality based on fear of external punishment, on the other hand, is associated with the mother's excessive use of power-assertive discipline, for example, physical punishment, deprivation of privileges, or the threat of these. There is also evidence that under certain conditions—when the child is openly and unreasonably defiant—the occasional use of power assertion by mothers who typically use induction may contribute positively to moral internalization.[2]

This research is limited because it is correlational, and it may seem as plausible to infer that the child's moral orientation affects the parent's discipline, as the reverse.[3] I have argued, however, that although the child does influence the parent's behavior, this is most true in infancy because of the parent's sensitivity to cues indicating

1. For a critical review of the research on parent discipline, see Martin L. Hoffman, "Moral Internalization: Current Theory and Research," in *Advances in Experimental Social Psychology*, vol. 10, ed. Leonard Berkowitz (New York: Academic Press, 1977).

2. Martin L. Hoffman, "Conscience, Personality, and Socialization Techniques," *Human Development* 13, no. 2 (1970): 90-126.

3. Richard Q. Bell, "A Reinterpretation of the Direction of Effects in Studies of Socialization," *Psychological Review* 75 (March 1968): 81-95.

the child's helplessness and need for attention.[4] By two years the parent shifts dramatically from primarily a caretaker to a disciplinarian. From then on, through early adolescence, the child has little control and is frequently compelled by the parent to change behavior against his will. Furthermore, the inner states aroused in the child by different disciplinary techniques (for example, self-blame, fear) are similar to those aroused by moral encounters in internalized and noninternalized persons (guilt, fear). Since early disciplinary encounters predate internal moral development, it follows that inductive discipline is more of an antecedent than a consequence of moral internalization. Final resolution of this issue awaits research employing appropriate (for example, cross-lagged longitudinal) designs. (The laboratory research on discipline has little relevance, since the subjects were young children.)

I recently proposed a theoretical explanation of the findings.[5] First, most disciplinary techniques have power-assertive and love-withdrawing properties, which comprise the motive-arousal component needed to get the child to stop and pay attention to the inductive component that may also be present. Second, the child may be influenced cognitively and affectively (through arousal of empathy and guilt) by the information in the inductive component and thus experience a reduced sense of opposition between desires and external demands. Third, if there is too little arousal, the child may ignore the parent; if there is too much, the resulting fear or resentment may prevent effective processing of the inductive content. Techniques having a salient inductive component ordinarily achieve the best balance. Fourth, the ideas in inductions (and the associated empathy and guilt) are encoded in "semantic" memory and retained a long time, whereas the details of the setting in which they originated are encoded in "episodic" memory and soon forgotten. Fifth, eventually, lacking a clear external referent to which to attribute the ideas, the child may experience them as originating in the self.

4. Martin L. Hoffman, "Moral Internalization, Parental Power, and the Nature of Parent-child Interaction," *Developmental Psychology* 11 (March 1975): 228-39.

5. Martin L. Hoffman, "Parental Discipline and Moral Internalization: A Theoretical Analysis," Developmental Report No. 85 (Ann Arbor, Mich.: University of Michigan, 1976).

PARENT AS MODEL

It has been assumed, since Freud, that children identify with their parents and adopt their ways of evaluating one's own behavior. The intriguing question is, why does the child do this? Psychoanalytic writers stress anxiety over physical attack or loss of the parent's love. To reduce anxiety, the child tries to be like the parent—to adopt the parent's behavioral mannerisms, thoughts, feelings, and even the capacity to punish oneself and experience guilt over violating a moral standard. For other writers, the child identifies to acquire desirable parent characteristics (for example, privileges, control of resources, power over the child).

The research, which is sparse, suggests that identification may contribute to aspects of morality reflected in the parent's words and deeds (for example, type of moral reasoning, helping others). It may not contribute to feeling guilty after violating moral standards,[6] however, perhaps because parents rarely communicate their own guilt feelings to the child, children lack the cognitive skills needed to infer guilt feelings from overt behavior, and children's motives to identify are not strong enough to overcome the pain of self-criticism.

In the early 1960s Bandura suggested that identification is too complex a concept; imitation is simpler, more amenable to research, yet equally powerful as an explanatory concept. Numerous experiments followed. Those studying the effects of adult models on moral judgment and resistance to temptation in children are especially pertinent. They have found that children will imitate an adult model who yields to temptation (for example, leaves an assigned task to watch a movie), as though the model serves to legitimize the deviant behavior; but they are less apt to imitate a model who resists temptation. The research also suggests that when a child who makes moral judgments of others on the basis of consequences of their acts is exposed to an adult model who judges acts on the basis of intentions, the child shows an increased understand-

6. Martin L. Hoffman, "Identification and Conscience Development," *Child Development* 42 (October 1971): 1071-1082.

ing of the principle of intentions, and the effect may last up to a year.[7]

It thus appears that identification may contribute to the adoption of visible moral attributes requiring little self-denial, which may become internalized in the sense that the child uses them as criteria of right and wrong in judging others, but identification may not contribute to the use of moral standards as an evaluative perspective for examining one's own behavior.

THE ROLE OF THE FATHER

The research reviewed thus far does not indicate a crucial role for fathers except as models for boys. Fathers are important socialization agents, however, and their absence must create an enormous gap in the child's life. The special role of fathers in moral development, furthermore, is suggested in both Parsons's view that they bring the larger society's normative standards into the home, and Freud's view that by identifying with them boys acquire society's standards and the motivational and control systems that assure adherence to them.

There is evidence that fathers play an important, although perhaps an indirect role in moral socialization. In a study where the factors of intelligence and social class were controlled, young adolescent boys without fathers obtained significantly lower moral internalization scores and were rated by teachers as more aggressive than was the case for a group of boys who had fathers.[8] These effects appear to be more pronounced than the effects of not identifying with a father who is present. No differences were obtained for girls. These and other findings suggest that the negative effects of the father's absence on boys may be attributable in part to the lack of a paternal model, perhaps mediated by the effects of the father's absence on the mother's child-rearing practices.

7. For a critical review of the identification and imitation research, see Martin L. Hoffman, "Moral Development," in *Carmichael's Handbook of Child Psychology*, vol. 2, 3d ed., ed. Paul H. Mussen (New York: John Wiley and Sons, 1970), pp. 261-359.

8. Martin L. Hoffman, "Father Absence and Conscience Development," *Developmental Psychology* 4 (May 1971): 400-406.

SEX-ROLE SOCIALIZATION

Contrary to Freud and others, females appear to be more morally internalized than males. In a national survey, fourteen- to sixteen-year-olds were asked why parents made rules and what would happen if there were none. Boys more often said parents made rules to keep children out of trouble.[9] In an experimental study based on the Milgram obedience paradigm, females more often resisted pressure to violate a norm against harming others,[10] which is the more remarkable since females typically more often conform in experiments not bearing on moral issues.[11] And, in a field experiment females more often returned valuable items found in the street when no witnesses were present; when others were present, there was no sex difference.[12]

In a developmental study young, middle-class female adolescents (grades five to seven) gave strong evidence of having more internalized moral orientations than males. Moral transgressions were more often associated with guilt in females, and fear of punishment in males. Females also revealed a more humanistic moral orientation (for example, they placed a greater value on going out of one's way to help others); and the higher value placed on achievement by males appeared to reflect an egoistic rather than a moral orientation.[13]

The sex differences may be due partly to child-rearing differences. Parents of girls more often use inductive discipline and

9. Elizabeth M. Douvan and Joseph B. Adelson, *The Adolescent Experience* (New York: John Wiley and Sons, 1966).

10. Wesley Kilham and Leon Mann, "Level of Destructive Obedience as a Function of Transmitter and Executant Roles in the Milgram Obedience Paradigm," *Journal of Personality and Social Psychology* 29 (May 1974): 696-702.

11. Michael Wallach and Nathan Kogan, "Sex Differences and Judgment Processes," *Journal of Personality* 27 (December 1959): 555-64.

12. Alan E. Gross, "Sex and Helping: Intrinsic Glow and Extrinsic Show" (Paper presented at meetings of the American Psychological Association, Honolulu, September 1972).

13. Martin L. Hoffman, "Sex Differences in Moral Internalization and Values," *Journal of Personality and Social Psychology* 32 (October 1975): 720-29.

express affection.[14] But the same pattern of sex differences was also obtained for the parents. This suggests the need for a broader explanation. One possibility is that since females have been traditionally socialized into the "expressive" role—to give and receive affection and be responsive to other people's needs—they are well equipped to acquire humanistic moral concerns. Boys are socialized this way too, but as they approach adolescence they are increasingly instructed in the "instrumental" character traits and skills needed for occupational success, which may often conflict with humanistic moral concerns. Since females may now be receiving more instrumental socialization than formerly, the sex difference in morality may soon diminish.

The Influence of Peers

Despite the interest, there is little theorizing and still less research on the effects of peers. The theories about peer effects on moral development boil down to three somewhat contradictory views. One, since gross power differentials do not exist in unsupervised peer interactions, everyone is allowed the kind of experiences (spontaneous role-taking, rule-making, rule-enforcing experiences) needed to develop a morality based on mutual consent and cooperation among equals.[15] Two, unsupervised peer interactions may release inhibitions and undermine the effects of prior socialization—a view reflected in William Golding's novel *Lord of the Flies* and Le Bon's notions about collective behavior.[16] Three, both of these views are possible, and which one prevails depends, among other things, on the hidden role of adults (for example, the first may operate when the children come from homes characterized by frequent affection and inductive discipline).[17] Parents may

14. John U. Zussman, "Relationship of Demographic Factors to Parental Discipline Techniques," *Developmental Psychology* 14 (November 1978): 685-86.

15. Jean Piaget, *The Moral Judgment of the Child* (New York: Harcourt, Brace and Co., 1932).

16. Gustav Le Bon, *The Crowd: A Study of the Popular Mind* (New York: Viking Press, 1960).

17. Martin L. Hoffman, "Adolescent Morality in Developmental Perspective," in *Handbook of Adolescent Psychology*, ed. Joseph Adelson (New York: Wiley Interscience, in press).

also play a more direct, "coaching" role, as when they do not just take their child's side in his argument with another child but sometimes provide perspective on the *other* child's point of view.

The research indicates that parental influence wanes and peer groups become more influential as children get older.[18] The direction of the influence is less clear. Some studies report broad areas of agreement between peer and adult values.[19] Others show disagreement—radical disagreement, as in the finding that newly formed unsupervised groups of preadolescent boys may undermine the preexisting morality of some members,[20] or modest differences in emphasis, as in high school subcultures stressing athletics and popularity rather than academic achievement.[21] There is also evidence that young adolescents are more apt to endorse peer-sponsored misbehavior than are younger children, and that this may reflect a growing disillusionment with the fairmindedness and good will of adults rather than an increasing loyalty to peers, whose credibility may actually suffer a decline.[22] Finally, the peer-model research suggests that exposure to a peer who behaves aggressively or yields to temptation and is not punished increases the likelihood that a child will do the same; if the model is punished, the subject is more likely to behave as though there were no model.[23] These findings suggest that if children deviate from adult moral norms without punishment, as often happens outside the home, this may stimulate a child to deviate; if they are punished, however, this may not serve as a deterrent. The immediate impact of peer behavior

18. Edward C. Devereux, "The Role of Peer-group Experience in Moral Development," in *Minnesota Symposia on Child Psychology*, vol. 4, ed. John P. Hill (Minneapolis: University of Minnesota Press, 1970), pp. 94-140.

19. Russell L. Langworthy, "Community Status and Influence in a High School," *American Sociological Review* 24 (August 1959): 537-39.

20. Muzafer Sherif et al., *Intergroup Conflict and Cooperation: The Robber's Cave Experiment* (Norman, Okla.: Univerity Book Exchange, 1961).

21. James S. Coleman, *The Adolescent Society* (New York: Free Press of Glencoe, 1961).

22. V. Edwin Bixenstine, Margaret S. DeCorte, and Barton A. Bixenstine, "Conformity to Peer-sponsored Misconduct at Four Grade Levels," *Developmental Psychology* 12 (May 1976): 226-36.

23. Hoffman, "Moral Development," in *Carmichael's Handbook of Child Psychology*, ed. Mussen.

may thus be more likely to weaken than to strengthen one's inhibitions.

Television

The burgeoning research on effects of television on aggression is tangential to mainstream moral development research, but any assessment of social influences would be incomplete without reference to it. It may also be useful to provide an alternative to the frequent assumption that important effects have been demonstrated.[24] To begin, the correlations between watching violent television and behaving aggressively are inconclusive because the causality is unclear. In the one study that used a cross-lagged design, it was found that a childhood preference for violent programs relates to aggressive behavior in adolescence,[25] but that study may have serious flaws.[26]

Numerous experiments, done mainly in the 1960s, showed that children exposed to a live or filmed model behaving aggressively—or helping or sharing—are apt to behave like the model shortly afterwards. It thus appeared that television program content might affect children's moral development. To demonstrate this convincingly, however, may require controlling the television-viewing experience of children and observing their social behavior over an extended time in a natural setting. This has been done in several studies. In one study employing young adolescent subjects, the television viewing of 625 ethnically and socio-economically heterogeneous nine- to fifteen-year-old boys attending seven residential schools and institutions (three private preparatory schools and four "boys homes") was controlled. For six weeks they were required to watch television for at least two hours a day. Half watched regularly broadcast programs with aggressive content (for example, "Gunsmoke"); the other half watched nonaggresssive programs (for example, "The Dick Van Dyke Show"). Several

24. Aletha H. Stein and Lynette K. Friedrich, "The Impact of Television on Children and Youth," in *Review of Child Development Research*, vol. 5 ed. E. Mavis Hetherington et al. (Chicago: University of Chicago Press, 1975), pp. 183-256.

25. Leonard D. Eron et al., "Does Television Violence Cause Aggression?" *American Psychologist* 27 (April 1972): 253-63.

26. Robert M. Kaplan, "On Television as a Cause of Aggression," *American Psychologist* 27 (October 1972): 968-69.

indices of aggression were used but the most important were ratings by trained observers who had frequent contact with the boys. No evidence was found that television violence leads to an increase in aggressive behavior. Indeed, *less* aggression was found among highly aggressive lower-class boys, and also among a group of low-intelligence, hyperactive boys who had watched the violent television programs. The authors conclude, however, that because of imperfections in the study the most valid interpretation of the findings is that, for the population sampled, viewing of televised aggression does not lead to an increase in real-life violence.[27]

In a partial replication that eliminated some design flaws, no significant differences in aggressive behavior were found between boys exposed to the aggressive and nonaggressive television diets.[28] Further research is needed, perhaps using more subtle measures of aggression. It is possible, however, that even the most sophisticated designs may not reveal long-term effects, because the effects may be overridden by one's overall television experience (including newscast violence) and actual socialization experiences, as well as other pressures and frustrations to which one is exposed, which may be impossible to control. The *measurable* effects of television on behavior may thus be largely momentary.

Cognitive Conflict and Moral Thought

About fifty years ago, Piaget suggested that the experience of conflict between one's existing moral views and new stimulus events contributes to maturity of moral thought. This view continues to stimulate theory and research. Building upon Piaget's formulations, Kohlberg sees morality as developing in a series of six stages beginning with a premoral one, in which the child obeys to avoid punishment, and ending with a universal sense of justice or concern for reciprocity among individuals.[29] Each stage is a

27. Seymour Feshbach and Robert D. Singer, *Television and Aggression* (San Francisco: Jossey Bass, 1971).

28. William D. Wells, "Television and Aggression: Replication of an Experimental Field Study" (unpublished manuscript, Graduate School of Business, University of Chicago, 1973).

29. Lawrence Kohlberg, "Moral Stages and Moralization: The Cognitive-Developmental Approach," in *Moral Development and Behavior*, ed. Thomas Lickona (New York: Holt, Rinehart and Winston, 1976), pp. 31-53.

homogeneous, value-free, moral cognitive structure or reasoning strategy; moral reasoning within a stage is consistent across different problems, situations, and values. Each stage builds upon, reorganizes, and encompasses the preceding one, and provides new perspectives and criteria for making moral evaluations. People in all cultures move through the stages in the same order, varying only in how quickly and how far they progress. The impetus for movement comes from exposure to moral structures slightly more advanced than one's own. The resulting cognitive conflict is resolved by integrating one's previous structure with the new one.

The following criticisms have been made of Kohlberg's theory: the stages do not appear to be homogeneous, or to form an invariant sequence; there is no evidence that exposure to appropriate levels of moral reasoning inevitably leads to forward movement through the stages, or that it leads to "structural" rather than value conflict; although low positive correlations exist between moral reasoning and moral behavior, the stages are not associated with distinctive patterns of behavior.[30] These problems may be due to the codes used in scoring the children's moral reasoning responses. Future research with the new coding system may produce different results.[31] The theory has also been criticized, however, for neglecting motivation, which may be needed to translate abstract moral concepts into action;[32] for claiming universality though actually based on Western thought (for example, stage 5 makes sense only in a constitutional democracy and stage 6 requires a level of abstract thought that may disqualify most people in the world);[33]

30. Martin L. Hoffman, "Moral Internalization: Current Theory and Research"; William M. Kurtines and Esther B. Greif, "The Development of Moral Thought: Review and Evaluation of Kohlberg's Approach," *Psychological Bulletin* 81 (August 1974): 453-70.

31. Lawrence Kohlberg et al., "Assessing Moral Stages: A Manual" (Unpublished manuscript, Center for Moral Education, Harvard University).

32. William P. Alston, "Comments on Kohlberg's 'From Is to Ought,'" in *Cognitive Development and Epistemology*, ed. Theodore Mischel (New York: Academic Press, 1971), pp. 269-84.

33. Elizabeth L. Simpson, "Moral Development Research: A Case Study of Scientific Cultural Bias," *Human Development* 17, no. 2 (1974): 81-106.

and for having a male and a "romantic individualistic" bias.[34]

Whether or not cognitive conflict theory is confirmed, it has called attention to the individual's own active efforts to draw meaning from experience. And, although Kohlberg's stages may not form a universal invariant sequence, they may nevertheless provide a valid description of the changes in moral thought that occur with age in our society. His measure may thus afford the best available means of comparing adolescent with pre- and post-adolescent morality. Finally, apart from its scientific value, Kohlberg's work has led to a new approach to moral education: different moral stages are assumed to be represented in the classroom; in discussing moral dilemmas, lower-stage children are thus exposed to higher-stage reasoning; and in handling the resulting conflict their moral levels advance.[35] This approach appeals to educators partly because they do not have to make moral judgments or state their values. They need only present moral dilemmas, foster discussion, and occasionally clarify a child's statement.

The evaluation research needed to assess this approach has not been done. There is some laboratory research that may be pertinent, however, and since the subjects were young adolescents, it will be discussed in some detail.

In a study done by Turiel, seventh-grade boys were assigned moral stage scores based on their responses to six Kohlberg dilemmas. The experimental subjects were given other dilemmas and instructed to take the role of the central figure and "seek advice" from the experimenter. To produce cognitive conflict, the experimenter gave arguments on both sides of the issue, based on moral concepts that were one or two stages above the subject's stage ($+1$ or $+2$) or one stage below (-1). The subjects were retested a week later. The hypothesis that one's stage limits how far one can go was confirmed: the $+1$ condition had a greater effect than $+2$. The more important hypothesis was that, since each stage

34. Edward E. Sampson, "Scientific Paradigms and Social Values: Wanted —A Scientific Revolution," *Journal of Personality and Social Psychology* 36 (November 1978): 1332-43; Robert Hogan, "Theoretical Egocentrism and the Problem of Compliance," *American Psychologist* 30 (May 1975): 533-40.

35. Lawrence Kohlberg, "The Implications of Developmental Psychology for Education: Example from Moral Development," *Educational Psychologist* 10 (Winter 1973): 2-14.

is a reorganization of the preceding one, and a tendency exists to move forward, +1 subjects will shift in the +1 direction to a greater degree than —1 subjects will shift in the —1 direction. The findings were the opposite. The control group, however, inexplicably showed more backward than forward movement and, as a result, the net shift (experimental minus control) was greater— almost significantly—for the +1 than the —1 group. Thus it is only due to the control group's strange response that the findings may be construed as providing some support for the hypothesis.[36]

In a later, similar study seventh-grade children at stage 1 and 2 (but not the higher-stage children) shifted more toward higher than lower moral levels. They also obtained high scores on social desirability, which in turn correlated with shift in moral judgment. Since these subjects were externally oriented to begin with, the findings suggest that direct social influence processes rather than cognitive conflict may account for their shift in judgment.[37]

The studies of comprehension and preference for higher moral levels, which also follow Turiel's format,[38] appear to have other problems. The findings were that comprehension was high, up to the subject's own predominant stage, then fell off rapidly; and the highest stage comprehended was the most preferred of those comprehended. Stage 6 statements, however, were the most preferred of all, even by subjects who did not comprehend it, which means that the subject's predominant stage did not predict his preference. This finding raises questions about the design of all these studies. The investigators apparently constructed the statements of "advice," and despite their attempts to balance each pro-con pair for stage, attitude, and issue, the high-stage statements, as I have suggested elsewhere,[39] may have been inadvertently

36. Elliot Turiel, "An Experimental Test of the Sequentiality of Developmental Stages in the Child's Moral Judgments," *Journal of Personality and Social Psychology* 3 (June 1966): 611-18.

37. James J. Tracy and Herbert J. Cross, "Antecedents of Shift in Moral Judgment," *Journal of Personality and Social Psychology* 26 (May 1973): 238-44.

38. James R. Rest, "The Hierarchical Nature of Moral Judgment: A Study of Patterns of Comprehension and Preference of Moral Stages," *Journal of Personality* 41 (March 1973): 86-109.

39. Hoffman, "Moral Internalization: Current Theory and Research."

phrased more attractively than low-stage statements. This would introduce a spurious element into the subjects' choices. Indeed, there is recent evidence that this may have happened.[40]

All in all, the research does not augur well for the view that moral education programs relying on interventions that produce cognitive conflict will foster moral growth, at least as measured by Kohlberg's scheme. Perhaps other moral indices would reveal an effect. For example, the degree to which a person senses the moral dimension in complex situations may be a better indicator of his behavior in real-life situations, in which moral issues are not as visible as in Kohlberg's dilemmas. I might also note that, besides being exposed to conflicting moral views, the children in Kohlberg's program are encouraged to participate in decisions about making rules and assigning punishments for violating them. Should this program prove effective, it will therefore still remain for research to determine if arousal of cognitive conflict is a necessary ingredient.

Psychoanalytic Concepts

In the psychoanalytic account of conscience development, which was worked out mainly for males, the child experiences many frustrations, some due to parental intervention, which contribute to hostile feelings. The child also desires close bodily contact, especially with the mother, for whom his main rival is the father. The child's hostile and erotic behavior is often punished, resulting in anxiety over loss of love. To avoid anxiety the child may repress his hostile and erotic feelings. To maintain the repression, and also keep the parents' love, the child adopts the rules and prohibitions emanating from them. He also develops a generalized motive to emulate them and adopt their inner states. This includes the capacity to punish oneself after violating a prohibition—thus turning inward the hostility orginally felt toward the parent. This self-punishment is experienced as a guilt feeling, which is dreaded because of its intensity and resemblance to the earlier anxiety. The child thereafter tries to avoid guilt by acting in accord with the

40. Joseph J. Moran and Andrew J. Joniak, "Effect of Language on Preference for Responses to a Moral Dilemma," *Developmental Psychology* 15 (May 1979): 337-38.

internalized parental prohibitions, and erecting defense mechanisms against the awareness of contrary impulses. This basic process of conscience or superego formation is accomplished by age five or six and solidified in the latency period—the remaining, relatively calm years of childhood.

The general view among psychoanalytic writers is that the impulse control achieved during the latency period is disrupted at puberty by the emergence of intense sexual drives, and the child is plunged again into an oedipal situation. The writers stress different consequences of this oedipal revival. One postulates a "rebellion against the superego," in which the young adolescent rejects both the parents' standards and the part of the self that has unreflectively adopted them.[41] Another suggests that the superego mellows with age and loses some of its "exaggerated idealism" due to ego maturity, particularly after the "tempest of instinctual conflicts during adolescence has subsided."[42] With the aid of the "neutralized energy" then available to it, the superego can operate on the basis of more reasonable goals, mature moral judgments, and tolerance. And still another stresses a big difference between the revived and original oedipal situations: the existence in adolescence of legitimate substitute love objects for the mother, which frees the child to express erotic impulses.[43] This enables him to establish more realistic moral values and controls (for example, he may identify with the father but not as a global defense against an overpowering rival, since the father is no longer a rival in the same crucial way).

As for peers, one writer suggests that as the childhood superego loses its hold the adolescent may long for experiences that will bolster it and form a bulwark against regressive tendencies.[44] This longing may be felt as a need to act in accord with certain lofty ideals and to join groups in order to borrow strength from

41. Peter Blos, *On Adolescence* (New York: Free Press, 1962).

42. Edith Jacobson, *The Self and the Object World* (New York: International Universities Press, 1964). See especially the chapters in Part II, "Superego Formation and the Period of Latency," pp. 89-155.

43. Douvan and Adelson, *The Adolescent Experience.*

44. Albert J. Solnit, "Youth and the Campus: the Search for a Social Conscience," *Psychoanalytic Study of the Child* 27 (1972): 98-105.

their cohesiveness and identifications. Another argues that the superego is "reexternalized" in adolescence, that is, its values are made available to conscious appraisal, reassessed, played out, tested and challenged in discussions mainly with peers, and sometimes in action.[45] The values seen as mythical and unreal are discarded. Others are retained and "reincorporated" into the superego. As a result, the superego, which formerly represented only the traditional and cultural values held by the parents, now represents the values and ideals that are unique and appropriate at the time. This reappraisal is triggered by the contradictions, duplicities, and uncertainties that abound in society and by the fact that adults in contemporary society are unsure of their values, which deprives the young of the security that may come from the conviction of the older generation. Adolescents may thus feel pressed to contruct their own system of guiding ideals. For those not exposed to society's contradictions (for example, those who are not under immediate pressure to assume adult responsibilities), the childhood superego may remain relatively intact.

Finally, Erikson suggests there are three broad stages of moral development: specific moral learning in childhood; ideologies experienced in adolescence; and ethical consolidation in adulthood. Erikson's main concern is the search for an identity, which requires a sense of purpose. If in the face of overwhelming evidence the adolescent becomes disillusioned with the moral and religious beliefs acquired in childhood, then there is a loss of purpose, which may lead to a desperate search for an ideology to fill the gap. To be acceptable, the ideology must fit both the "evidence" and the adolescent's high cognitive level. And if the ideology is shared by others it is even more attractive because it provides community. For Erikson, then, ideology is the "guardian of identity" because it provides a sense of purpose, helps tie the present to the future, and contributes meaning to action.[46]

These formulations are all interesting, but there has been no attempt to show the connections between them, and they lack

45. Calvin F. Settlage, "Cultural Values and the Superego in Late Adolescence," *Psychoanalytic Study of the Child* 27 (1972): 57-73.

46. E. H. Erikson, "Reflections on the Dissent of Contemporary Youth," *International Journal of Psychoanalysis* 51 (1970): 11-22.

empirical support. The writers either give no evidence, or, more typically, cite an example or two, drawn from case files, which provide at best a superficial level of support. They also fail to come to grips with certain critical theoretical issues. If the child-hood superego is indeed based on repression, then it is not enough to say that it mellows with age and is enriched by values acquired on a more cognitive basis in adolescence. The crucial, ignored question is, how can cognitively acquired values be incorporated into a largely unconscious mental structure? On the other hand, to say that the repression is lifted due to development of the ego, which then takes over the superego's function, appears to abandon the concept of conscience entirely, since the ego can serve immoral as well as moral purposes. The crucial question that is begged is, what makes the person utilize his ego capacities for moral rather than egoistic ends?

In short, what seems to be missing in the psychoanalytic, as in the cognitive conflict view, is a concept of a mature motive force that may underlie moral action. What follows are beginning attempts to fill this gap.

Empathy and Prosocial Behavior

Empathy, the vicarious emotional response to another person, has long interested social thinkers. Philosophers like David Hume and Adam Smith, and early personality theorists like Stern, Scheler, and McDougall all saw its significance for social life. Despite the interest, there has been little theory or research. The topic will be discussed here, nevertheless, because it bears on the affective side of morality, which has long been neglected. The focus thus far has been on the response to someone in distress, since this seems central to morality. A brief summary of a developmental theory of empathic distress follows.[47]

When empathically aroused, older children and adults know that they are responding to something happening to someone else,

47. What follows is a summary of a theoretical model presented in two articles: Martin L. Hoffman, "Developmental Synthesis of Affect and Cognition and Its Implications for Altruistic Motivation," *Developmental Psychology* 11 (September 1975): 607-22; idem, "Empathy: Its Development and Prosocial Implications," in *Nebraska Symposium on Motivation*, vol. 25 (Lincoln, Neb.: University of Nebraska Press, 1977), pp. 169-217.

and they have a sense of what the other is feeling. At the other extreme, infants may be empathically aroused without these cognitions. Thus, the experience of empathy depends on the level at which one cognizes others. The research suggests at least four stages in the development of a cognitive sense of others: for most of the first year, a fusion of self and other; by eleven to twelve months, "person permanence" or awareness of others as distinct physical entities; by two to three years, a rudimentary awareness that others have independent inner states—the first step in role taking; by eight to twelve years, awareness that others have personal identities and life experience beyond the immediate situation.

Empathy thus has a vicarious affective component that is given increasingly complex meaning as the child progresses through these four stages. Four levels of empathic distress may result from this coalescence of empathic affect and the cognitive sense of the other. The first three levels, which pertain to infancy and early childhood, will be mentioned briefly to provide a developmental context for the last. At the first level the infant's empathic response lacks an awareness of who is actually in distress. For example, an eleven-month-old girl, on seeing a child fall and cry, looked like she was about to cry herself and then put her thumb in her mouth and buried her head in her mother's lap, which is what she does when she is hurt. With "person permanence," at the second level, one is aware that another person and not the self is in distress, but the other's inner states are unknown and may be assumed to be the same as one's own. For example, an eighteen-month-old boy fetched his own mother to comfort a crying friend, although the friend's mother was also present. With the beginning of role taking, at the third level, empathy becomes an increasingly veridical response to the other's inner states in the situation. By early adolescence, at the fourth level, owing to the emerging conception of self and other as continuous persons with a separate history and identity, one becomes aware that others feel pleasure and pain not only in the situation but also in their larger life experience. Consequently, although one may continue to react to another's immediate distress, one's reaction is intensified when the distress is not transitory but chronic. This stage thus combines empathically aroused affect with a mental representation of another's general level of distress or deprivation. If this representation falls short of the observer's idea of a minimal standard of well-being, an empathic distress response may result even if contradicted by the other's apparent momentary state, that is, the representation overrides contradictory situational cues.

To summarize, the young adolescent is capable of a high level of empathic distress. He can process various types of information gained from his own vicarious affective reaction, from immediate situational cues, and from general knowledge about the other's life. He can act out in his mind the emotions and experiences suggested by this information, and introspect on all of this. He may thus gain an understanding and respond affectively in terms of the circumstances, feelings, and wishes of the other, while maintaining the sense that this is a separate person from the self.

It also seems likely that with further cognitive development, but still within the period of early adolescence, one can comprehend the plight of an entire class of people (for example, poor, oppressed, retarded). Although one's distress experience differs from theirs, all distress has a common affective core, which allows for a generalized empathic distress capability. Empathic affect combined with the perceived plight of an unfortunate group may be the most advanced form of empathic distress.

These levels of empathic response are assumed to form the basis of a motive to help others; hence their relevance to moral development. The findings from research may be summarized as follows: (a) very young children (two to four years) typically react empathically to a hurt child, although they sometimes do nothing or act inappropriately; (b) older children and adults react empathically too, but this is usually followed by appropriate helping behavior; (c) the level of empathic arousal and the speed of a helping act increase with the number and intensity of distress cues from the victim; and (d) the level of arousal drops following a helping act but continues if there is no attempt to help.

These findings fit the hypothesis that empathic distress is a prosocial motive. Some may call it an egoistic motive because one feels better after helping. The evidence suggests, however, that feeling better is not the usual *aim* of helping. Regardless, any motive for which the arousal condition, aim of ensuing action, and basis for gratification in the actor are all contingent on someone else's welfare must be distinguished from obvious self-serving motives like approval, success, and material gain. It thus seems legitimate to call empathic distress a prosocial motive, with perhaps a quasi-egoistic dimension.

Qualifications are in order. First, although helping increases with intensity of empathic distress, beyond a certain point empathic distress may become so aversive that one's attention is directed to the self, not the victim. Second, empathic distress and helping are positively related to perceived similarity between observer and victim: children respond more empathically to others of the same race or sex. Adults do, too, and they also respond more empathically to others perceived as similar in abstract terms (for example, similar "personality traits"). This is probably true of young adolescents as well, since they are capable of such abstractions. These findings suggest that empathic morality may be particularistic, applied mainly to one's group; but they also suggest that moral education programs that point up the similarities among people, at the appropriate level of abstraction, may help foster a universalistic morality.

Despite the qualifications, any human attribute that can transform someone else's misfortune into one's own distress demands the attention of social scientists and educators, not only for its relevance to moral development but also for its potential significance in bridging the gap between the individual and society.

Interpersonal Guilt

The reemergence of interest in affective and motivational aspects of morality includes a revived interest in guilt. I have suggested a relation between guilt and empathy that can be summarized as follows.[48] The attribution research suggests a human tendency to make causal inferences about events. One can thus be expected to make inferences about the cause of a victim's distress, which serve as additional inputs in shaping one's affective empathic response. If one is the cause of the distress, one's aware-

48. Martin L. Hoffman, "Empathy, Role-taking, Guilt, and Development of Altruistic Motives," in *Moral Development and Behavior*, ed. Lickona, pp. 124-43.

ness of this may combine with the empathic affect aroused to produce a feeling of guilt (not the Freudian guilt that results, as noted earlier, when repressed impulses enter consciousness).

There is no developmental theory of guilt, but the possible importance of empathic distress and causal attribution suggests (a) that there may be guilt stages corresponding to the empathy stages, and (b) that research is needed on certain neglected aspects of cognitive development, such as awareness that one has choice over one's actions and that one's actions have an impact on others, and the ability to contemplate or imagine an action and its effects (necessary for anticipatory guilt and guilt over omission).

A summary of the findings to date with young adolescent subjects follows. As noted earlier, discipline that points up the effects of the child's behavior on others contributes to guilt feelings, which may be taken as modest support for a connection between empathic arousal and guilt. There is recent experimental evidence for the view that arousal of empathic distress intensifies guilt feeling.[49] The next three findings were attained in story-completion research. By early adolescence, children are capable of experiencing guilt feelings following acts of omission as well as commission.[50] Guilt arousal is usually followed by a reparative act toward the victim or toward others and, when neither is possible, a prolongation of the guilt. Guilt arousal sometimes triggers a "metacognitive" process involving a self-examination and reordering of value priorities, together with a resolution to act less selfishly in the future.[51] Interestingly, this last type of response to guilt, which should contribute importantly to moral development, might be missing in children who are too "good" to transgress and consequently do not feel guilt.

In sum, guilt is associated with empathy, and it may serve as a motive both to act morally in the immediate situation and to contemplate acting more morally in the future. It thus appears, somewhat paradoxically, that guilt, which results from immoral action, operates as a moral motive.

49. Ross Thompson and Martin L. Hoffman, "Empathic Arousal and Guilt in Children," *Developmental Psychology*, in press.

50. Hoffman, "Sex Differences in Moral Internalization."

51. Hoffman, "Adolescent Morality in Developmental Perspective."

Summary and Conclusions

All the theories, with the possible exception of social-learning theory, view the young child's morality as limited or deficient in some respect. In the psychoanalytic view, the child's superego is rigid, primarily unconscious, and often harsh. For cognitive conflict theory, the child is not truly moral, his acts being based on reward-punishment contingencies or on a thoughtless allegiance to authority. In the empathy-based conception, the child's feeling for others is confined to simple emotions experienced in the immediate situation.

To explain the advances in adolescence, the theories rely on inevitable physical and cognitive changes. Psychoanalytic theory stresses (a) hormonal changes and the associated drives and emotions that disrupt the delicate impulse control system developed earlier; (b) anxiety resulting from loss of both the control system and the close, dependent relation to parents that supported it; and (c) pressures to construct a more mature moral stance or to erect defenses to ward off impulses and maintain the earlier control system.

Cognitive conflict theory stresses the adolescent's thinking, which is no longer tied to the concrete and immediate. This enables one to (a) reason logically and deductively, compare the actual with the ideal, and construct contrary-to-fact propositions; (b) relate oneself to the distant past and future and understand one's place in society, history, and the universe; and (c) conceptualize one's own thought, and take one's mental constructions as objects and reason about them (for example, only by age eleven to twelve do children spontaneously introduce concepts of belief, intelligence, and faith when discussing their religion). Consequently, when one moves from grade school to the more heterogeneous high school (and eventually college) environment, one is ripe for recognizing that one's earlier acquired moral system is but one of many, with no clear basis for deciding which is superior, and often at odds with real-world demands. The adolescent may thus begin to question and perhaps reject his former moral system and, sometimes taking years in the process, construct a more viable one.

The theory of empathic morality relies on some of these same cognitive advances, but the focus is on other cognitive dimensions: the integration of the young adolescent's capacity for vicarious arousal, which he or she has had all along, with the newly emerging cognitive awareness of others as well as oneself as individuals having an identity, life circumstances, and inner states. I have also suggested elsewhere that the perceived contrast between one's own well-being and that of other persons or groups, of which one may first become aware in early adolescence, may at times produce a type of guilt feeling that provides a force toward moral action.[52]

It seems clear that none of the theories has a monopoly on explanation, nor are there obvious contradictions among them. Each bears mainly on a particular dimension of moral development and one or another aspect of the new world faced by the young adolescent. My conclusion is in the form of an overall framework for adolescent moral development that attempts to integrate the findings and the most promising hypotheses, provides a developmental perspective, and takes account of the competitive egoistic processes often ignored.

1. People often assume that their acts are under surveillance. This fear of ubiquitous authority may lead them to behave morally even when alone. The socialization experiences leading to this orientation may include frequent power-assertive and perhaps love-withdrawing discipline, which results in painful anxiety states becoming associated with deviant behavior. Subsequently, kinesthetic and other cues produced by the deviant act may arouse anxiety, which is avoided by inhibiting the act. When the anxiety becomes diffuse and detached from conscious fears of detection, the inhibition of deviant action may be viewed as reflecting a primitive form of internalization (perhaps analogous to the Freudian superego).

2. The human capacity for empathy may combine with the cognitive awareness of others, and how others are affected by one's behavior, resulting in an internal motive to consider others. As contributing socialization experiences, the research suggests exposure to inductive discipline by parents who also provide adequate affection and serve as models of prosocial moral action (for

52. Ibid.

example, they help and show empathic concern for others rather than blame them for their plight). Reciprocal role taking, especially with peers, may also help heighten the individual's sensitivity to the inner states aroused in others by one's behavior; having been in the other's place helps one know how the other feels.

3. People may cognitively process information at variance with their preexisting moral conceptions and construct new views that resolve the contradiction. When they do this, they will very likely feel a special commitment to, and in this sense internalize, the moral concepts they have actively constructed.

These three processes are not stages. The first, in one form or another, may be pervasive at all ages, including adolescence. Anxiety over retribution by God, for example, often provides the major motive for moral action in traditional society. This is true to some degree in our country as well, though mainly in young children. Adolescents often question the existence of God,[53] and sometimes lose their only moral motive in the process—although there is evidence that some moral beliefs in early adolescence are totally independent of degree of religious commitment.[54] The second, empathy-based process may also be prevalent at all ages, although primarily in humanistically oriented groups. If linked to religion, we might expect it to be the value-prescription aspect (how one should behave toward others) rather than fear of retribution by a deity. The third, more cognitive process may be the one most limited to adolescence, although perhaps only applicable to a relatively small number of those for whom intellectually attained values have special importance.

The three processes may develop independently, since their presumed socialization antecedents differ. They may sometimes complement each other, as when the rudimentary moral sense,

53. Raymond G. Kuhlen and Magda Arnold, "Age Differences in Religious Beliefs and Problems During Adolescence," *Journal of Genetic Psychology* 65 (December 1944): 291-300. See also, Mary C. Jones, "A Comparison of the Attitudes and Interests of Ninth-grade Students over Two Decades," *Journal of Educational Psychology* 51 (August 1960): 175-86.

54. Derek Wright and Edwin Cox, "Changes in Moral Belief among Sixth-form Boys and Girls over a Seven-year Period in Relation to Religious Belief, Age, and Sex Difference," *British Journal of Social and Clinical Psychology* 10 (September 1971): 332-41.

originating in the child's early capacity for empathy and in disciplinary encounters, contributes direction for resolving moral conflicts in adolescence. And, conversely, resolving moral conflicts in adolescence may help account for the progression from that rudimentary moral sense to more complex moral orientations. The processes may sometimes be noncomplementary, as when an early anxiety-based inhibition prevents a nonmoral behavior from occurring later, when its control might be acquired through moral conflict resolution. Perhaps they are best viewed as three components of a moral orientation, with people varying as to which one predominates, and individual differences being due to variations in cognitive abilities and socialization.

A mature orientation in our society, then, would be based predominantly on empathic and cognitive processes, and minimally on anxiety. The challenge is to find ways to foster this morality. Whether this is possible in the context of the prevailing competitive-individualistic ethic is problematic. A recent finding brings into bold relief the dilemma that may confront many parents and educators in their efforts to socialize children for both morality and achievement.[55] It also demonstrates that under high achievement pressure parents may communicate to their children that, when success and honesty are in conflict, it is more important to succeed than to be honest.

55. Roger V. Burton, "Cheating Related to Maternal Pressures for Achievement" (unpublished manuscript, 1972).

CHAPTER X

Extending Rights and Responsibilities

STEVEN SELDEN

In his essay on the history of the family and childhood, Aries proposed that the *idea* of childhood is a relatively new one.[1] In the middle ages, for example, children past infancy, past seven years of age, were considered as miniature adults. The child's welcome into the adult community carried with it the presumption of social and legal competence. By the twentieth century in industrialized nations, however, the concept of childhood had changed and had been fully differentiated from that of adulthood. Further, an educational system had been designed to meet the particular needs of this group, which were different from adults' needs. Here the presumption associated with this age group is of social and legal incompetence.

This concept of the incompetent child leads to tensions as different groups articulate visions of the meaning of schooling for the last two decades of the twentieth century. Two groups exemplifying this tension are educators concerned for minimum competencies and those concerned for student rights. For the first group, education is to be preparation for adult life and the child is presumed incompetent; for the second, education is seen as part of life and in particular legal senses there is a presumption of competence. For this second group, the advocates of students' rights and responsibilities, the assumption of incompetence is seen as both wrong and dangerous. It has "profound significance not just because children are reliant on adults to exercise their rights for them, but because a child denied the opportunity to exercise responsibilities is effectively denied the opportunity to mature into

1. Philip Aries, *Centuries of Childhood: A Social History of Family Life* (New York: Vintage Books, 1962).

a responsible adult." [2] Proposing an expansion of students' rights, these advocates have taken their pleas to the courts, which "have consistently rendered decisions which increase the protection of the individual." [3] In many of these cases the young persons argued that they had been denied a particular Bill of Rights protection or that improper procedures had been used against them. They claimed protection offered by the Fourteenth Amendment. This amendment serves as a focus for the application of federal constitutional guarantees in state contexts and is leading to a redefinition of both childhood and students' rights—a redefinition that moves toward the assumption of legal competence.

The Fourteenth Amendment

It will be useful to give brief consideration here to the legal and historical development of the Fourteenth Amendment.[4] Prior to the Civil War, Americans viewed themselves first as citizens of their respective states and then as citizens of the nation. After the war, there was a substantial change in the *legal* view of this membership. The legal ordering was reversed and the instrument of this revolution was the Fourteenth Amendment, which states:

All persons born or naturalized in the United States and subject to the jurisdiction thereof, are citizens of the United States and of the state wherein they reside. No state shall make or enforce any law which shall abridge the privileges or immunities of citizens of the United States.

The ratification of the amendment was a prerequisite for readmission of the Southern states to the Union after the Civil War. It was designed to protect the newly freed slaves from arbitrary state action since they were now "citizens of the United States

2. Hillary Rodham, "Children's Rights: A Legal Perspective," in *Children's Rights: Contemporary Perspectives*, ed. Patricia A. Vardin and Ilene N. Brody (New York: Teachers College Press, 1979), p. 19.

3. David C. Carter, "Children and Student Rights: A Legal Analysis," *Urban Education* 11 (July 1976): 185.

4. For an excellent analysis of the educational impact of this amendment, see Michael LaMorte, "The Fourteenth Amendment: Its Significance for Public Education," *Educational Administration Quarterly* 10 (Autumn 1974): 1-19. See also, William R. Hazard, *Education and the Law: Cases and Materials on Public Schools*, 2d ed. (New York: Free Press, 1978), pp. 302-19.

and of the state wherein they reside." The amendment further stated that no state can "deprive any person of life, liberty, or property, without due process of law, nor deny to any person within its jurisdiction the equal protection of the laws."

Embodied in this paragraph is the issue of fairness in applying the law. In addition to the ideas that the state may not deny a citizen federally guaranteed rights are the dual notions of due process and equal protection. It is on the basis of these two legal constructs that much of the litigation on students' rights is constructed; and it is in the judicial interpretation of the Constitution that the federal case law is created. Decisions in particular cases, in a sense, make the law and the interpretations upon which such decisions are based have changed over time. For example, the Supreme Court has reinterpreted the equal protection clause of the Fourteenth Amendment in relation to education and specifically in relation to the legality of de jure segregated schools. Initially, in the case of *Plessy* v. *Ferguson* (1896) the Court judged that equal protection was being afforded black Americans through "separate but equal" educational facilities.[5] The inequality of these facilities was to remain legally permissible for fifty-seven years until the revolutionary *Brown* decision in 1954. It is useful here to let the Court itself speak:

We conclude that in the field of public education the doctrine of "separate but equal" has no place. Separate educational facilities are inherently unequal. Therefore we hold that . . . [those] for whom the actions have been brought are, by reason of the segregation complained of, deprived of the equal protection of the laws guaranteed by the Fourteenth Amendment."[6]

While the consequence of the reversal of *Plessy* by *Brown* is of educational importance on its face, it has wider implications for students' rights, since it raises the issue of appropriateness of particular classifications. For in *Brown* it was judged that race is not a justifiable basis for educational differentiation. Where school authorities today attempt to exclude married or pregnant students from the school program, they will have to show (in the case of

5. *Plessy v. Ferguson*, 163 U.S. 537 (1896).

6. *Brown v. Board of Education of Topeka*, 347 U.S. 483, 495.

"fundamental interest") that the categories are reasonable and not capricious with respect to the educational objectives of the school. Students who find themselves excluded from particular school activities and programs due to these classifications or others can be expected to protest on the basis of the equal protection clause of the Fourteenth Amendment, claiming that the classifications are unreasonable. But equal protection is only one aspect of the attempt in the Fourteenth Amendment to achieve national unity and the protection of black Americans. The amendment also states that no person shall be deprived of "life, liberty, or property without *due process* of law." (italics added)

While more difficult to define than equal protection, due process continues the emphasis upon fair treatment. It implies that one individual will be treated in the same manner as any other individual under similar circumstances where life, liberty, or property are to be curtailed. Here one can see the importance of the amendment as its interpretations serve as arbiters between the rights of the individual and the state, between students and the schools. "Under this concept, government action may not be unreasonable or capricious and when clients are not treated alike there must be a sound basis for dissimilar treatment." [7] Again, to foreshadow a later discussion of specific issues related to students' rights, when the school chooses to curtail certain rights in the area of freedom of speech, grooming, dress, or hair length, one can expect ensuing legal discussions to pivot in part on the due process clause of the Fourteenth Amendment. Further, where the separation of church and state is an issue, as in litigation on school prayers, one can again expect to find the due process clause appropriately cited.

The amendment serves as a magnifying glass to focus federal constitutional rights in state contexts. And it further aids in the redefinition of what it means, in the legal sense, to be a child or youthful student in America. Recent court decisions have extended explicit Bill of Rights protections to juveniles and to the viewing of students as "persons." In two cases—*In Re Gault* and *Tinker* v. *Des Moines Independent School District*—there were landmark

7. LaMorte, "The Fourteenth Amendment," p. 5.

decisions in the redefinition of the rights of youth and of students. We turn now to a consideration of those cases.

Gault and Tinker: Landmark Cases in Rights of Young Persons

As a creation of the Progressive Era, the juvenile court system was designed to protect minors from the negative effects of the adult system. The hope was that minors would be treated so that they would be rehabilitated by a benevolent and noncapricious system. Questions of due process did not take a significant place in the proceedings and excesses did take place. In many cases, neither justice nor the accused were well served. One such case was that of Gerald Gault. As a consequence of a Supreme Court decision on his treatment by the juvenile justice system, certain procedural due process guarantees are now applicable to juveniles.

In re Gault: THE ISSUE OF PROCEDURAL DUE PROCESS

On June 8, 1964, Gerald Gault, a fifteen-year-old, was taken into custody with a friend by the sheriff of Gila, Arizona. The sheriff was acting on a complaint by a neighbor alleging that Gerald had made several telephone calls to her during which lewd or indecent remarks had been made. Neither of Gerald's parents was at home when the sheriff arrived and no notice was left at the house indicating that he was in custody nor was an attempt made to notify the parents of their son's arrest. When the mother did arrive home, neighbors told her that her son was at the detention home.

A hearing was scheduled at the detention home for the following day. While a probation officer filed a petition relating to the case, neither Gerald nor his parents were given a copy. Gerald was again remanded to the detention home. No record was kept of these proceedings and another hearing was scheduled for six days later. As it was the presiding judge's opinion at this hearing that the mother's presence was unnecessary, she was not contacted by him, but was merely telephoned once by the probation officer. It was also not until after this hearing that the charge of "lewd phone calls" was officially made and no record of this charge was forwarded to the Gaults. And so, after being placed in custody without being charged, and after being detained without being charged, Gerald Gault had his day in court—without benefit of counsel or the right to cross-examine his accusers. As a consequence of these "procedures," Gerald was sentenced to the Arizona State Industrial School for the period of his minority, that is, for six years. Had Gerald been an adult, and had he been found guilty, Arizona law would have demanded no more than a fine of fifty dollars and/or two months in jail.

When the Gaults sought consideration of the case by the Arizona Supreme Court, they were informed that their complaint, that Gerald had been denied due process protection, was inapplicable. As a minor, the Court explained, Gerald *had no such protections.*

The case was then brought before the U.S. Supreme Court, where Mr. Justice Fortas pointedly noted that "Juvenile Court history has again demonstrated that unbridled discretion, however benevolently motivated, is frequently a poor substitute for principle and procedure." With clear reference to the case before the Court, he continued, "departures from established principles of due process have frequently resulted not in enlightened procedure, but in arbitrariness." It was just this concern for the avoidance of arbitrariness when dealing with juveniles that led to the extension of Fourteenth Amendment protections to juveniles. Noting that "neither the Fourteenth Amendment nor the Bill of Rights is for adults alone," the Court specified guarantees applicable to juveniles facing commitment to state institutions. These guarantees include (for both parent and child): "timely notice, in advance of the hearing of the specific issues they must meet"; the right to be represented by counsel; protection against self-incrimination; and opportunity for cross-examination of witnesses.[8]

While decided in the context of juvenile justice, the message was clear for school authorities: the juveniles attending our schools are also likely to have constitutional protections similar to those identified in *Gault*. In *Goss* v. *Lopez* (1975), the Supreme Court ordered that children could not be expelled or suspended from school (for up to ten days) without an adequate opportunity to respond to the charges made against them.

8. *In Re Gault*, 387 U.S. 1 (1967).

The issue we have considered here pertains to one form of due process—*procedural* due process. Essentially the Court ruled that certain guarantees as to the *way* in which adults were to be treated also applied to young persons. There is also another due process issue, that of *substantive* due process. As Koenings and Ober note, "substantive issues are involved with the reasons behind the rule or the details of the discipline. They center around the 'why' or 'what', concerning themselves with rights to free speech, rights to privacy, or rights to personal liberty." [9]

Tinker: THE ISSUE OF SUBSTANTIVE RIGHTS

A landmark decision with respect to students' *substantive* due process rights was handed down in *Tinker* v. *Des Moines Independent School District.* Dealing with the issue of freedom of speech, it was the "sole high court case pointedly involving the rights of secondary school students under the First Amendment." [10]

In December 1965, at the time of escalating involvement of the United States in Southeast Asia, a number of students and adults in Des Moines, Iowa met to plan a strategy for protest. The decision was made to wear black arm bands from December 16 until New Year's Eve. Hearing of the students' intentions, the principals of the Des Moines schools instituted a preemptory plan of their own. It required that students wearing such arm bands to school remove them under penalty of suspension. Readmission to school would be possible only if the arm bands were removed. John Tinker, Christopher Eckhardt, and Mary Beth Tinker, all aware of the regulation, wore black arm bands and were suspended. The case went to litigation and lower courts found in favor of the school district. An appeal was taken to the U.S. Supreme Court.

Justice Fortas, as in *Gault,* delivered the majority opinion and, unlike the lower courts, upheld the students' right to wear the arm bands. Limiting itself to the specifics of the case, the Court ruled that the wearing of arm bands "was closely akin to 'pure

9. Sharon L. Koenings and Steven Ober, "Legal Precedents in Student Rights Cases," in *Schooling and the Rights of Children,* ed. Michael W. Apple and Vernon Haubrich (Berkeley, Calif.: McCutchan Publishing Co., 1975), p. 133.

10. Ibid., p. 144.

speech' which . . . the Court has repeatedly held is entitled to comprehensive protection under the First Amendment." [11] The landmark language continued as the Court noted that "recognizing special characteristics of the school . . . it can hardly be argued that . . . students . . . shed their constitutional rights to freedom of speech or expression at the schoolhouse gate." [12] And lastly, in language that seems to revise the meaning of the term "student," the Court noted that "students in school as well as out of school are '*persons*' under our Constitution." [13]

Yet the Court was not saying that the constitutionally guaranteed right of freedom of speech was without the potential for regulation in the schools. In *Tinker*, it offered a standard on the grounds of which restraint could be rationalized:

Conduct by the student, in class or out of it, which for any reason— whether it stems from time, place, or type of behavior . . . materially disrupts classwork or involves substantial disorder or invasion of the rights of others, is, of course, not immunized by the Constitutional guarantee of freedom of speech.[14]

In practice, then, this standard gives the school administration the power to curtail free expression in cases of "material or substantial disruption." A restriction of First Amendment guarantees, however, is a restriction of what is known as a "fundamental" right (for example, speech, dress, religion) and this cannot be done lightly. The Court has placed the burden of justifying this restraint *on the school*:

In order for the State in the person of school officials to justify prohibition of a particular expression or opinion, it must be able to show that its action was caused by something more than a mere desire to avoid the discomfort and unpleasantness that always accompany an unpopular viewpoint.[15]

11. *Tinker v. Des Moines Independent Community School District*, 393 U.S. 503 (1969).

12. Ibid., p. 506.

13. Ibid., p. 508. (italics added)

14. Ibid., p. 513.

15. Ibid., p. 509.

In subsequent cases that closely parallel *Tinker*, the courts have supported the student, while in those that vary from *Tinker* the student's position has not always been upheld. While the Court has identified students as persons who do not leave their constitutional protections at the schoolhouse gate, the exact nature and number of these protections are still to be specified. When constitutionally guaranteed adult rights are being sought by juveniles, the courts have offered various interpretations. For example, in considering recent action in the area of procedural due process, Rodham notes that within a period of three years the U.S. Supreme Court decided two "apparently conflicting cases as to a child's rights within schools." In one case, the Court ordered that a child could not be expelled or suspended "without being given an adequate chance to respond to the charges against him." In the area of substantive rights, however, the Court reviewed a case in which a student challenged severe corporal punishment inflicted upon him. The Court ruled that "absent excessive physical harm, corporal punishment was permissible under the Eighth Amendment of the Constitution." [16]

It would seem that, while the Court has specified procedural due process protections applicable to juveniles, there is less clarity in reference to whether students possess the same Bill of Rights protections as adults. For example, as indicated above, the Court decided that corporal punishment was permissible under the Eighth Amendment. It did not say, however, that it was required. In schools in Maryland, for example, corporal punishment is dealt with by county, with some counties choosing not to permit educators to beat their children. The point here is that citizens need not employ litigation in all cases. A change in the Maryland Educational Statutes, for example, brought by community political action, could deny corporal punishment in all counties. We shall return to the question of alternatives to litigation at the conclusion of this chapter.

SUBSTANTIVE RIGHTS: IMPLICATIONS OF *Tinker*

We move now to a consideration of a number of other substantive issues, those of prior restraint, dress/hair codes, and patri-

16. Rodham, "Children's Rights: A Legal Perspective," p. 17.

otic exercises. As we shall see, the *Tinker* decision sets an important precedent for many of these cases.

Prior restraint. One would not be surprised to see a person on any city street selling or giving away privately printed newsletters, leaflets, or broadsides supporting particular social or political movements. Nor would one be surprised to hear oral presentations of these same views. Such behavior is, after all, protected by the First Amendment. Yet is was not until 1969 with *Tinker* that this protection of the Constitution was extended to students in schools. Providing that they did not "materially or substantially" disrupt school activities, students were free to express their opinions on any subject. In cases, however, where students express these views and other students strongly disagree, many school administrators feel bound to honor group order over individual rights. It is here that the issue of distribution of non-school-sponsored publications leads to the question of prior restraint. Specifically, if students wish to distribute a non-school-sponsored publication, must they submit it to the school principal for approval prior to its distribution?

The answer to this question is not as singular as one might wish.[17] There are general tendencies in the court decisions, yet the courts have not spoken with one voice and local regulations reflect this variation. While *Tinker* guarantees free expression to students, local boards have required that:

If a student desires to . . . make a distribution of free literature which is not officially recognized as a school publication, the student shall submit such . . . material to the principal for review and prior approval.[18]

While this position may be consistent with decisions of certain U.S. circuit courts (the Second, Fourth, and Fifth Circuits) other circuit courts (the First and Seventh) have rejected the concept of

17. In *Fujishima v. Board of Education*, 460 F.2d 1355 (7th Cir., 1972), the court found the prior review invalid, while in *Baughman v. Freienmuth*, 478 F. 2d 1345 (4th Cir., 1973) and *Nitzerg v. Parks*, Civil No. 74-1839 (4th Cir., April 14, 1975) Clearing House No. 17,267, the courts denied the specific prior review procedures but indicated they would permit prior review in principle.

18. *Student Responsibilities and Rights* (Chestertown, Md.: Kent County Public Schools, 1974), p. 5.

prior approval as a violation of the prohibition of censorship.[19] Consistent with these decisions, Montgomery County, Maryland notifies its students that non-school-sponsored publications "may be halted and disciplinary action taken by the principal *only after* the distribution has begun." [20] My position is that this latter guideline is the more desirable one and furthermore that it is consistent with the spirit of the Supreme Court, which noted that "any prior restraint on expression comes to this Court with a 'heavy presumption' against its Constitutional validity." [21] Essentially, it is proposed here that prior review is an unnecessary and unwise policy that is in conflict with the spirit if not the letter of the *Tinker* decision and with the implied due process protection of the Fourteenth Amendment. Even in those circuits where prior review is permitted, it is not required. Local districts have options. As Levine and Cary note, "even without court orders, such large urban school districts as Philadelphia and New York have decided on their own that it would not be proper to require students to submit literature for advance approval." [22]

We have focused narrowly here on the issue of prior review. As with other questions of this sort, *Tinker* has been interpreted in various ways. Where the interpretation has been made to increase such freedom, it is assumed that students will accept responsibility for their actions. So it should be, for the extension of rights to students must imply an expansion of their responsibilities,

19. For a more complete listing of these cases and those supporting the concept of prior approval, see *The Constitutional Rights of Students: Analysis and Litigation Materials for the Student's Lawyer*, ed. P. M. Lines (Cambridge, Mass.: Center for Law and Education, 1976), pp. 62-66. This excellent volume is potentially useful to anyone advocating the rights of students in school.

20. *Student Rights/Responsibilities wtih Staff Implementation Guidelines* (Montgomery County, Maryland: Montgomery County Public Schools, 1975), p. 12. (italics added)

21. *Carroll v. President and Commissioners of Princess Anne*, 393 U.S. 175, 181 (1968), as cited in *The Constitutional Rights of Students*, ed. Lines, p. 62.

22. Alan H. Levine and Eve Cary, *The Rights of Students: The Basic ACLU Guide to a Student's Rights* (New York: Avon Books, 1977), p. 36. See also, Tobyann Boonin, "The Benighted Status of U.S. School Corporal Punishment Practice," *Phi Delta Kappan* 60 (January 1979): 395-96.

and responsible behavior in the context of guaranteed rights is one measure of the mature citizen that schools are mandated to produce.

Hair length and dress codes. As with prior restraint one also finds various interpretations by the courts of students' rights pertaining to personal appearance. In twenty-four states it is unconstitutional to restrict hair length unless (in terms of *Tinker*) the school can show it would substantially or materially disrupt the school activity or that there is a rational relationship between the rule and some educational purpose. In another twenty-four states, schools are permitted but not mandated to develop such codes. Again, the courts have not spoken with one voice. Some have found for the student;[23] others have supported the school.[24] In Green's view, the issue is covered by the Fourteenth Amendment, the regulation of hair length being seen as "an arbitrary infringement prohibited by the due process and/or equal protection clause."[25] To date the Supreme Court has refused to hear cases dealing with hair length, leaving the issue to the lower courts. As a consequence, one can expect students' success in cases involving hair length and dress codes to depend greatly upon the jurisdiction in which the student resides. Such cases can be avoided, however, by local school districts recognizing the students' responsibility for their own grooming and dress. For example, one student guide leaves this responsibility to the student:

Student dress and grooming are the responsibility of students and their parents, except in situations where the standard of dress and grooming is a reasonable requirement of a course or activity, is necessary for reasons of health and safety, or disrupts school proceedings.[26]

This policy seems both reasonable and consistent with those

23. *Richards v. Thurston*, 424 F.2d 1281 (1st Cir. 1970), *Sims v. Colfax Community School District*, 307 F. Supp. 485 (S.D. Iowa, 1970), *Bannister v. Paradis*, 316 F. Supp. 185 (D. N. Hamp. 1970).

24. *Gene v. Stanley*, 453 F.2d 205 (3d Cir. 1972), *Hatch v. Goerke*, 502 F.2d 1189 (10th Cir. 1975).

25. Lawrence G. Green, "Hair Length," in *The Constitutional Rights of Students*, ed. Lines, p. 205.

26. *Student Rights/Responsibilities with Staff Implementation Guidelines*, p. 19.

cases in which the decisions have found for the student. For students who live in states that permit restrictive hair/dress regulations or in districts where court decisions have found in the schools' favor, litigation may not be the wisest choice. In these cases, it can be more fruitful to propose that a committee of students, community persons, and school staff be formed. Such a committee could advocate the creation of a code more representative of the Fourteenth Amendment's protections as interpreted above.

Patriotic exercises: Flag salute. Two cases precede *Gault* and *Tinker* in the area of student rights. Both deal with students who refused to participate in flag salute ceremonies and were expelled. In the first case, decided in 1940, the U.S. Supreme Court found for the school.[27] But in 1943, in the heat of World War II, the Court reversed itself, setting a precedent that protects students today. Citing the free speech and religious freedom protections of the First Amendment, the Court charged that a compulsory flag salute "invades the sphere of intellect and spirit which it is the purpose of the First Amendment of the Constitution to preserve from all official control." [28] Subsequent cases in lower courts have extended this protection so that students may now sit quietly during both the flag salute and the national anthem (without leaving the room) and they may do so on grounds of conscience as well as religious conviction.[29] A representative guideline reflects these protections when it specifies that both "teachers and pupils cannot be compelled to pledge allegiance to the flag nor be required to participate in patriotic exercises; and they may not be penalized or embarrassed for failure to do so." [30]

Yet almost every day in the child's public school experience begins with patriotic exercises. Mandated as they are in most states by law, they develop a certain "taken for granted" quality about them in classroom life. As such they are not likely to be seen by

27. *Minersville School District v. Gobitis*, 310 U.S. 586 (1940).

28. *West Virginia Board of Education v. Barnette*, 319 U.S. 624, 643 (1943).

29. *Goetz v. Ansell*, 477 F.2d 636 (2d Cir. 1973), *Sheldon v. Fannin*, 221 F. Supp. 766 (D. Ariz. 1963).

30. *Students Rights/Responsibilities with Staff Implementation Guidelines*, p. 32.

the student as activities about which choice exists. Participating in opening exercises each day is not just something one *learns* in school—it *is* school. Raising the issue of one's right not to be compelled to participate then provides an excellent occasion to begin discussions with students on their substantive rights.

PROCEDURAL DUE PROCESS ISSUES: IMPLICATIONS OF *Gault* AND *Goss*

As a consequence of *Gault*, specific procedural protections were extended to juveniles. The context for *Gault*, however, was the juvenile justice system and not the schools. For due process rights in a school setting, we will need to consider another case heard before the U.S. Supreme Court, the case of *Goss v. Lopez*.

The particulars in this case deal with blanket suspensions given to groups of students during the racially tense spring of 1971 in Columbus, Ohio. Nine students, including Dwight Lopez, were suspended for ten days from the Columbus Public Schools without benefit of prior hearing. They appealed to the district court, where they were supported. When the case was brought before the U.S. Supreme Court, the Court decided in the students' favor.[31]

Citing *Barnette*, the Court noted that, "The Fourteenth Amendment . . . protects the citizen against the State itself and all of its creatures . . . Boards of Education not excepted." Further, the Court identified access to public education as a property right and in the words of the Fourteenth Amendment, one cannot be deprived of property without due process:

The State is constrained to recognize a student's legitimate entitlement to a public education as a property interest which is protected by the Due Process clause, . . . and this interest cannot be taken away . . . without adherence to the minimum procedures required by that clause.[32]

In the case of *Goss* these minimum procedures applied to suspensions of ten days or less. They include presenting an oral or written statement of charges, permitting the student an opportunity for denial, and a presentation of evidence allowing the stu-

31. *Goss v. Lopez*, 419 U.S. 565 (1975).
32. Ibid., p. 573.

dent to present "his side of the story." [33] Reflecting an understanding of the real world of schools, the Court noted that students posing a threat to themselves or others may be removed immediately, allowing the above procedures to follow "as soon as practicable." While it did not deal directly with suspensions of longer than ten days, the Court did suggest that "more formal" procedures might be needed in such instances. In Maryland, for example, state statutes differentiate between short-term suspensions of less than five days, which require the procedures cited above, and suspensions of five days or more. In these latter cases the following provisions are added:

1. The student shall be informed, in writing, of the charges against him/her, including a summary of the evidence upon which the charges are based.
2. The student shall be informed of his/her right to be represented or advised during the proceedings by a person or persons of his or her choosing.
3. The student shall be given reasonable time to prepare a case.

In response to numerous lower court decisions that have focused on the suspension and expulsion procedures employed, many states have passed statutes guaranteeing due process rights to students. The above procedures are a county interpretation of such a state law.[34] In many cases local school districts, working within the guidelines of *Goss*, have developed standards of behavior warranting suspension or exclusion in addition to the appropriate procedures.[35] It seems reasonable that where administration, staff, parents, and *students* are involved in developing these guidelines, they will be more easily enforced. Further, there is a greater likelihood that in the development of fair procedures such a group would also develop fair rules, thereby combining both the procedural and substantive dimensions of the due process clause.

33. Ibid., p. 581.

34. *Public School Laws of Maryland*, Article 77, Section 956.

35. See the guidelines developed and distributed by the public schools of Prince George's County, Maryland, for a very extensive and specific listing.

EQUAL PROTECTION: THE ISSUE OF APPROPRIATE
CLASSIFICATIONS

A third protection offered by the Fourteenth Amendment, after due process and federal citizenship, is that of equal protection. Specifically, the amendment notes that no state may "deny any person within its jurisdiction equal protection of the laws." The significance of this clause can be seen in decisions dealing with classifications and particularly those considered to be unreasonable. As noted earlier in the *Brown* decision, the Court denied the use of race as an acceptable basis for classification, making de jure segregated schools illegal.

The issue of the appropriateness of student classifications—of equal protection—has been dealt with in cases concerning exclusion based upon marriage, pregnancy, and parenthood. In general, the courts have found in favor of the students and their rights to education. Given the importance that society places upon education, these exclusionary categories have been ruled invalid. Levine and Cary report that "a Kentucky court held that there was no reason to suppose that the marriage of a student would diminish the need of that student for an education—indeed just the contrary would appear the case." [36] LaMorte notes that "decisions in federal courts have overthrown rules excluding a married student from extracurricular activities, excluding an unwed mother from attending public school, and denying equal educational treatment to an unmarried pregnant senior." [37]

Those who have most recently gained access to education in schools have been the exceptional children. The landmark decision came in 1971 in the case of *Pennsylvania Association for Retarded Children (PARC)* v. *Commonwealth of Pennsylvania*, in which the equal protection clause of the Fourteenth Amendment was extended to the exceptional child.[38] The decision held that no mentally retarded child could be denied admission to a public school without notice and opportunity for a hearing. Many of

36. Levine and Cary, *The Rights of Students*, p. 102.

37. LaMorte, "The Fourteenth Amendment," p. 13.

38. *Pennsylvania Association for Retarded Children (PARC) v. Commonwealth of Pennsylvania*, 243 F. Supp. 279 (1972).

these cases have dealt with the issue of insufficient funding for programs for the handicapped.

It is clear that the judicial trend is toward supporting the inclusion of children with handicaps in the school. While the courts have been activist in this area, local boards often lag behind. In the landmark case of *Mills* v. *Board of Education of the District of Columbia*, the court found that the district had failed to provide education and training for exceptional children in 1972 and ruled that they must do so. Three years later, in 1975, further action was taken and the court found the mayor and the school board in contempt for "failure to place forty-three children in appropriate classes." [39] The passage of PL 94-142, the Education for All Handicapped Children Act (1975), has now added to the judicial standards of *PARC* and *Mills* the potential for enforcement through fiscal sanctions of the Department of Health, Education, and Welfare.[40] For the middle-school student in the 1980s, the composition of the student body will likely change as the exceptional child is physically and socially integrated into the school. It will be a difficult integration yet one based on a sense of what is just. To the extent that middle-school students recognize that the school is just, they are likely to ask for justice in future personal and institutional relations. In this way the Fourteenth Amendment, initially a legal guideline for human relations, will become curriculum content for the middle school.

Conclusion

It has been proposed here that the meaning of childhood, youth, and student have been changing. Recent changes in students' rights and responsibilities have been motivated by court actions that in many cases have extended both the substantive and procedural rights of students. One can expect that the future will bring continued consideration of students' substantive rights, for they are currently the least well defined. Where school people assume competence on the part of students, as is appropriate in

39. *The Constitutional Rights of Students*, ed. Lines, p. 174.

40. For an analysis of PL 94-142, see Don R. Barcovi and Richard W. Clellend, *Public Law 94-142: Special Education in Transition* (Arlington, Va.: American Association of School Administrators, n.d.).

the case of the middle-school student, one can expect substantive protections to be extended. In the 1980s, however, this expansion may be as successfully achieved through the actions of local advocates of students' rights and responsibilities as through the courts. Concerning procedural due process, it has been argued that all students should be guaranteed these protections. Where these procedures are clearly stated, publicly available, and publicly agreed upon, all concerned will benefit. Furthermore, it is reasonable to expect that these protections will be applied to students in the upper elementary and middle schools. After all, it does seem difficult to imagine many situations (excluding emergencies) in which due process should be denied to any student, or in the words of the Supreme Court, to any "person." Indeed, the middle school has the potential to judge students, faculty, and parents as persons in this sense and to move toward the creation of a morally and legally just institution.

CHAPTER XI

Promoting Cognitive and Psycholinguistic Development

MORRIS E. ESON AND SEAN A. WALMSLEY

The terms "cognitive" and "psycholinguistic" may have come to suffer from the phenomenon known as semantic satiation, that is, a loss of meaning resulting from constant repetition. It would be useful, therefore, to consider the range of meanings of these terms at the outset of our discussion.

Cognition and Psycholinguistics

The term "cognitive" became popular in psychology with the increased attention given to Piaget's formulations in "genetic epistemology." It refers to thought processes, to ways of understanding, and to processes involved in deriving meaning. A synonym for cognitive, related to its Latin root *cognoscere*, is "knowing." Beyond this, the term has taken on a meaning within the discipline of psychology, indicating a school of thought in opposition to behavioristic psychology, with its attention to overt measurable stimuli and responses. A cognitive-structuralist view seeks to understand human function in terms of "mental structures" or assumed organized internal processes within the person. In studying developmental changes, the cognitive structuralist seeks to understand how children in different periods of development organize or structure their experiences or their encounters with the world. Adopting such a view, as opposed to an associationist or behaviorist view, has some significant implications for the study of development and, more importantly, it suggests a role for the teacher that is organized around the understanding of the pupil rather than that of intervention and determined modification of the learner's behavior. It is the cognitive-structuralist view that will guide us in our discussion throughout this chapter.

The term "psycholinguistic" came into use a few decades ago with the aim of reuniting linguistics and psychology. The initial attempts at forging such a union were designed in part to bring about more comprehensive approaches to educational problems. Miller notes that:

Psychologists have long recognized that human minds feed on linguistic symbols. Linguists have always admitted that some kind of psychosocial motor must move the machinery of grammar and lexicon. Sooner or later they were certain to examine their intersection self-consciously. Perhaps it was also inevitable that the result would be called "psycho-linguistics." [1]

Miller goes on to point out that it was hoped that developments in this "hybrid" discipline would bring about improvements in methods for teaching reading and writing, or for second-language teaching. The emergence of interest in psycholinguistics coincided with the exciting revolution in linguistics initiated in large part by the work of Noam Chomsky. This coincidence of the re-awakened interest in the interrelationship of language and psychology and of Chomsky's renascent view of the centrality of grammatical rules in language function, actually resulted in a narrowing of efforts in psycholinguistics. Most of the early work addressed itself to the testing of psychological hypotheses derived from transformational-generative grammar.

More recently the research in psycholinguistics has achieved a new balance, with a lesser emphasis on the linguistic side of the compound and an increased attention to the psychological functions involved in dealing with linguistic phenomena. This shift in emphasis has been particularly evident in the area of developmental psycholinguistics, where the study of cognitive development has been joined to the study of age or stage changes in language function. In a discussion of child language, Suppes has noted the need for such a corrective balance: "Too great an emphasis has been placed on grammar or syntax and too little on semantics." [2] Some of the areas of cognitive-linguistic function that

1. George A. Miller, "The Psycholinguists: On the New Science of Language," *Encounter* 23 (Winter 1964): 29.

2. Patrick Suppes, "The Semantics of Children's Speech," *American Psychologist* 29 (February 1974): 103.

need attention in understanding how children change in their comprehension and interpretation of utterances are the following: growth of the appreciation of metaphor and synonymy; increasing mastery of complex grammatical structures, such as logical connectives; changes in the structure of concepts with concomitant changes in understanding of polar opposites and antinomy; development of the ability to recognize and cope with ambiguity and the appreciation of humor; development of communication skills and the ability to use language for the promotion of social solidarity.[3]

In this chapter we consider the ways in which cognition is presumed to change between ages ten and fifteen, the ways in which these cognitive developments are related to the changes in linguistic skills, and the implications of these developmental changes for teachers and teaching.

Metacognitive Changes During the Period of Semiformal Operations

According to cognitive-structure theory the child passes through a series of stages, each with a characteristic mode of structuring and interpreting the world. In Piaget's formulation there are four major stages with substages within each. Since the major concern of this chapter is with the third and fourth stages, we shall only comment briefly on the characteristics of the child's thought processes just prior to entering the third stage.

In the latter part of the preoperational period, just prior to school entry, the child's thought patterns are characterized as intuitive. Although concepts and the attributes that define them are relatively stable, the child's thinking tends to be highly impressionistic, and bound by the appearance of things. Intuitive thought seems to attend in a kind of saccadic way to this or that aspect of a display, gaining only impressionistic understanding of an experience. The child's interpretation of language tends to be relatively literal and when pressed to explain a metaphor or a proverb, for example, he will resort to syncretic, almost free associative, responses.

3. Morris E. Eson, "Cognitive Function and Interpretive Semantics: Psychological Components of Psycholinguistics," *International Journal of Psycholinguistics* 7 (1977): 67-76.

The transition from the preoperational period to the period of concrete operations is marked by some striking cognitive and linguistic changes. White has compiled an impressive list of studies that document what has come to be known as the five to seven shift.[4] He cites, for example, the work of Hofstaetter who found, in a factor analysis of longitudinal intelligence test data, that a factor III accounts for a majority of the variance from age five onward.[5] Hofstaetter characterizes this factor by the terms "planning," "provisional action," and "abstract behavior." Another change shown during this age period is the shift in the type of response given in a word association task. The younger children tend to respond with words that would ordinarily be found before or after the stimulus word in a sentence (for example, short—pants); the older children tend to respond with a word from the same lexical class, and in the case of adjectives, the response is likely to be the antonym (short—long). This, along with evidence from other sources, would indicate that as the child enters the concrete operational period he acquires a more thorough understanding of the concept. The word "short" is no longer merely a descriptive term but is appreciated more abstractly as one end of a bipolar continuum. In communication the younger child displays an inability to take into account the perspective of the other, while the older child begins to be aware of other perspectives and begins to shape the message and to interpret it in terms of these perspectives.

As the child enters the period of concrete operations, at about six or seven, he begins to be capable of engaging in cognitive processes that Piaget calls operations. The term "operations" as applied to cognition means that the thought is differentiated from preoperational thinking in several ways. First, operational thinking is capable of imagining a sequence of events as being reversible, for example, the recognition that the process of addition and subtrac-

4. Sheldon H. White, "Evidence for a Hierarchial Arrangement of Learning Processes," in *Advances in Child Development and Behavior*, vol. 2 ed. Lewis P. Lipsitt and Charles C. Spiker (New York: Academic Press, 1965), pp. 187-220.

5. Peter R. Hofstaetter, "The Changing Composition of 'Intelligence': A Study in *T*-Technique," *Journal of Genetic Psychology* 85 (September 1954): 159-64.

tion are the same operation carried out in opposite directions. Second, operational thinking is conducted in such a way as to keep in balance the relationship between change and constancy, variance and invariance, in understanding an event. For example, in the usual test for the presence of operational thought, the conservation task, the child indicates that the amount of clay in a transformed shape has remained the same even though the shape has changed. A third characteristic of operational thought is that operations themselves are linked so that, for example, the addition-subtraction operation is linked to multiplication, classification, ordering, and so on. It is because of this that the various cognitive skills that characterize the concrete operational period emerge at or near the same time; children begin to show a conservation response, they develop the ability to handle classification schemes, and in a relatively short time they become capable of systematically ordering events along a continuum.

In most of the Piagetian literature the period of concrete operations, from about seven to twelve years, is considered to be relatively homogeneous. It is our position here that in the latter half of this period there occurs a transformation in the child's thinking. The evidence for this transformation is in our estimation strong enough to warrant the designation of "shift," a ten to twelve shift analogous to the five to seven shift. The thought process at the conclusion of this transformation is not as well organized as Piaget describes it when he characterizes it as formal operational. The thought process is similar in part to that of the period of formal operations, to be discussed below, but it lacks certain qualities so that it would not properly be called formal. We would characterize the thinking during this period as semiformal. The primary characteristic of the thinking and the language function of this period is that it is metacognitive and metalinguistic, that is, the child is able to think about thinking and is able to consider language as a system and thus observe and consider language phenomena at a distance, as it were. These attributes of cognitive and linguistic function are of considerable importance and we shall discuss them in some detail.

The final stage of cognitive development is termed "formal

operations," and, according to Flavell and to Neimark,[6] is characterized by the following: (a) the ability to subordinate the real world within the realm of possible worlds (in other words, to approach problems hypothetico-deductively by generating sets of possible hypotheses to account for observed data, rather than "empirico-inductively" by ordering or interrelating properties or features of the observed data;[7] (b) the ability to conceptualize and test the logical relationships between propositions, not merely those that relate propositions to real objects and events (this ability is typically thought of as knowledge and use of the sixteen possible combinations of binary propositions of the form PQ [P and Q], $\overline{P}Q$ [not P, Q], P$\overline{Q}$ [P, not Q], $\overline{PQ}$ [not P, not Q]); (c) the ability to generate all possible combinations and permutations; (d) the ability to combine inverse and reciprocal relationships; and (e) the ability to adopt consciously planful, efficient strategies for organizing and retrieving information.

Several points need to be made about formal operational thinking during adolescence. First, although most adolescents have progressed beyond concrete operations, not all of them attain formal operational thinking in the sense that Piaget and his followers have defined it. Just exactly how many do not reach this stage seems to depend on the kind of task used to determine formal operational thinking. In fact, Piaget's definition of formal operations and the methods by which he has examined adolescent formal thought[8] are not without their critics. For example, Ennis takes Piaget to task for what he considers to be serious flaws in the logic of the combinations of the sixteen binary propositions;[9] and some of these combinations are in fact impossible to test.

6. John H. Flavell, *Cognitive Development* (Englewood Cliffs, N.J.: Prentice-Hall, 1977); Edith D. Neimark, "Intellectual Development During Adolescence," in *Review of Child Development Research*, vol. 4, ed. Frances D. Horowitz (Chicago: University of Chicago Press, 1975), pp. 541-94.

7. Flavell, *Cognitive Development*, pp. 103-7.

8. See, for example, Bärbel Inhelder and Jean Piaget, *The Growth of Logical Thinking from Childhood to Adolescence* (New York: Basic Books, 1958).

9. Robert H. Ennis, "Children's Ability to Handle Piaget's Propositional Logic: A Conceptual Critique," *Review of Educational Research* 45 (Winter 1975): 1-41.

Staudenmeyer argues that there are both linguistic (for example, semantic and syntactic) and nonlinguistic (for example, response bias strategies, interpretation of task requirements) factors that may interfere with the adolescent's performance on a formal operational task.[10] Wason and Johnson-Laird suggest that the kind of logical thinking used in typical everyday tasks may not be the same as that required in experimental situations.[11] Thus formal operational thinking, not being necessarily the most efficient or preferred method of solving most problems, including those that are amenable to being solved "formally," has to be specially recruited for tasks in which it is expected by examiners to be used.

A constant problem faced by researchers in this area is that subjects in experiments are often not aware that they are being asked to apply "formal" reasoning. In a recent study, Stone and Day have shown that there is a large number of latent users of formal operational strategies who would have been misclassified as nonformal operational by traditional procedures.[12] Their results suggest that it would be useful to employ the notion of levels of availability in making individual and developmental differentiations in the use of formal operational strategies. While there is little disagreement that adolescent thinking is characterized by more mature intellectual reasoning than that exhibited in the earlier period of concrete operations, there continues to be disagreement as to the precise nature of formal operational thought, and the extent of the utility of this type of thinking in the kinds of reasoning tasks typically demanded in the adolescent years.

In summary, the universality of formal operations, in the strict definition of the term, is highly questionable. However, as anyone who has dealt with children within the age range of seven to thirteen will testify, the thinking of children in the early stages

10. Herman Staudenmeyer, "Understanding Conditional Reasoning with Meaningful Propositions," in *Reasoning: Representation and Process in Children*, ed. Rachel J. Falmagne (Hillsdale, N.J.: Lawrence Erlbaum Associates, 1975), pp. 55-79.

11. Peter C. Wason and Philip N. Johnson-Laird, *Psychology of Reasoning: Structure and Content* (Cambridge, Mass.: Harvard University Press, 1972).

12. C. Addison Stone and Mary C. Day, "Levels of Availability of a Formal Operational Strategy," *Child Development* 49 (December 1978): 1054-65.

of concrete operations differs qualitatively from that of children in the later stages. If it is not that they have become formal operational, then what is it that characterizes the difference? It is our contention here, as noted previously, that the thinking becomes semiformal operational. The major characteristic of this kind of thinking is that it becomes metacognitive and metalinguistic.

COGNITION

The child's ability to think about the thought process itself changes the nature of his thinking. One limitation of the child's thought before becoming metacognitive is judging the adequacy or correctness of a response. Children in the early stage of concrete operations seem incapable of reflecting on their own thinking. It is almost as if they were not fully aware of their own thinking. This quality is sometimes seen in the child's lack of awareness that the solution he has offered needs to be verified. Even bright children of seven or eight will fail the Plan of Search items in the *Stanford-Binet Intelligence Scale* because of the absence of metacognitive skills. In this item the child is shown a diamond-shaped figure with a small gap. The examiner gives the child a pencil and says: "Let's suppose that your purse with a lot of money in it has been lost in this big field. Take this pencil and start here (pointing) at the gate and show me where you would go to hunt for the purse so as to be sure not to miss it."[13] Children whose thinking is preoperational are likely to indicate that the diamond representing the field is too small. In the early concrete operational period they often draw a single line and say, "Here it is." A more sophisticated concrete operational response, one that is not yet semiformal operational, would run somewhat as follows, "I'd go look for it where I lost it" and the child would draw a small circle in a restricted portion of the field. We must confess that this response is truly the most practical response and there is a high probability that it corresponds to the actual response that even Piaget would give were he to lose a purse with a lot of money in a field. What the item is calling for, however, is a demonstration of the child's ability spontaneously to raise the

13. Lewis M. Terman and Maud A. Merrill, *Stanford-Binet Intelligence Scale* (Boston: Houghton Mifflin, 1960), p. 102.

problem to an abstract level, to think about it and to question the adequacy of his response.

In the younger child, once a solution has been reached, no further deliberation seems called for. The younger child, when faced with disconfirming evidence, distorts the evidence to support his conclusion. The child whose thinking is operational at a semiformal level is more willing to reconsider his conclusion and operates with a willingness, or even an obligation, to test his own formulation.

We noted earlier that in the Piagetian formulation the entire period of concrete operations is considered relatively homogeneous. This is not entirely correct. In discussing simple multiplication or intersection as an operation, Inhelder and Piaget indicate that in carrying out this operation a 75 percent level of success is not reached until ages nine or ten.[14] We feel that Piaget and Inhelder have underestimated the importance of this achievement. In our estimation the intersection task marks a significant qualitative change in the child's thought. In that task the subject is presented a row of red objects (for example, an apple, a book, a hat, a flower) and a row of butterflies of various colors (for example, green, blue, yellow, purple) at right angles to the row of objects. An empty space is left at the point at which the two rows intersect and the subject is asked to fill this cell, the answer being the derivation of the constant feature in the row of objects (redness) and the constant feature in the row of butterflies (butterfliness), resulting in a red butterfly. The skill in performing this task seems to mature during the period of semiformal operations, and it seems to be the hallmark of the child's metacognitive ability.

MEMORY

Several authors have pointed out that the basically involuntary operations and processes of memory (for example, recognition, representation) appear to remain stable over age.[15] However, there

14. Bärbel Inhelder and Jean Piaget, *The Early Growth of Logic in the Child* (New York: Harper and Row, 1964).

15. See, for example, John H. Flavell and Henry M. Wellman, "Metamemory," in *Perspectives on the Development of Memory and Cognition*, ed. Robert V. Kail and John W. Hagen (Hillsdale, N.J.: Lawrence Erlbaum Associates, 1977), pp. 3-33, and Neimark, "Intellectual Development During Adolescence."

are many developmental changes in general memory ability (for example, immediate memory span), in the voluntary and deliberate strategies (for example, rehearsal, mnemonic schemes) used by children to assist them in remembering things both immediately and for future retrieval, and in the knowledge and awareness of memory itself, which Flavell terms "metamemory."

Kreutzer et al. interviewed children in kindergarten and in grades one, three, and five about their knowledge of memory, and found that kindergarten and first-grade children know something about the meanings of the words "learn," "remember," and "forget," and know that meaningless, rote-learned items (for example, phone numbers) are very quickly forgotten if not used often.[16] They also are able to make some plans for future retrieval of information, such as writing down a telephone number when asked to remember it for a future occasion. The older children, however, especially the eleven-year-olds, are much more planful in their mnemonic strategies, partly, it appears, because they have far more of them available, partly because they are "more sensitive to the presence of existing relations among items (to be retrieved) and aware of their powerful effects upon item retrievability."[17] Paris compared the memory organization skills of second-grade and sixth-grade children.[18] The older children showed significantly more spontaneous reconstruction of remembered information and displayed "constructive memory-monitoring" skills. In another study Paris and Lindauer showed that eleven- and twelve-year-old children were better able than six- and seven-year-olds to derive new cognitions from old ones through inference.[19] The increased demands on memory made by the typical late elementary and early secondary school curriculum also presumably contribute

16. Mary Anne Kreutzer, Sister Catherine Leonard, and John H. Flavell, *An Interview Study of Children's Knowledge about Memory*, in *Monographs of the Society for Research in Child Development* 40, no. 1 (1975), Serial No. 159.

17. Ibid., p. 54.

18. Scott G. Paris, "Memory Organization During Children's Repeated Recall," *Developmental Psychology* 14 (January 1978): 99-106.

19. Scott G. Paris and Barbara K. Lindauer, "The Role of Inference in Children's Comprehension and Memory for Sentences," *Cognitive Psychology* 8 (April 1976): 217-27.

to the development of more efficient ways of organizing information in memory.[20]

COMPREHENSION

While Piaget and Inhelder's demonstrations of the nature of adolescent thinking are derived primarily from responses to scientific problems (for example, the pendulum and the chemical mixing experiments), Peel uses more discursive material describing problematic situations in which adolescents demonstrate their maturity of judgment.[21] In brief, his procedure consists of constructing short passages dealing with a topical, social, or intellectual problem. Each passage is followed by a question about some aspect of the passage, and it always is itself followed by the question, "Why do you think so?" The passages are so constructed that the first question cannot be answered solely by reference to the passage; the adolescent must draw on his own experiences as well. Levels of the maturity of the judgments are derived through analysis of the explanation given by the adolescent to the second question, "Why do you think so?"

Peel has proposed three levels of explanation, which he terms "restricted," "circumstantial," and "imaginative." The restricted type of explanation, given by children under eleven, is tautological, premise-denying, and frequently irrelevant. The second type of explanation, the circumstantial, offered by students between ages twelve and thirteen plus, is bound solely by the content of the passage, often taking account of only one factor in the situation. The highest type of explanation, the imaginative-comprehensive, shown by subjects older than thirteen and a half, invokes independent ideas yet takes into account the premises set by the problem.

In Peel's scheme, the adolescent begins with a somewhat restricted set of explanations, but is able gradually to put distance between himself and the problem presented, and to be able to weigh the various competing hypotheses that have to be generated to account for the explanation offered. His findings suggest that

20. Neimark, "Intellectual Development During Adolescence."

21. Edward A. Peel, *The Nature of Adolescent Judgment* (New York: John Wiley and Sons, 1971).

although there are many substages between his circumstantial and imaginative levels of explanation, these are attributable for the most part to the specific variables encountered in the passage; he concludes, however, that "thought during and after adolescence reveals itself chiefly in the range of circumstantial and imaginative-comprehensive judgments."[22]

Metalinguistic Changes During the Period of Semiformal Operations

After reviewing the work of several investigators of syntactic development beyond age five, Palermo and Molfese conclude that two trends describe the changes in language skills between kindergarten and seventh grade.[23] First, there appears a general but gradual consolidation of language structures. Second, and more important from our point of view, there appear to be abrupt shifts in performance occurring between kindergarten and first grade (at the onset of the concrete operational period) and between the fifth and seventh grades (in the latter part of the concrete operational period, the period we have called semiformal operational). Palermo and Molfese point out that similar abrupt changes occur in semantic development. Thus, for example, at about ten to twelve years children begin to differentiate the meanings of words such as "good," "pretty," and "happy," where earlier they treated them as synonymous. They also begin to provide abstract definitions for words in place of concrete functional definitions. In regard to this latter point, it is interesting to note that items in the Stanford-Binet test of intelligence calling for abstract definitions (pity, curiosity, grief, surprise) first appear at the age ten level.

From a social-communicative point of view the child changes in several ways as a result of acquiring metalinguistic skills. Alvy has shown that communication between children improves markedly between the ages of six and eight and again between eight and eleven. He found that egocentric communications, those that fail

22. Ibid., p. 42.

23. David S. Palermo and Dennis L. Molfese, "Language Acquistion from Age Five Onward," *Psychological Bulletin* 78 (December 1972): 409-28.

to take into account the other's point of view, decrease with age.[24] Being able to draw inferences about what others are thinking brings about a more effective understanding of the communication process and results in the ability to share social reality. This shared intersubjectivity, as Rommetveit calls it,[25] forms an integral part of the metalinguistic ability and transforms large segments of private experience into shared cognitive-emotive events.

METAPHOR

The development of metalinguistic ability during the period of semiformal operations is most clearly demonstrated in the production and interpretation of metaphor. Every lexical item changes its meaning as it is used in different contexts. Metaphor, however, represents a special case of variation and extension of meaning. It is a pervasive feature of language, and it adds novelty and interest to language. In order to understand a metaphor in the same terms that the adults of a language community understand it, the child needs to have developed two semantic principles, namely, the *reality principle* and the *cooperative principle*. When a listener interprets an utterance according to the reality principle, he proceeds on the assumption that the speaker is referring to a situation or concepts out of which the listener can make sense. The application of the cooperative principle leads the listener to assume that the speaker is observing four maxims: the maxim of quality (not saying anything that is known to be false); the maxim of quantity (telling all that needs to be known and no more); the maxim of relation—(saying things that are relevant); the maxim of manner (avoiding obscurity and ambiguity).[26] A metaphor can only be appreciated as a metaphor when the reality and the cooperative principles guide the participant in the communication

24. Kerby T. Alvy, "Relation of Age to Children's Egocentric and Co-operative Communication," *Journal of Genetic Psychology* 112 (June 1968): 275-86.

25. Ragnar Rommetveit, *On Message Structure: A Framework for the Study of Language and Communication* (New York: John Wiley and Sons, 1974).

26. H. Paul Grice, "Logic and Conversation," in *Syntax and Semantics*, vol. 3, *Speech Acts*, ed. Peter Cole and J. L. Morgan (New York: Seminar Press, 1975), pp. 41-58.

process. Encountering a metaphor means that the listener recognizes the possibility that the reality and cooperative principles have been violated and only by extending the meaning of the figurative term can he undo the apparent violation and reestablish the fundamental principles of the communication. Loewenberg suggests that no one produces or understands a metaphor unless he understands it *as* a metaphor.[27] In this way the production and adequate interpretation of a metaphor is truly a metalinguistic undertaking.

While metaphor is a pervasive feature of language, the study of how children develop metaphoric competence had been very much neglected until quite recently. Several of the recent studies have shown that children go through a series of distinct changes in their ability to interpret metaphor and do not treat metaphor *qua* metaphor until they reach the period of semiformal operations.[28] Children between the ages of five and seven usually give syncretic responses when asked to tell the meaning of a metaphor. Thus, Eric (age five years, eight months and preoperational) gives a typically syncretic response to the metaphor "The wind whispered to him all night long," in stating: "The wind don't whisper, it goes 'wsshhoo'—it can't whisper cause its just standing, lying down going to sleep and that's why it don't want to bother the quiet trees." In contrast, a child in the early concrete operational period (Stacy, age six years, four months) responded to the same metaphor by saying: "It means the wind is blowing and it sounds like when someone is talking real quiet to me." Although children in the early stages of concrete operations can provide a reasonable paraphrase of the metaphor, they are unable to explain the way the metaphor works. Laura (age seven years, two months and in

27. Ina Loewenberg, "Identifying Metaphors," *Foundations of Language: International Journal of Language and Philosophy* 12 (1975): 315-38.

28. See, for example, Solomon E. Asch and Harriet Nerlove, "The Development of Double Function Terms in Children: An Exploratory Investigation," in *Perspectives in Psychological Theory*, ed. Bernard Kaplan and Seymour Wapner (New York: International Universities Press, 1950), pp. 47-60; Richard M. Billow, "A Cognitive Developmental Study of Metaphor Comprehension," *Developmental Psychology* 11 (July 1975): 415-23; Ellen Winner, Anne Rosenstiel, and Howard Gardner, "The Development of Metaphoric Understanding," *Developmental Psychology* 12 (July 1976): 289-97; and Michael S. Cometa and Morris E. Eson, "Logical Operations and Metaphor Interpretation: A Piagetian Model," *Child Development* 49 (September 1978): 649-59.

the early stage of concrete operations) paraphrases the metaphor, "When the wind blew, the leaves began to dance" as follows: "They move all around and go back and forth." When asked to explain her paraphrase she remarked, "Well, I don't know. People aren't the same as leaves! People have eyes and mouths and leaves don't really dance—they don't have feet!" The child who has reached the stage of semiformal operations, as demonstrated by succeeding at the intersection task, is able to explain his paraphrase. For example, Patrick (age ten years, two months) explains this paraphrase of the same metaphor ("It means they moved and blew back and forth") as follows: "It describes it pretty good. Cause people shake back and forth when they dance, so it's like the leaves do when the wind pushes them." This illustrates well the child's growth in metalinguistic ability.

Cometa and Eson, from whom the above illustrations have been drawn, were able to show that children who could not perform on the intersection task, without exception also could not provide an adequate explanation of the metaphor.[29] Although some of the children who could perform successfully on the intersection task were also incapable of explaining metaphor, the analysis of the data revealed that the intersection skill was a necessary, although not sufficient, condition for metalinguistic appreciation of the metaphor. The onset of formal operations produced little change in the ability to handle metaphor. Children who had not reached the stage of semiformal operations had zero percent explanations, those who had reached this stage as evidenced by performance on the intersection task but who were not formal operational gave 80 percent adequate explanations, and children who were formal operational gave 95 percent adequate explanations.

HUMOR

Paralleling the development of metaphor comprehension is the development of the appreciation of humor. In fact, it may be argued that the cognitive processes underlying both are the same. Enjoyment of the various forms of humor depends upon the level of cognitive development. Thus, a child who has mastered the conservation task and demonstrated that he has begun to use con-

29. Cometa and Eson, "Logical Operations and Metaphor Interpretation."

crete operations will appreciate the following kind of joke: "Mr. Jones went into a restaurant and ordered a whole pizza for dinner. When the waiter asked if he wanted it cut into six or eight pieces, Mr. Jones said: 'Oh, you had better make it six: I could never eat eight.'" [30] But it is not until the child has reached the stage of semiformal operations that he will show the understanding of what is funny about the following: "A man went one day to the post office and asked if there was a letter waiting for him. 'What is your name?' asked the postmaster. 'Why,' said the man, 'you will find my name on the envelope.'" [31]

Sheppard proposes developmental levels for the appreciation of humor somewhat analogous to those of the explanation of metaphor. [32] Sheppard indicates that there is a preexplanatory stage for the appreciation of humor, when children can enjoy an incongruity but cannot explain why the matter is funny. This corresponds to the preoperational stage. In the early stages of concrete operations the child will be able to say with reference to the pizza joke: "It makes no difference how many pieces he cuts the pizza into; he will get the same amount." In the later stages of concrete operations, in the semiformal period, the humor will be characterized by the ability "to incorporate self-reference, to apply a metaphorical interpretation to events, and to discover social truths in humor and satire." [33]

LOGICAL CONNECTIVES

An aspect of psycholinguistic development that has received considerable attention is children's and adolescents' understanding and use of logical connectives. Connectives are syntactic structures, such as "and," "if," and "or," that signal underlying logical

30. Paul E. McGhee, "Children's Appreciation of Humor: A Test of the Cognitive Congruency Principle," *Child Development* 47 (June 1976): 420-26.

31. From the verbal absurdities item at years IX and XII of the Stanford-Binet Intelligence Scale.

32. Alice Sheppard, "Developmental Levels in Explanations of Humor from Childhood to Late Adolescence," in *It's a Funny Thing, Humor,* ed. A. J. Chapman and H. C. Foot (Oxford, England: Pergamon Press, 1977), pp. 225-28.

33. Ibid., p. 227.

propositional relationships.[34] Certain connectives have received more than usual attention because they signal particular logical relationships of interest to cognitive psychologists; for example, "and" signalling *conjunction*, and "or" *disjunction*.[35] There has also been interest, however, in how adolescents understand and use connectives in the normal course of reading, writing, or speaking.[36] In these instances, connectives are more broadly conceived as signalling relationships of time (after, before); conjunction and co-ordination (and); comparison (like, similarly); contrast or anti-thesis (but, although); cause (therefore, because); conditionality (if, provided that); emphasis (indeed, moreover); and elaboration (for example, in summary).[37]

Many of these connectives are learned and used very early in a child's linguistic development, for example, "and" signifying conjunction.[38] Others, such as "but" and "because," are gradually acquired over the course of the elementary school years and are generally well known by age twelve or so. On the Stanford-Binet, for example, in Minkus Completion 1, children in year XII have to understand conjunction, contrast, and cause. Some connectives appear to be learned somewhat more slowly. Watts provides evidence that "although" is not fully understood even at age fifteen.[39] Other connectives, however, have multiple meanings (for example, "or" signifying exclusive disjunction [meaning one or the other, but not both] and inclusive disjunction [meaning one or the other

34. Henry F. Olds, *An Experimental Study of Syntactic Factors Influencing Children's Comprehension of Certain Complex Relationships*, Final Report (Cambridge, Mass.: Center for Research and Development in Educational Differences, 1968).

35. Henry Beilin and Barbara Lust, *Studies in the Cognitive Basis of Language Development* (New York: Academic Press, 1975).

36. See Walter Loban, *Language Development: Kindergarten through Grade Twelve*, Research Report No. 18 (Urbana, Ill.: National Council for Teachers of English, 1976).

37. Michael A. K. Halliday and Ruqaiya Hasan, *Cohesion in English* (London: Longman, 1976).

38. Evelyn W. Katz and Sandor B. Brent, "Understanding Connectives," *Journal of Verbal Learning and Verbal Behavior* 7 (April 1968): 501-9.

39. Albert F. Watts, *The Language and Mental Development of Children: An Essay in Educational Psychology* (London: George G. Harrap and Co., 1944).

or both]); in these cases, children frequently learn one meaning first, and then gradually acquire the other. In the case of "or," the inclusive disjunction meaning is apparently not mastered until late adolescence.[40]

It has been argued that the qualitative change in children's understanding of such connectives as "or" that occurs in adolescence is a function of the onset of formal operational thinking.[41] This raises several questions, however. First, of what consequence is this late acquisition of certain logical connectives? Given the rarity of inclusive disjunction relationships in materials typically read by adolescents, even in science-related matter,[42] one might argue that adolescents have little need for such sophisticated understanding, even though it might be indicative of their ability to think at the level of formal operations.

Second, we know little about the development of adolescents' understanding of the large number of connectives that signal less formal logical operations, for example, those that signal comparison, contrast, emphasis, and elaboration. Although these occur increasingly in secondary school reading materials,[43] their understanding and use by adolescents has only been partially investigated.[44] Such studies imply, however, a gradual increase in the range of use and depth of understanding.

Third, we know little about how an understanding of connectives relates to the comprehension of written text.[45] Despite the in-

40. Edith D. Neimark and Nan S. Slotnick, "Development of the Understanding of Logical Connectives," *Journal of Educational Psychology* 61 (December 1970): 451-60.

41. Beilin and Lust, "Studies in the Cognitive Basis of Language Development"; Neimark and Slotnick, "Development of the Understanding of Logical Connectives."

42. Paul L. Gardner, "Logical Connectives in Science: A Preliminary Report" (Paper presented at the Sixth Annual Conference of the Australian Science Education Research Association, May 1975).

43. Denis Rodgers, "Which Connectives? Signals to Enhance Comprehension," *Journal of Reading* 17 (March 1974): 462-66.

44. See, for example, Loban, *Language Development.*

45. Sean A. Walmsley, "Children's Understanding of Linguistic Connectives: A Review of Selected Literature and Implications for Reading Research," in *Reading: Theory, Research, and Practice,* Twenty-sixth Yearbook of the National Reading Conference, ed. P. David Pearson (Clemson, S.C.: National Reading Conference, 1977): 292-98.

creased number of connectives in secondary school reading materials, their function in assisting readers to gain access to the meaning of passages is not well known.

Metacognition and Metalinguistic Awareness in Reading and In Oral and Written Discourse

We are struck by the congruence of the evidence from disparate sources suggesting that during the late elementary school years children are increasingly able to reflect on the cognitive and linguistic systems they use. Myers and Paris provide evidence for the development of metacognitive and metalinguistic awareness of reading between the ages of six and twelve.[46] From interviews conducted with second and sixth graders, they concluded that (a) second graders appear to perceive reading as an orthographic-verbal translation problem, whereas sixth graders regard it as a meaning-construction and comprehension task, and (b) that second graders are relatively insensitive to semantic dimensions of sentences and paragraphs, and to goals and methods of comprehension, while sixth graders are relatively sensitive to these metacognitive and metalinguistic variables. What occurs between the ages of six and twelve, according to Myers and Paris, is the acquisition of metacognitive knowledge about reading that facilitates the selection of reading strategies and allows the reader deliberately to ignore information not relevant to the task of comprehension.

Children's stories, whether told orally or written down, appear to share similar features in their development in this period. Gardner notes that five- to seven-year-olds are not accomplished storytellers, but have mastered some "formal aspects of the literary realm," [47] a finding corroborated by the work of Leondar and of Sutton-Smith.[48] A group of six- to fifteen-year-olds, when asked

46. Meyer Myers and Scott G. Paris, "Children's Metacognitive Knowledge about Reading," *Journal of Educational Psychology* 70 (October 1978): 680-90.

47. Howard Gardner, *The Arts and Human Development* (New York: John Wiley and Sons, 1973).

48. Barbara Leondar, "Hatching Plots: Genesis of Storymaking," in *The Arts and Cognition,* ed. David Perkins and Barbara Leondar (Baltimore: Johns Hopkins University Press, 1977), pp. 172-91; Brian Sutton-Smith, "The Importance of the Storytaker: An Investigation of the Imaginative Life," *Urban Review* 8 (Summer, 1975): 82-95.

by Gardner to complete two stories without endings (that had very different styles), did so in a way that characterizes this development of storytelling ability:

The six-year-olds tended to give a *brief*, one sentence ending to the story, completing it in the simplest possible way, as if supplying the last strip in a comic. The eight-year-olds gave *picaresque* endings. These were long, detailed, complex, often filled with high adventure, drama, and excitement, but not always appropriate to the demands of the stories. The sixth graders appeared to be at the *watershed* of literary creativity: they revealed a great deal of promise in their endings, and the best of them were extremely sensitive to the style of the original, clever in their endings, and faithful to the original. The ninth graders were, as a group, competent, even *professional*, in the task: they executed it adequately, but few, if any, revealed notable originality or sensitivity to style. They gave what was called for, nothing more, and appeared to have lost the promise of the sixth graders.[49]

These results bear a striking resemblance to Sutton-Smith's analysis of oral stories made up by five- to ten-year-olds; between these years, children develop what Sutton-Smith terms "narrative competence," in other words, they go through a series of stages in inventing narrative plots.[50] Stories become more complex and more coherent in their narrative structure. Leondar also has examined children's written stories and finds similar developmental trends; she concludes that the late elementary child learns to distance himself from outward events and eventually learns to distance himself from, and thus to observe, internal processes of mind.[51] This growth of complexity and coherence in written discourse is related to the developmental changes in "person perceptions," that is, the way in which children construct inferences about people's personalities and general behaviors. Barenboim found that age ten to fourteen children increasingly refer to affective and cognitive processes in describing individuals and they show an increasing tendency to employ statements that organize relationships, such as contrast, attempted explanations of behavior, or relating general

49. Gardner, *The Arts and Human Development*, pp. 211-12.

50. Sutton-Smith, "The Importance of the Storytaker."

51. Leondar, "Hatching Plots," p. 165.

dispositions to specific behaviors.[52] Barenboim concludes that during this period children form an implicit personality theory through which they organize their perceptions. It is reasonable to assume that this would be reflected in written discourse.

Further evidence of this emerging cognitive competence may be found in the writing of school children examined by Britton and his associates in England.[53] Most of the writing that children aged eleven to eighteen do in school is what Britton calls transactional (that is, writing that informs or persuades), and most of it has as its audience the teacher, or teacher-as-examiner. Of interest to us, however, is the finding that over the course of the years eleven to eighteen, children increasingly construct more abstract generalizations about the topics on which they write. The percentage of protocols in which the writer "reports" events that have happened, either directly or vicariously, steadily decreases beyond the age of thirteen, to be replaced with protocols in which the writer "increases the distance between himself and his material," and is able increasingly to make classificatory statements and to present sequences of such statements. In other words, the writer is able to write about "what happens," not merely "what happened." [54] Britton found very few protocols, even amongst the eighteen-year-olds, that demonstrated the writer's ability to write speculatively or tautologically (that is, the construction of and testing of hypotheses, the building of "theories"). Such writing would be typically associated with formal operational thinking and its infrequent occurrence supports our contention and the contention of others that formal operational thinking is by no means a universal stage.

Implications for Teaching

Our description of the cognitive and linguistic changes during the period of transition into adolescence has centered on the in-

52. Carl Barenboim, "Developmental Changes in the Interpersonal Cognitive System from Middle Childhood to Adolescence," *Child Development* 48 (December 1977) 1467-74.

53. James Britton et al., *The Development of Writing Abilities, 11-18* (London: Macmillan, 1975).

54. James Moffett, *Teaching the Universe of Discourse* (Boston: Houghton Mifflin, 1968).

creasing self-awareness and awareness of others. The thinking of the ten- to twelve-year-old transescent begins to know itself, as it were. What are some of the conditions that foster this development? Piaget asserts:

Only by means of friction against other minds, by means of exchange and opposition does thought come to be conscious of its own aims and tendencies. . . . This is why every act of socialized intelligence implies not only consciousness of a definite thought direction (as, for instance, of problem) but also consciousness of the successive statements of a narrative (relations of implication) or of those between successive images of the objects of thought (causal relations).[55]

One factor, then, which accounts for the transescent's advance in cognitive and linguistic function is the constant interaction with other minds. In the course of this interaction the child is compelled to confront other interpretations of an event, other points of view that differ from his own. These confrontations eventually lead him to the stable construction of other people's minds and thus to the position where he can think about his own thinking and understand how language serves as a means for him to communicate with other minds. This suggests that classrooms in which this kind of intellectual confrontation takes place are the kinds of places where children can become metacognitive and metalinguistic.

In a recent discussion of the impact of the development of the written form of language on the human mind, Olson argues that "schooling, particularly learning to read, is the critical process in the transformation of children's language from utterance to text." [56] Utterance, according to Olson, is the use of language in a community with only an oral tradition. Text is the term Olson applies to cultures with a strong bias toward written language. In a text-dominated culture such as ours, assumptions and premises are made explicit, formal rules of logic are observed, and individuals operate on careful definitions; all of this "produces an instrument of considerable power for building an abstract coherent theory of reality." Olson goes on to argue:

55. Jean Piaget, *Judgment and Reasoning in the Child* (New York: Harcourt, Brace and Co., 1928), pp. 11-12.

56. David R. Olson, "From Utterance to Text: The Bias of Language in Speech and Writing," *Harvard Educational Review* 47 (August 1977): 257-81.

The formal uses of text provide a poor fit to daily, ordinary practical and personally significant experience. Oral language with its depth of resources and its multitude of paths to the same goal, while an instrument of limited power for exploring abstract ideas, is a universal means of sharing our understanding of concrete situations and practical actions.[57]

The cognitive and linguistic abilities that mature during the period of semiformal operations represent a balance of the two trends, the forms of thought that partake of the formal and the logical and those that are reasonably bound to the concrete here and now; the forms of thought that are relatively free of gross egocentrism but are still concerned with the specific self and the specific other. The period of transescence is a crucial one insofar as the school is concerned. The challenge it presents is to provide the child with the kinds of educational opportunities that will enable him to continue to enjoy the subjective and the intersubjective life while at the same time to examine his experience from an objective, formal, and abstract vantage point.

57. Ibid., p. 278.

CHAPTER XII

Enhancing the Acquisition of Knowledge

DAVID P. AUSUBEL

Cognitive development is an important aspect of transescence, both in its own right and for its significance for progress toward autonomy, especially in moral development. (See chapters 2, 9, and 11.) Because of its reciprocal relationship with learning, it is of central concern to schools. (See chapter 4.) Acquisition of new meanings is essential to cognitive development and, conversely, the level of such development influences the instructional methods that can be used to promote meaningful learning.

Two cautions must be observed in considering appropriate teaching procedures for middle and junior high schools. One is that the great variation in cognitive development clearly calls for such diversity of instructional strategies that none can be considered truly characteristic of this level. The other caution is that the basic principles of learning are the same at this level as at others. Any adaptations made in recognition of developmental characteristics and individual differences therein must rest on a sound and thorough understanding of how meaningful learning takes place. Unfortunately, much instructional advice is based on conceptions of learning that are not especially applicable to the kind of knowledge acquisition with which schools are primarily concerned. Therefore, the bulk of this chapter is devoted to one theoretical framework that bears specifically on meaningful verbal learning, with only a brief consideration of the instructional adjustments that are appropriate for transescent learners.

It is extremely important here to distinguish between the phenomenon of *development*, with its long time frame, and that of *learning*, which manifests itself in events taking place at a particular time. Knowledge of Piaget's invariant stages of intellectual development may be helpful in deciding what instructional adjustments are suitable for transescents, but with respect to learning theory per se, Piaget has little or nothing to say. Indeed, many features of Piaget's system tend to give it an antieducational flavor. In his emphasis on spontaneous or incidental experience, he discounts the role of education in promoting cognitive development and in facilitating the transition from one cognitive stage to another.[1]

Any attempt to understand the historical development and current theoretical status of the psychology of learning and instruction must, of necessity, begin with an examination of the contrasting views of cognitive and neobehavioristic theorists about the nature of cognitive processes and phenomena. There are a number of other eclectic and, in my opinion, "pseudo-cognitive" positions that for various reasons cannot readily be identified with either the neobehavioristic or cognitive point of view or even placed on the same continuum with them. These include (a) a variant of the cybernetic or information theory approach, based on a computer model of cognitive organization and functioning;[2] (b) an approach to meaning based on associative relations;[3] and (c) various information-processing models based on so-called semantic network theories.[4] Although often labeled "cognitive," these latter positions

1. For additional evidence of Piaget's antieducational stance, see David P. Ausubel, Joseph D. Novak, and Helen Hanesian, *Educational Psychology: A Cognitive View*, 2d ed. (New York: Holt, Rinehart and Winston, 1978).

2. See Allen Newell, James C. Shaw, and Herbert A. Simon, "Elements of a Theory of Human Problem Solving," *Psychological Review* 65 (May 1958): 151-66; Daniel E. Berlyne, *Structure and Direction in Thinking* (New York: John Wiley and Sons, 1965); Robert M. Gagné, *Conditions of Learning*, 3d ed. (New York: Holt, Rinehart and Winston, 1977); George A. Miller, Eugene Galanter, and Karl H. Pribram, *Plans and the Structure of Behavior* (New York: Holt, Rinehart and Winston, 1967).

3. See George A. Miller, "The Magical Number Seven, Plus or Minus Two: Some Limits on Our Capacity for Information Processing," *Psychological Review* 63 (March 1956): 81-97; James E. Deese, *The Structure of Associations in Language and Thought* (Baltimore, Md.: Johns Hopkins University Press, 1965); Donald T. Campbell, "Systematic Error on the Part of Human Links in Communication Systems," *Information and Control* 1 (December 1958): 334-69; John R. Anderson and Gordon H. Bower, *Human Associative Memory* (Washington, D.C.: V. H. Winston, 1973).

4. See Ronald E. Johnson, "Meaningfulness and the Recall of Textual Prose," *American Educational Research Journal* 10 (Winter 1973): 49-58; Ulric Neisser, *Cognitive Psychology* (New York: Appleton-Century-Crofts, 1967); Peter H. Lindsay and Donald A. Norman, *Human Information Processing*, 2d ed. (New York: Academic Press, 1977); Endel Tulving, "Episodic and Semantic Memory," in *Organization of Memory*, ed. Endel Tulving and Wayne D. Donaldson (New York: Academic Press, 1972), pp. 381-403.

either focus more on perceptual than on cognitive phenomena, pertain to rote learning as much as to meaningful learning, or assume in the learner some quite nonhuman features, such as virtually unlimited capacity to assimilate discrete items of information and static processing operations unmodifiable by either development or creativity. Unfortunately, space limitations rule out a more thorough critique of these positions, which, insofar as they deal with meaningful learning, must be recognized as possible alternatives to the cognitive theory that is contrasted here with the neobehavioristic viewpoint.

Neobehavioristic versus Cognitive Orientations

The differences between these two theoretical orientations are as fundamental as they can possibly be and cannot be explained away by saying that each group of theorists is essentially interested in elucidating basically different kinds of psychological phenomena.

It is true, of course, that over the years neobehaviorists have devoted most of their attention to such problems as classical and operant conditioning, rote verbal learning, instrumental learning, and discrimination learning, whereas cognitive psychologists have been traditionally preoccupied with such problems as thinking, concept formation, and the acquisition of knowledge. Nevertheless, representatives of both schools have attempted to extend their views to encompass the entire field of psychology.

In fact, controversy exists about the psychology of cognition precisely because neobehaviorists have extended their views "upwards" to include the more complex cognitive processes, whereas their theoretical antagonists have extended their views "downwards" to include simpler kinds of learning. In this chapter we are largely concerned with the convergence of these two theoretical currents on the more complex kinds of cognitive phenomena generally referred to as "the higher mental processes."

NEOBEHAVIORISM

Like the behavioristic position from which it was derived, the neobehavioristic view focuses on objectively observable responses and their environmental instigators and reinforcers as the proper objects of investigation in psychology. Consciousness is regarded as a "mentalistic" concept that is both highly resistive to scientific inquiry and not very pertinent to the real purposes of psychology as a science. It is considered an epiphenomenon that is important neither in its own right nor as a determinant of behavior. Furthermore, say the neobehaviorists, it cannot be reliably (objectively) observed; and it is so extremely idiosyncratic as to render virtually impossible the kinds of categorization necessary for making scientific generalizations.

Exponents of the cognitive viewpoint, on the other hand, take precisely the opposite theoretical stance. Using perception as their model, they regard differentiated and clearly articulated conscious experience (for example, knowing, meaning, understanding) as providing the most significant data for a science of acquiring potentially meaningful bodies of knowledge. Instead of focusing mechanistically on stimulus-response connections and their "organismic" mediators, they endeavor to discover psychological principles of organization and functioning governing these differentiated states of consciousness and the underlying cognitive processes (for example, meaningful learning, abstraction, generalization) from which they arise.

From the standpoint of cognitive theorists, the attempt to ignore conscious states, or to reduce cognition to mediational processes reflective of implicit behavior, not only removes from the field of psychology what is most worth studying, but also absurdly oversimplifies highly complex psychological phenomena. Mediational processes are viewed as tortuous, implausible, and unparsimonious constructs made necessary both by the neobehaviorists' stubborn refusal to recognize the centrality of consciousness in cognitive processes and by their attempt to reduce cognition to a set of implicit stimulus-response correlations that are applicable only to much simpler kinds of behavior.

Cognitive theorists acknowledge that serious difficulties inhere in the objective study of states of consciousness, but feel that this approach does not present insuperable obstacles and, if successful, can yield a much richer harvest of scientific understanding in the field of cognition. They point out, in addition, that even many neobehaviorists rely on verbal reports of conscious states (such as Osgood's widely used semantic differential procedure[5]) in study-

5. Charles E. Osgood, George C. Suci, and Paul H. Tannenbaum, *The Measurement of Meaning* (Urbana, Ill.: University of Illinois Press, 1957).

ing cognitive phenomena, despite referring to such reports as "instrumental linguistic *responses*."

Advocates of the neobehavioristic position had little trouble explaining such phenomena as classical and instrumental conditioning or rote verbal learning, but initially experienced considerable difficulty with cognitive phenomena and processes, particularly those involving symbols. At first, the only principles they could offer in explaining how responses could be evoked by stimuli that were not originally associated with them by means of contiguity and reinforcement were the concepts of stimulus and response generalization. But this kind of transfer mechanism obviously depends on physical (or perceptual) similarity within the sets of stimuli or responses in question; hence it could not be applied to such problems as symbolic representation (that is, equivalence in meaning between signs and significates), the inclusion of physically dissimilar exemplars within the same conceptual category, and problem solving involving the transfer of a given principle from one physically dissimilar situation to another.

Neobehaviorists attempted to solve these problems of symbolic representation, conceptual equivalence, and transfer by proposing a hypothetical mediational process that could render physically dissimilar situations equivalent by virtue of constituting the common organismic response evoked by each situation. This mediational process was considered a form of implicit behavior (internal, stimulus-producing response) related to Hull's "fractional anticipatory goal response" and "pure stimulus act."[6] Different modern neobehavioristic conceptions of meaning have been offered by Osgood, Berlyne, Gagné, and Staats.[7]

One major issue hinges on whether the essential psychological attributes of meaning are *connotative* in nature and can therefore be conceptualized adequately in terms of implicit motor or affec-

6. Clark C. Hull, *Principles of Behavior* (New York: Appleton-Century, 1943).

7. Osgood, Suci, and Tannenbaum, *Measurement of Meaning*; Daniel E. Berlyne, "Knowledge and Stimulus-Response Psychology," *Psychological Review* 61 (July 1954): 245-54; idem, *Structure and Direction in Thinking*; Gagné, *The Conditions of Learning*; Arthur W. Staats, "Verbal Habit-Families, Concepts, and the Operant Conditioning of Word Classes," *Psychological Review* 68 (May 1961): 190-204.

tive responses, as Osgood maintained,[8] or whether they are basically *denotative* in nature and must necessarily be reflective of differentiated cognitive content. A related issue has to do with the applicability of the conditioning paradigm to the process whereby meanings are acquired, that is, whether the acquisition process is purely automatic or involves some implicit awareness and various active cognitive operations.

Having thus accounted for symbolic representation in neobehavioristic terms, Berlyne[9] and Osgood[10] then go on to propose that knowledge can be conceptualized as an organization of habits mediated by "believed," designative implicit responses. These responses are purportedly organized within the individual in particular hierarchies that reflect their association (contiguous occurrence) in his past experience. Berlyne and Osgood carry the argument one step further by proposing various behavioristic mechanisms whereby new knowledge is generated, as in thinking and problem solving, by means of sequences of symbolic responses or "trains of thought."[11] These authors regard as crucial for thinking the factors that determine the sequence of symbolic responses once they are initiated, suggesting such mechanisms as Hull's "habit-family hierarchy," "convergence," "divergence," "patterning," and "symbolic transformation."

Partially consonant with this formulation is Piaget's proposition that logical operations, at least in terms of their ontogenesis (developmental history), represent internalizations of those actions through which one external situation is transformed into another.[12] Cognitive theorists, however, consider this interpretation of thinking much too mechanistic and reflexive. They maintain that the problem of thought is not primarily a matter of accounting for the

8. Osgood, Suci, and Tannenbaum, *Measurement of Meaning.*

9. Berlyne, "Knowledge and Stimulus-Response Psychology."

10. Charles E. Osgood, "A Behavioristic Analysis of Perception and Language as Cognitive Phenomena," in *Contemporary Approaches to Cognition: A Symposium Held at the University of Colorado* (Cambridge, Mass.: Harvard University Press, 1957), pp. 75-118.

11. See also Irving M. Maltzman, "Thinking from a Behavioristic Point of View," *Psychological Review* 62 (July 1955): 275-86.

12. Berlyne, "Knowledge and Stimulus-Response Psychology."

automatic sequencing of connections between symbolic responses when an individual is confronted with a problem situation; it is rather a problem of explaining how existing propositional units in his cognitive structure are consciously reorganized and recombined as complexly articulated, conscious solutions to meet the ideational demands of a new means-end relationship.

THE COGNITIVE POSITION: ASSIMILATION THEORY

In contrast to the neobehavioristic approach we have just considered, the cognitive position with respect to the psychology of learning and meaning has a decidedly ideational and, by behavioristic standards, "mentalistic" flavor. Meaning is not an implicit response but a clearly articulated and precisely differentiated conscious experience that emerges when potentially meaningful signs, symbols, concepts, or propositions are related to, and incorporated within, a given individual's cognitive structure on a nonarbitrary and substantive basis.[13] The acquisition of new meanings is thus held to be coextensive with meaningful learning, a process that is considered qualitatively different from rote learning in terms of the nonarbitrary and substantive relatability of the content of what is to be learned to existing ideas in cognitive structure.

Progressive differentiation. The human nervous system as a data-processing and storing mechanism is regarded as so constructed that new ideas and information can be meaningfully learned and retained only to the extent that appropriately relevant and typically more inclusive concepts or propositions are already available to serve a subsuming role or provide ideational anchorage.[14] Subsumption thus largely accounts for the acquisition of new meanings (the accretion of knowledge); for the extended retention span of meaningfully learned materials; for the very psychological organization of knowledge as a hierarchical structure in which the most inclusive concepts occupy a position at the apex of the structure and subsume progressively more highly differentiated sub-

13. David P. Ausubel, "A Subsumption Theory of Meaningful Verbal Learning and Retention," *Journal of General Psychology* 66 (April 1962): 213-14.

14. David P. Ausubel, *The Psychology of Meaningful Verbal Learning* (New York: Grune and Stratton, 1963).

concepts and factual data; and for the eventual occurrence of forgetting.

This latter process (forgetting) is conceptualized as the second or "obliterative" phase of subsumption, in which the distinctive import and substance of a subsumed idea is first dissociable from the anchoring idea that subsumes it and is then gradually assimilated by the more general meaning of its more stable and inclusive subsumer.[15] Hence, forgetting is interpreted as a progressive loss in the dissociability of new ideas from the ideational matrix in which they are embedded and in relation to which their meaning emerges. This theory of meaningful learning and retention is referred to as assimilation theory.[16]

Discovery and reception in meaningful learning. A sharp distinction has been made between the rote-meaningful and the reception-discovery dimensions of learning.[17] Contrary to the traditional position of progressive education, autonomous discovery, as part of a problem-solving approach to the learning of subject matter, is *not* considered a prerequisite for the acquisition of meaning (understanding), as long as the learner employs a meaningful learning set and studies potentially meaningful material. Nevertheless, simply because in reception (expository) learning the context of what is to be learned is presented rather than discovered, we cannot assume that it is a purely passive phenomenon. It is still necessary for the learner to relate the new material to relevant, established ideas in his own cognitive structure; to apprehend in what ways it is similar to, and different from, related concepts and propositions in his structure of knowledge; to translate it into a personal frame of reference consonant with his idiosyncratic experience and vocabulary; and often to formulate what is for him a completely new idea requiring much reorganization of existing knowledge.[18]

Presenting the case for the problem-solving approach to learn-

15. Ibid.

16. Ausubel, Novak, and Hanesian, *Educational Psychology: A Cognitive View.*

17. David P. Ausubel, "In Defense of Verbal Learning," *Educational Theory* 11 (January 1961): 5-25.

18. Ausubel, *The Psychology of Meaningful Verbal Learning.*

ing, Bruner argues that discovery is necessary for "real possession" of knowledge, has certain unique motivational advantages, organizes knowledge effectively for later use, and promotes retention.[19] Elsewhere I have denied some of these specific claims, but I agree that the discovery method does offer some unique motivational advantages, is a useful adjunctive technique under certain educational conditions, and is necessary for the development of problem-solving abilities and for learning how new knowledge is discovered.[20] But the discovery method is not an indispensable condition for the occurrence of meaningful learning and is much too time consuming to be used efficiently as a primary method of transmitting subject matter in typical classroom situations.

Cognitive structure. Such theorists as Bruner, Gagné, and I not only agree that the learner's acquisition of clear, stable, and organized bodies of knowledge is the major long-term objective of education, but also insist that these bodies of knowledge, once acquired, constitute, in their own right, the most significant independent variable influencing the meaningful learning and retention of new subject matter.[21] Hence control over meaningful learning can be exercised most effectively by identifying and manipulating significant cognitive structure variables. This can be done in two ways: (a) *substantively*, by showing concern for the "structure" of a discipline (that is, using for organizational and integrative purposes those unifying concepts and propositions that have the widest inclusiveness, explanatory power, generalizability, and relatability to the subject matter of that discipline); and (b) *programmatically*, by employing suitable principles of organizing and ordering the sequence of subject matter, constructing its internal logic and organization, and arranging practice trials (review).

Three factors in existing cognitive structure self-evidently play

19. Jerome S. Bruner, "The Act of Discovery," *Harvard Educational Review* 31 (Winter 1961): 21-32.

20. David P. Ausubel, "Learning by Discovery: Rationale and Mystique," *Bulletin of the National Association of Secondary School Principals* 45 (December 1961) 18-58; idem, *The Psychology of Meaningful Verbal Learning*, pp. 139-75.

21. Jerome S. Bruner, *The Process of Education* (Cambridge, Mass.: Harvard University Press, 1960); Robert M. Gagné, "The Acquisition of Knowledge," *Psychological Review* 69 (July 1963): 355-65; Ausubel, *The Psychology of Meaningful Verbal Learning*.

important programmatic roles in affecting the extent to which new ideas are assimilable by the learner: (a) the availability of relevant and more inclusive anchoring ideas in the learner's structure of knowledge; (b) their degree of discriminability from the new learning material; and (c) their relative degree of stability and clarity. The extent to which these variables can be manipulated by the nature of prior learning experience (that is, programmatically) determines in large measure the extent to which new knowledge can be acquired. The most significant substantive aspect of antecedent learning experience, on the other hand, is the degree of explanatory and unifying value it has for a given discipline, as well as the degree of inclusiveness characterizing the particular concepts and principles that are present in the learner's cognitive structure.

Conditions of Meaningful Learning

In order for new learning material (potential knowledge) to be assimilated it is necessary that the learner exhibit a meaningful learning set (a disposition to relate such material nonarbitrarily and substantively to his cognitive structure) and that the new material be potentially meaningful. This latter characteristic, in turn, presupposes (a) that the material is sufficiently nonrandom and sensible to be related in nonarbitrary and substantive fashion to ideas that at least some human beings possess in their structure of knowledge and (b) that it is similarly relatable to ideas that exist within the cognitive structure of the *particular* learner.

The first of these latter two conditions may be referred to as a property of the material itself and is rarely lacking in school learning tasks. It may be termed "logical meaning."[22] Subject matter, therefore, can at best manifest logical meaning. This is transformed into "psychological meaning" when it interacts with relevant ideas in a particular learner's cognitive structure to produce an idiosyncratic interactional product.

22. This does not necessarily imply that such material must be logically or empirically valid. To exhibit logical meaning, material simply must seem plausible or reasonable rather than consist of randomly paired relationships (for example, paired adjectives, scrambled sentences). Many meanings simply abound in faulty logic and are grounded in empirically invalid data (for example, the phlogiston theory of combustion), yet exhibit impressive meaning.

All phenomenological (psychological) meaning is, by definition, idiosyncratic in nature, since no two persons have identical cognitive structures. Psychological meaning never occurs in the abstract sense of the term; it invariably emerges in a particular individual.

It follows, therefore, that the more idiosyncratic a meaning is the more thoroughly it reflects the unique qualities of the particular learner's structure of knowledge, and hence the more intimately he has reformulated it and incorporated it into his unique ideational frame of reference and language usage. Nevertheless, meanings are seldom so idiosyncratic as to preclude communication within a given culture. This is so both because most individuals share some degree of commonality of cognitive experience and because they are exposed to more or less the same body of logical meanings.

No matter how much potential meaning may inhere in a given proposition, it will be learned by rote as an arbitrary and meaningless series of words if the learner manifests a rote learning set; and, conversely, no matter how meaningful an individual's learning set may be, nothing can be meaningfully learned unless it is potentially meaningful. Nonarbitrariness presupposes the existence of some plausible, nonrandom or sensible, connection between concept words. Substantiveness (or nonverbatimness), on the other hand, assumes that the same proposition expressed in equivalent language conveys precisely the same meaning as the original expression.

THE ROTE-MEANINGFUL AND RECEPTION-DISCOVERY CONTINUA

Both the rote-meaningful and reception-discovery dimensions of learning exist on a continuum rather than being dichotomous in nature. As will be explained shortly, representational learning is much closer to the rote end of the continuum than is concept or propositional learning. Also, it is quite possible to exhibit a rote and meaningful set simultaneously or successively (for example, learning the multiplication table; an actor who first learns his lines meaningfully before memorizing them). Similarly, discovery learning may be entirely autonomous, as in the case of a research scientist, or wholly contrived or arranged, as in the case of a typical science student performing a laboratory experiment.

Much confusion has arisen in the past regarding the relationship between the reception-discovery and the rote-meaningful dimensions of learning. Discovery enthusiasts have tended to regard reception and rote learning, on the one hand, and meaningful and discovery learning, on the other, as virtually synonymous. Actually these two dimensions of learning are entirely independent, that is, orthogonal to each other.[23] Depending on the conditions of learning, reception and discovery learning may each be rote or meaningful. Advocates of discovery learning have been quick to recognize rote instances of reception learning but have been less disposed to recognize that many "cookbook" laboratory exercises and "type problem" solutions in mathematics conform to all of the criteria of rote learning.

Actually, discovery learning exhibits many features of the reception mode. The only real difference between the two is that in reception learning the principal content of what is to be learned is presented to the learner, whereas in discovery learning, the problem-setting proposition and relevant background knowledge in the learner's cognitive structure must be reorganized to meet the demands of a means-end relationship. This latter generation and testing of problem-solving hypotheses is really the only true aspect of so-called discovery learning.

KNOWLEDGE AS SUBSTANTIVE CONTENT OR AS PROBLEM-SOLVING CAPABILITY

Both Gagné and Bruner differ from me in their conception of the role of cognitive structure in transfer.[24] This difference stems in part from their more behavioristic conception of the nature of knowledge as consisting of the capability of performing different classes of problem-solving tasks.

Thus, in fostering transfer, Gagné focuses on the learner's possession of the component or subordinate problem-solving capabilities required for manifesting a given higher-order problem-solving capability.[25] Concentrating more on the deductive aspects of trans-

23. Ausubel, *The Psychology of Meaningful Verbal Learning*, chapter 14.

24. Gagné, "The Acquisition of Knowledge"; Bruner, *The Process of Education*.

25. More recently, Gagné has recognized verbalizable knowledge but discounts its importance relative to intellectual skills. See Robert M. Gagné, "Learning Hierarchies," *Educational Psychologist* 6 (Winter 1968): 1-3, 6, 9.

fer, Bruner emphasizes "generic learning" because it can facilitate derivative problem solving, that is, the solution of problems that involve particular exemplars of a more general proposition.

On the other hand, I view knowledge as largely a substantive (ideational) phenomenon, rather than as a problem-solving capability, and I regard the transfer functions of cognitive structure as applying more significantly to reception learning than to problem solving in the typical classroom situation.[26] Moreover, I advocate the learning of generic concepts and propositions more to provide stable anchorage for correlative materials (for example, extensions, elaborations, modifications, and qualifications of established ideas in cognitive structure) than to make possible the regeneration of forgotten derivative instances. The main problem of transfer in acquiring a body of knowledge involves the stabilization (through the substantive and programmatic procedures specified above) of those stored, discriminable, and correlative ideas in the learner's cognitive structure (constituting his representation of the flesh and blood of a discipline) that would otherwise undergo obliterative subsumption; much less crucial for transfer is enhancement of the ability to solve on demand those problems that can be successfully handled if the learner retains a bare skeleton of generic principles (derivative subsumption).

KINDS OF MEANINGFUL LEARNING[27]

The most basic kind of meaningful learning is representational learning (that is, the kind of learning that occurs when names are acquired for objects, events, concepts, persons, and so forth) and when these names come to signify to the individual whatever their referents do. This is the simplest form of meaningful learning because it satisfies the criterion of nonarbitrary and substantive relatability to the learner's cognitive structure. All particular new names are acquired by a process of representational equivalence in which name and referent are equated in meaning by being related as exemplars to the general proposition in cognitive structure that everything has a name and that the name signifies to the learner whatever its referent does.

26. Ausubel, *The Psychology of Meaningful Verbal Learning*, pp. 139-75.

27. This section is adapted from Ausubel, *Educational Psychology: A Cognitive View.*

Naming is also substantive in the sense that the learner implicitly understands that synonomous native-language terms and second-language equivalents signify the same things that the original word does. Unlike conditioning and rote associative learning, often only a single pairing of symbol and referent are necessary (instead of multiple pairings) to establish representational equivalence. However, since the choice of a word to represent a symbol is purely arbitrary (except for words derived from a previously known root), and must be reproduced verbatim, representational learning is the type of meaningful learning that is closest to rote learning.

"Concept formation" involves learning what is common among multiple instances of a category of objects, events, situations, and ideas that differ along dimensions other than the relevant one(s) in question. During the preschool years the critical attributes of a concept are generally discovered by a problem-solving process of hypothesis-generation and testing, until the essence of the critical attributes are abstracted and later refined by the removal of originally overinclusive attributes and the addition of originally under-inclusive attributes. Typically such concepts include categories that have similar perceptible referents (for example, house, dog, fish), except for such simple second-order abstractions as "vegetable" that include perceptually dissimilar categorical members (for example, carrots, beans, lettuce, spinach).

During the school years and thereafter, concept formation gradually is displaced by "concept assimilation": new concepts are, for the most part, acquired through definition and context, that is, their criterial attributes are presented to, rather than discovered by, the learner.

In both concept formation and concept assimilation, concept acquisition is followed by representational learning in which the newly acquired concept meaning is equated in signification with the word that represents it.

"Propositional learning" consists of assimilating facts and principles in sentence form that, in turn, consists of concept words which have both denotative and connotative meanings, as well as syntactic functions. A proposition, therefore, expresses more than the sum of its component words.

Propositional learning can be either subordinate (subsumptive), superordinate, or combinatorial. "Subsumptive learning" occurs when a "logically" meaningful proposition in a particular discipline is related meaningfully to specific superordinate concepts or propositions in the learner's structure of knowledge. Such learning may be called "derivative" if the learning material simply exemplifies or supports an idea already existing in cognitive structure. It is called "correlative" if it is an extension, elaboration, modification, or qualification of previously learned concepts or propositions.

"Superordinate propositional learning" occurs when a new proposition is related to specific subordinate ideas already established in the student's cognitive structure that can be subsumed under it. Both superordinate and subordinate concept learning also occur.

Finally, combinatorial propositional learning refers to instances where a potentially meaningful proposition cannot be related to specifically relevant subordinate or superordinate ideas in the learner's cognitive structure but is relatable to a broad background of generally relevant content in such structure.

The Significance of Meaningful Learning in the Acquisition of Knowledge

Meaningful reception learning is of tremendous importance in acquiring and storing large bodies of subject-matter knowledge. The acquisition and storage of such knowledge is really a very impressive phenomenon, considering (a) that human beings, unlike computers, can apprehend and remember only a few (about seven) discrete items of information that are presented only a single time, and (b) that memory for rote-learned lists receiving multiple presentations is notoriously limited both over time and with respect to length of list, unless greatly overlearned.

The tremendous efficacy of meaningful learning inheres in its two principal characteristics: nonarbitrariness and substantiveness. When, on the other hand, learning material (even if its components are already meaningful) is arbitrarily related to cognitive structure, no direct use can be made of existing knowledge in the learner's cognitive structure for assimilating the learning task as a whole. At the very best, already meaningful constituent units can be related to isolated, unitary, and discrete elements in cognitive structure; but this in no way either makes the newly internalized arbitrary associations themselves relatable as a whole to established content in cognitive structure or makes them usable in acquiring new knowledge. And because the human mind is not efficiently designed to assimilate and store arbitrary associations, this approach permits only limited amounts of such material to be acquired and retained, and then only after much effortful repetition.

RETENTION

The fact that a new idea becomes a meaningful entity in cognitive structure (after it is meaningfully assimilated) makes it intrinsically less vulnerable than internalized arbitrary associations are to interference from other arbitrary associations, and hence makes it more retainable. Furthermore, the maintenance of this same nonarbitrary relatability advantage (through the anchorage of the new meaning to its corresponding established idea during the storage period) further extends the span of retention and decreases forgetting.

Moreover, the substantive or nonverbatim nature of thus relating new material to, and incorporating it within, cognitive structure, circumvents the drastic limitations imposed by the short item-retention and time-spans of rote memory on the processing and storage of information. Much more can obviously be assimilated and retained if the learner is required only to assimilate the substance of ideas rather than the precise words used in expressing them.

Another suggested means of overcoming the discrete item-span limitations in the acquisition and retention of the human brain has been called "chunking" by Miller and is derived from information theory.[28] "Chunking" refers to the process of rearranging the stimulus input successively into a smaller number and more efficiently organized sequences of bits or units. Miller suggests that linguistic recoding is the most powerful device that human beings possess for extending the amount of information they can process and remember, and thus, for acquiring large bodies of knowledge.

28. Miller, "The Magical Number Seven, Plus or Minus Two: Some Limits on Our Capacity for Information Processing."

It is quite clear, however, that compensatory mechanisms such as chunking merely increase the learner's rote capacity for apprehending and retaining information. This is the case because in such experiments as Miller and Selfridge's the experimentors demand rote recall.[29] Thus, because of their rote learning set, the subjects never have a fair opportunity to demonstrate that meaningful learning of prose material is superior to the rote learning of meaningless but linguistically connected prose.

Many different kinds of explanations have been proposed for the demonstrable superiority of meaningful learning and retention over rote learning and retention. In my opinion, however, the only tenable explanation reflects the underlying process differences between the two kinds of learning, that is, the internalization of discrete and isolated rote learning tasks that are not meaningfully anchored as a whole to relevant ideas in the learner's structure of knowledge (and their subsequent vulnerability to proactive and retroactive interference) versus nonarbitrary and substantive relatability (assimilation by) in particular ways to relevant ideational systems in existing cognitive structure (followed by the gradual loss of dissociability or forgetting of the newly acquired meanings from their anchoring ideas).

Many studies of long-term retention of subject matter dispute the widely held view that meaningfully learned material exhibits limited longevity. Much of the rapid forgetting characterizing school learning, however, is reflective of: (a) rote learning of potentially meaningful material; (b) poorly organized and programmed subject matter; (c) inadequate subject-matter and developmental readiness; (d) correctable ambiguity and confusion in the presentation of ideas; (e) failure to correct misconceptions and misapprehensions promptly; (f) inadequate pacing and review of material (for example, cramming); (g) expository teaching techniques that present facts without organizing and explanatory principles; (h) measuring devices that encourage rote memorization of facts and steps in problem solving, and (i) insufficient motivation. If these abuses of reception learning were corrected, there is good

29. George A. Miller and Jennifer A. Selfridge, "Verbal Context and the Recall of Meaningful Material," *American Journal of Psychology* 63 (April 1950): 176-85.

reason to believe that pupils would remember the basic ideas of a given discipline over the better part of a lifetime.[30]

EVIDENCE OF MEANINGFUL LEARNING[31]

Genuine evidence of meaningful learning is difficult to obtain. Through long experience, most students are adept at mouthing abstract ideas they do not really understand with an appearance of genuine comprehension. Very often, in testing for comprehension, one merely elicits rotely memorized verbalizations. At the very least, therefore, test questions must be phrased in different language than that in which the material was first encountered, and teachers must give credit for answers that are substantively rather than verbatimly correct.

A second approach is to require students to solve problems presupposing understanding of the relevant concepts and principles involved. But here caution is indicated. A student may really understand the latter concepts and principles involved but be unable to apply them successfully in solving problems because he either exhibits neurotic anxiety or lacks such traits as problem-sensitivity, improvising ability, resourcefulness, venturesomeness, resilience, persistence, and a systematic approach to problem solving. Thus inability to solve problems related to a given principle does not necessarily imply lack of understanding of the principle in question. Contrariwise, pupils may "solve" problems merely by memorizing steps in the solution of type problems, or in the manipulation of symbols, without any comprehension whatsoever.

Major Issues and Competing Proposed Solutions

PROGRESSIVE DIFFERENTIATIONS VERSUS LEARNING HIERARCHIES

Perhaps the most pervasive issue in the acquisition of knowledge is whether new knowledge is assimilated from the "top downwards" or from the "bottom upwards." As we have seen above, assimilation theory assumes the former and Gagné's "learning hierarchies" approach assumes the latter. Actually, this is not an all-

---

30. Ausubel, *The Psychology of Meaningful Verbal Learning.*

31. Adapted from Ausubel, *The Psychology of Meaningful Verbal Learning.*

or-none matter. In superordinate learning, for example, more inclusive ideas are anchored to existing subordinate concepts and propositions in the learner's structure of knowledge. When the new superordinate ideas become stable, however, they tend to subsume and supersede in stability the subordinate ideas that originally anteceded them in cognitive structure.

It follows, therefore, that cognitive structure is organized hierarchically (as to level of abstraction, generality, and inclusiveness) from the "top-downwards," with highly inclusive ideas occupying positions at the top of the pyramid and progressively subsuming more highly differentiated facts, concepts, and principles. This principle of progressive differentiation applies to the acquisition and retention of knowledge, as well as to its organization.

INTERPRETIVE RECONCILIATION VERSUS COMPARTMENTALIZATION

Interpretive reconciliation is facilitated in expository teaching if the teacher and/or instructional materials explicitly anticipate the confusable similarities and differences between newly presented and existing anchoring ideas in the learner's structure of knowledge, instead of unrealistically expecting students to do all the necessary cross-referencing themselves. This is particularly important where established and stable preconceptions exist, which can result in considerable resistance to, and conflict with, new, more valid ideas that students encounter in science, mathematics, the humanities, and so forth.

Such interpretive reconciliation pulls together similar ideas expressed in different contexts, avoids the confusing proliferation of terms that essentially represent the same concept, avoids the compartmentalization of these latter terms as separate isolated entities, and clarifies the real differences between confusably similar ideas. Unless the learner is able to perceive how A and A' are actually different, for example, he will tend to learn and remember them as identical. Only discriminably different variants of the same idea, in other words, can enjoy independent existence as separately identifiable entities in cognitive structure.[32]

32. Ausubel, Novak, and Hanesian, *Educational Psychology: A Cognitive View.*

ADVANCE ORGANIZERS

I have introduced "advance organizers" as pedagogic devices to help implement the principles of progressive differentiation and interpretive reconciliation by bridging the gap between what the learner already knows and what he needs to know if he is to learn new material most actively and expeditiously.[33]

Operationally, organizers are defined as relatively brief substantive introductions, differing from overviews in that the ideas they contain are (a) more abstract, inclusive, and general than the more detailed learning material they precede, and (b) relatable to, and incorporate, existing relevant ideas (including reconstructions) already present in cognitive structure. The latter criterion is necessary, of course, if the organizer itself is to be learnable.

Advance organizers operate on the same general principle as already existing antecedent material in cognitive structure, in that they are organized according to the principles of progressive differentiation and integrative reconciliation, and the new material to be presented is sequentially dependent upon them. However, their relevance to both the new learning material and to related ideas in cognitive structure is both more specific and explicit, as well as more particularly relevant and targeted to the learning task.

Equivocal findings on the effects of advance organizers reflect, in my opinion, both failure to adhere to their operationally defined criteria and to various methodological inadequacies both in measuring the significant independent variables defining an organizer and in satisfactorily controlling other contaminating variables.

RECEPTION VERSUS DISCOVERY LEARNING[34]

Few pedagogic devices in our time have been repudiated more thoroughly by educational theorists of all persuasions than the method of expository verbal instruction. In fact, almost all of the

33. David P. Ausubel, "The Use of Advance Organizers in the Learning and Retention of Meaningful Verbal Material," *Journal of Educational Psychology* 51 (October 1960): 267-72. See Ausubel, Novak, and Hanesian, *Educational Psychology: A Cognitive View*, for a more comprehensive treatment of this topic.

34. For a more comprehensive treatment of this issue, see Ausubel, Novak, and Hanesian, *Educational Psychology: A Cognitive View*, chapter 5.

new pedagogic techniques introduced during the last fifty years owe their popularity more to prevailing disenchantment with expository teaching than to their own intrinsic merits.

This disenchantment, of course, has not been without adequate foundation. The most prevalent cause of the dissatisfaction, in fact, has been that in most classrooms throughout the world potentially meaningful subject matter has been taught to pupils as if rote, rather than meaningful, learning were involved.

Another but less significant cause is that psychologists have tried to include all types of learning (no matter how different in goal or process) under a simple explanatory model, that is, associative learning or conditioning.

Thus, until the late 1950s and early 1960s, and Mandler's disavowal in 1967 of the behavioristic attempt to reduce complex mental processes to the rote verbal model,[35] almost all psychologists and educational psychologists implicitly accepted the proposition that comprehension, the acquisition and retention of knowledge, forgetting, concept formation, and problem solving could eventually be explained by the same principles involved in the learning and retention of nonsense syllables and paired adjectives. It is small wonder, then, that educators perceived subject-matter learning as an extension of rote learning and turned to such panaceas as "learning by discovery," "every child is a creative thinker," "process" approaches to the teaching of science, and so forth.

Despite the strident assertions on the part of discovery enthusiasts, most classroom teachers still appreciate that verbal exposition, supplemented where necessary by concrete-empirical props, is actually the most efficient way of teaching subject matter and leads to sounder and less trivial knowledge than when students serve as their own pedagogues.

They reject such hypotheses as (a) that children really understand what they learn only when they discover it autonomously by themselves; (b) that learning the general "heuristics of discovery" is more important for purposes of transferability (and because of the alleged rapid obsolescence of knowledge) than learning the content of the various disciplines (for example, the

35. George Mandler, "Verbal Learning," in *New Directions in Psychology III* (New York: Holt, Rinehart and Winston, 1967), pp. 3-50.

"process" approach to science teaching); (c) that learning by discovery should be the principal pedagogic device for transmitting the vast amount of knowledge that students must acquire, particularly in professional and preprofessional studies; and (d) that science students learn science best by acting as if they were scientists and by doing the same things that scientists do.[36] They reject the latter proposition because of major differences between scientists and students in their respective goals and levels of subject-matter sophistication.

Furthermore, the availability of relevant background concepts and principles in the student's cognitive structure accounts for most of the variance in problem-solving outcomes (apart from discipline-specific, largely genetically determined, and relatively unteachable cognitive and personality traits).[37] Thus, overemphasis on "discovery" or "problem-solving" approaches to teaching, to the exclusion or minimization of expository presentation of key concepts and principles, can only result in a thoroughgoing educational disaster comparable to that occurring from the 1930s to the middle 1950s. At that time the expository teaching of the concepts and principles in mathematics and physical sciences fell into disrepute largely due to the influence of progressive education, thereby resulting in overreliance on rote-learned solutions to "type problems" and on cookbook performance of laboratory exercises for transmitting the substantive or ideational content of these disciplines. In consequence, an entire generation of high school and college graduates were able to "solve" all of the required problems dealing, for example, with Ohm's Law, logarithms, exponents, functions, differential and integral calculus, molar and molecular solutions, and the like, without having the foggiest notions of the meaning of any of the concepts or principles in question.

All of this, of course, does not in the least detract from the legitimate use of contrived (arranged) discovery learning (for example, laboratory exercises) in teaching pupils scientific method

36. Bruner, "The Act of Discovery."

37. See, for example, Richard E. Mayer, "Information Processing Variables in Learning to Solve Problems," *Review of Educational Research* 45 (Fall 1975): 525-41, and Per Saugstad, "Problem Solving as Dependent upon the Availability of Functions," *British Journal of Psychology* 46 (August 1955): 191-98.

in the various disciplines and in providing them with some notion of how new knowledge in a given field comes into being.

Developmental Considerations: Implications for Instruction

Thus far we have considered the learner's acquisition, retention, and organization of knowledge as contemporaneously occurring phenomena, without regard to his developmental status or general level of cognitive functioning. It is true that the basic conditions, kinds, and properties of meaningful learning as a process, as well as the variables that influence it, apply to all stages of development. Nevertheless, as we have seen from the preceding chapter, developmental changes in psycholinguistic and cognitive abilities during the middle or junior high school years necessarily impinge on conditions affecting the learning process and hence on instructional practices and curricular goals.

It is during the period of transescence that the transition from concrete to abstract cognitive functioning typically begins to occur in cultures such as our own.[38] That is, pupils become increasingly less dependent on the concurrent availability of concrete-empirical props in relating new abstractions and abstract propositions to their existing cognitive structures. Increments in conceptual and propositional knowledge beginning at this age level therefore tend to be increasingly emptied of the particularity inherent in the use of such props and, thus, to consist of meanings that are more general and genuinely abstract (that is, less intuitive) in nature.

These latter developments during the junior high school years have at least two significant implications for the design of instruction. First, many pupils become ready for a new type of expository teaching in which examples drawn from concrete experience are used primarily for purposes of illustrative clarification, that is, to enhance the acquisition of truly abstract meanings only on those occasions when particularly difficult or unfamiliar concepts and propositions are introduced. This role of concrete examples contrasts sharply with instructional practice in the elementary school years, when such examples are routinely used to make possible the

38. Bärbel Inhelder and Jean Piaget, *The Growth of Logical Thinking from Childhood to Adolescence* (New York: Basic Books, 1958).

acquisition of the intuitive meanings characterizing school learning during that period.

Second, subject matter can now be meaningfully assimilated in greater depth both (a) because the time-consuming presentation of concrete-empirical props can be circumvented in most instances of reception learning and (b) because the greater number and more abstract and inclusive nature of higher-order concepts and propositions in the learner's cognitive structure make possible the assimilation of a much wider array of differentiated facts and subconcepts.

It would be extremely misleading, however, to suggest that the routine use of concrete-empirical props to enable the learner to acquire intuitive meanings is never necessary at the junior high school level or to deny that it is no more necessary than in the senior high school grades. For one thing, there are good reasons for believing that many pupils in American junior high schools do not undergo at all the transition from the concrete to the abstract level of cognitive functioning.[39] For another, even those pupils who do function intellectually at the abstract level in some or most of their subjects must still undergo this transition in other subject matter areas where such is not yet the case.[40] Thus, any decision regarding the appropriate use of concrete examples in this age group requires prior identification of the particular learner's level of cognitive functioning in each subject matter area and hence presupposes considerable individualization of instruction.

39. Floyd H. Nordland, Anton E. Lawson, and Jane B. Kahle, "A Study of Levels of Concrete and Formal Reasoning Ability in Disadvantaged Junior and Senior High School Science Students," *Science Education* 58 (October 1974): 569-75.

40. Mary Ann Stone and David P. Ausubel, "The Intersituational Generality of Formal Thought," *Journal of Genetic Psychology* 115 (December 1969): 169-80.

SECTION THREE

SOME APPROACHES TO RESEARCH

CHAPTER XIII

Methods in Clinical Research

THOMAS M. ACHENBACH

This chapter focuses on behavior disorders occurring between ages ten and fifteen. The title refers broadly to research on behavior of clinical concern rather than being restricted to research in clinical settings or to the unsystematic accumulation of clinical impressions sometimes known as clinical research. Defining the subject matter in terms of "behavior" disorders does not imply an exclusively stimulus-response model of etiology or treatment, but merely a focus on disorders of which maladaptive behavior is a significant aspect. Since only a skeletal treatment of most issues is possible here, the reader will be referred elsewhere for details.

Developmental Variables

Awareness of the developmental context is a prerequisite to understanding behavior disorders for the following reasons: (a) developmental transitions inevitably bring new stresses, adaptive tasks, and potentials, as well as changes in self-concept and in relations to significant others; (b) normal developmental stress and change need to be distinguished from problems that bode ill for future development; (c) the pathological significance of each behavior must be judged in relation to norms for the individual's agemates and social background; (d) the success of particular adaptive styles may vary with the cultural milieux of particular cohorts; (e) events occurring in earlier developmental periods may be responsible for behavior that first emerges during the period of interest. Developmental variables having particular significance for ten- to fifteen-year-olds will be summarized below in terms of biological, cognitive, social-emotional, and educational development.

BIOLOGICAL DEVELOPMENT

The most dramatic developmental event of this period is the onset of puberty, and it has often been blamed for the turmoil ascribed to early adolescents in modern western societies. There is no doubt that pubertal changes in physique confront adolescents with new images of themselves that may evoke very mixed feelings. Potentially more puzzling to adolescents are the less overt changes they experience in emotional and cognitive functioning brought about by increases in sex hormones.[1] Furthermore, the wide variation in the timing of pubertal changes produces marked disparities in the appearance and interests of agemates. The psychological effects of these disparities are most evident in those who mature especially early or late, but adaptive challenges also confront those who are closer to the norm, as girls begin to tower over boys and as long-time playmates find themselves suddenly out of phase with one another.

The degree to which puberty is necessarily a period of high risk for behavior disorders is being increasingly questioned in light of longitudinal findings of minimal changes in the rate of psychopathology in general population samples.[2] Although biological maturity may help to precipitate adult forms of antisocial behavior, schizophrenia, and depressive conditions that are seldom seen before puberty, there is evidence that some of these disorders have their roots in genetic and/or early perinatal determinants, rather than being caused by conditions associated with puberty per se.[3] The possible contribution of early predispositions therefore necessitates consideration of the prior developmental history as well as the immediate developmental context of disorders emerging in adolescence.

1. Anke A. Ehrhardt and H. F. L. Meyer-Bahlburg, "Psychological Correlates of Abnormal Pubertal Development," *Clinics in Endocrinology and Metabolism* 4 (March 1975): 207-222; Anne C. Petersen, "Physical Androgyny and Cognitive Functioning in Adolescence," *Developmental Psychology* 12 (November 1976): 524-33.

2. Daniel Offer and Judith B. Offer, *From Teenage to Young Manhood* (New York: Basic Books, 1975); Michael Rutter et al., "Adolescent Turmoil: Fact or Fiction?" *Journal of Child Psychology and Psychiatry* 17 (January 1976): 35-56.

3. *Genetics, Environment, and Psychopathology*, ed. Sarnoff A. Mednick et al. (New York: American Elsevier, 1974).

COGNITIVE DEVELOPMENT

Although often neglected in clinical portrayals of adolescents, normal cognitive developmental changes may underlie early adolescents' skepticism toward accustomed values and authority. These cognitive changes are evident in aspects of intellectual functioning construed by Piaget as a transition from the concrete operational to the formal operational period of cognitive development at about the age of eleven or twelve.[4] Research on cognitive development is presented elsewhere in this volume, but it is important to note here that the propositional logic of the formal operational period heightens adolescents' awareness of possibilities that transcend their own experience. This means that not only the kinds of problem-solving tasks posed by Piaget, but also parents' religious, ethical, and political values and a young person's own self-concept and world view can now be questioned in the harsh light of hypothetico-deductive relativism. Yet, formal operational reasoning seldom brings mature resolutions of questions of value and identity in early adolescence. Furthermore, it appears to depend more on individual and cultural characteristics than do earlier cognitive attainments. Nevertheless, the process of questioning self, parents, and society is a normal adolescent phenomenon that does not necessarily signify either psychopathology or alienation. In fact, the abilities that evoke this questioning enable the adolescent to conceptualize and strive for abstract ideals inconceivable to younger children, even if the consolidation of such abilities is still incomplete.

SOCIAL-EMOTIONAL DEVELOPMENT

Psychoanalytic writers have stressed the centrality of oedipal conflicts in adolescent turmoil. According to Freudian theory, genital maturation spurs an upsurge of sexual drive that breaks through the repression of the latency period. This rearouses whatever variant of the oedipal theme the adolescent experienced in early childhood and motivates a struggle with instinctual impulses that can produce hostile withdrawal from parents, ascetic self-denial, self-indulgence, delinquent rebellion, or an alternation among these reactions.

4. Jean Piaget, "Piaget's Theory," in *Carmichael's Manual of Child Psychology*, 3d ed., ed. Paul M. Mussen, vol. 1 (New York: John Wiley and Sons, 1970), pp. 703-732.

In revising psychoanalytic theory to emphasize interfaces between individual emotional development and the social milieu, Erik Erikson has redrawn the picture of adolescent psychodynamics in terms of a central conflict between development of a stable personal identity and the threats of identity diffusion in the areas of sex, vocation, and personal values.[5] This picture highlights the challenges adolescents face from the combination of biological changes and social pressures to make vocational choices and to assume more adult roles. Identity crises per se may be less central, however, for adolescents whose role choices are more limited than those depicted in Erikson's case histories. Furthermore, while there is some research support for a progression from identity diffusion to achievement of stable occupational and ideological identities among normal college students,[6] longitudinal studies of general population and clinical samples suggest that intense adolescent crises often reflect long-standing problems of adaptation more than turmoil intrinsic to adolescent psychosocial development.[7]

Psychodynamic interpretations aside, it is clear that several major transitions in social functioning typically occur during the middle-school period. From involvement primarily in rather fluid neighborhood peer groups, early adolescents move to more intense and intimate relationships with individual same-sex companions, with whom sexual secrets and fantasies are shared and homosexual impulses may be expressed, either overtly or covertly. The balance then shifts toward overtures to the opposite sex, dating, and eventually more prolonged heterosexual relationships. Late maturers and others slow to make this shift, however, often follow an alternative course of close involvement with a same-sex peer group centered in sports or other shared interests.

EDUCATIONAL DEVELOPMENT

During the early elementary school years, most mental health referrals originate with school problems, especially hyperactivity,

5. Erik H. Erikson, *Childhood in Society* (New York: W. W. Norton and Co., 1963).

6. Alan S. Waterman, Patricia S. Geary, and Caroline K. Waterman, "Longitudinal Study of Changes in Ego Identity Status from the Freshman to the Senior Year at College," *Developmental Psychology* 10 (May 1974): 387-92.

7. Rutter et al., "Adolescent Turmoil."

learning disabilities, and failure to conform to the school culture. By the middle-school years, the reasons for referral shift more to delinquency, withdrawal, drug use, anxiety, depression, and conflicts with parents, but poor school performance remains a problem for most referred youth. In some cases, the clinical problems of the middle-school years reflect cumulative school failure that was not adequately dealt with earlier. This is especially likely in rigidly age-graded schools where children who fail to acquire the basic skills fall progressively further behind their classmates to the point where they are more motivated to avoid exposing their deficiencies than to overcome them through active learning. In other cases, however, poor school performance may reflect home conditions or personal characteristics that interfere with the development of work habits needed as the educational focus shifts from the acquisition of specific responses to the organized effort required for homework and extended assignments.

In still other cases, school problems may be by-products of generalized adaptive problems that interfere with development on many fronts. Adoption of a delinquent identity, for example, conflicts with academic achievement because the school provides such an exquisite arena for flaunting countercultural values before an attentive audience of peers and adult authority figures. School failure and misbehavior can also serve as especially provocative means of retaliation against parents with whom an adolescent is in conflict. Where adaptive problems take on a more internalized, self-punitive pattern, they may leave little energy for school work, although maintenance of adequate and sometimes superior achievement is more common in disorders of this sort than in the delinquent and aggressive syndromes.

Types of Disorders

It has already been mentioned that adult forms of antisocial behavior, schizophrenia, and certain depressive conditions are rare before puberty. Even after puberty, these syndromes can seldom be diagnosed with confidence until deviant behavior has followed a consistent pattern for an extended period. Because behavioral norms are less clear-cut during adolescence than during childhood or adulthood, and because major developmental advances are still possible before the consolidation of an adult pattern, the adult diagnostic categories of antisocial personality, schizophrenia, and affective disorders are seldom applicable to early adolescents. Neither has the official psychiatric taxonomy of childhood disorders been well validated for early adolescents. It remains to be seen whether the latest revision of the American Psychiatric Association's official taxonomy will win more respect than the previous versions.[8] A detailed appraisal of the problems involved is presented elsewhere.[9]

SPECIFIC BEHAVIOR PROBLEMS

An alternative way of viewing behavior disorders is through surveys of specific problems. Table 1 presents survey findings on the ten problems reported most frequently for clinically referred children aged ten through fifteen. For the sake of comparison, findings are also presented for normal (that is, nonreferred) children matched to the referred children for age, sex, race, and socioeconomic status.

In addition to the problems that are most common across the ten- to fifteen-year age span, certain less common but clinically significant problems emerge during this period. One is anorexia nervosa, an extreme avoidance of food that is far more common in girls than boys and can be so severe as to end in death. Because anorexia often begins around puberty and anorexics express overconcern about being fat, it has been interpreted as an unconscious attempt to stave off sexuality by preventing the normal bodily changes of adolescence, although biochemical factors have been implicated as well.[10] Suicidal behavior also emerges for the first time on a significant scale in adolescence. Completed suicides remain rare until mid-adolescence and are then most common among males, but suicidal threats and gestures increase rapidly in early

8. American Psychiatric Association, *Diagnostic and Statistical Manual of Mental Disorders,* 3d ed. (Washington, D.C.: American Psychiatric Association, 1980).

9. Thomas M. Achenbach, *Developmental Psychopathology* (New York: Ronald Press, 1974; 2d ed., New York: John Wiley and Sons, forthcoming).

10. Kelly M. Bemis, "Current Approaches to the Etiology and Treatment of Anorexia Nervosa," *Psychological Bulletin* 85 (May 1978):593-617.

TABLE 1

Percent of Clinically Referred Ten- to Fifteen-year-olds for
Whom Certain Problems Were Reported Most Often and
Percent of Normal Ten- to Fifteen-year-olds for Whom
Those Problems Were Reported *

PROBLEM	BOYS		GIRLS	
	CLINICALLY REFERRED (N = 300)	NORMAL (N = 300)	CLINICALLY REFERRED (N = 300)	NORMAL (N = 300)
Argues a lot	89	57	92	57
Can't concentrate	82	35	(68)	(29)
Can't sit still, restless, hyperactive	70	30	(52)	(22)
Demands attention	69	26	72	26
Disobedient at home	76	33	82	26
Easily jealous	(51)	(28)	72	33
Impulsive, acts without thinking	74	35	(67)	(26)
Nervous, highstrung, tense	(67)	(23)	74	23
Poor school work	77	20	(62)	(5)
Secretive	(63)	(26)	74	30
Self-conscious, easily embarrassed	(63)	(44)	74	43
Showing off, clowning	69	46	(53)	(31)
Stubborn, sullen, irritable	79	37	85	43
Sudden mood changes	(57)	(22)	73	25
Temper tantrums, hot temper	68	26	(64)	(21)
Unhappy, sad, depressed	(61)	(8)	79	12

* Parentheses indicate that the item was not among the ten problems reported most often for clinically referred children of that sex.

Source: Based on data from Thomas M. Achenbach and Craig S. Edelbrock, "Behavioral Problems and Competencies Reported by Parents of Normal and Disturbed Children Aged Four through Sixteen," *Monographs of the Society for Research in Child Development,* in press.

adolescence, especially among girls.[11] School phobia is a problem of moderate frequency during the early school years but the frequency increases in early adolescence. Such phobias appear to be more circumscribed and easier to treat in young children than in adolescents, for whom they may reflect generalized withdrawal tendencies.[12] Drug abuse and delinquency attract more publicity than other problems during early adolescence, and they are responsible for shunting some disturbed adolescents into the juvenile court system rather than the mental health system. The pathologi-

11. National Center for Health Statistics, *Death Rates for Suicide by 5-Year Age Groups, Color, and Sex: United States* (Washington, D.C.: U.S. Department of Health, Education, and Welfare, 1977).

12. L. C. Miller, C. L. Barrett, and E. Hampe, "Phobias of Childhood in a Prescientific Era," in *Child Personality and Psychopathology: Current Topics,* vol. 1, ed. Anthony Davids (New York: John Wiley and Sons, 1974).

cal significance of these behaviors is often difficult to assess, however, because episodic incidents are not uncommon among normal adolescents. On the other hand, the legal sanctions and potential long-term consequences can make them more damaging than other transitory behavior problems.

EMPIRICALLY DERIVED SYNDROMES

Another alternative to the official taxonomy is to derive syndromes from empirically obtained correlations among behavior problems. This provides a picture of the patterns of problems that tend to occur together, and numerous studies have shown considerable convergence in the patterns thus identified.[13] However, because the age, sex, and other characteristics of the young people affect the incidence and patterning of their problems, it is important to distinguish between patterns that are relatively universal and those unique to particular groups.

Two patterns have been identified almost universally in studies utilizing different behavior checklists, informants, subject populations, and methods of analysis. One of these patterns comprises problems such as aggression, temper, disobedience, overactivity, and delinquency; it has been variously labeled "undercontrolled," "acting-out," "conduct disorder," and "externalizing." The other pattern features such problems as bodily complaints, fears, worrying, and social withdrawal, and has been labeled "overcontrolled," "overinhibited," "personality disorder," and "internalizing." Classification of disturbed youth according to these patterns has generally shown that those manifesting the externalizing pattern come from more overtly disrupted homes, demonstrate less social competence, and have poorer responses to traditional mental health services than those who manifest the internalizing pattern.[14]

Finer-grained analyses show that the broad band internalizing-externalizing dichotomy subsumes a number of narrow band syndromes, some of which are fairly universal, whereas others are

---

13. Thomas M. Achenbach and Craig S. Edelbrock, "The Classification of Child Psychopathology: A Review and Analysis of Empirical Efforts," *Psychological Bulletin* 85 (May 1978): 1275-1301.

14. Ibid.

peculiar to a particular sex or age group.[15] Syndromes labeled "somatic complaints," "hyperactive," "delinquent," and "aggressive," for example, have been found for both sexes throughout the elementary school years and adolescence, although the precise composition and incidence of these syndromes varies with age and sex. More pronounced sex differences in the patterning of problems are evident in a syndrome labeled "uncommunicative" that was found only for boys and a syndrome labeled "cruel" that was found only for girls. These empirically identified syndromes contradict stereotypes of "typical" male and female behavior patterns.

Age differences in patterning are evident in a syndrome labeled "depressed" that was found for both sexes during the elementary school years and syndromes characterized largely by immaturity in the adolescent years. In this case, the empirically identified syndromes may contradict traditional stereotypes of *age* differences in behavior. It should be noted that these syndromes and their summary labels are intended to reflect the patterns of behavior problems reported by parents and teachers rather than diagnostic categories. In the absence of a well-validated diagnostic system, however, empirically derived and operationally defined categories of behavior problems are prerequisites for most kinds of clinical research. If these categories differentiate among youth who differ in prognosis, responsiveness to treatment, or etiological factors, they may ultimately provide a better basis for diagnosis than traditional taxonomies do.

Research Strategies

In considering clinical research strategies, it is important to be aware of the baseline of knowledge, methodology, and services from which research must proceed, and then to formulate realistic goals for advancing this baseline. The flood of popular and professional literature, the rich array of theory, and the abundance of research on childhood and adolescence might suggest that developmental deviations are already well understood and readily amelio-

15. Thomas M. Achenbach, "The Child Behavior Profile: I. Boys Aged 6-11," *Journal of Consulting and Clinical Psychology* 46 (June 1978): 478-88; Thomas M. Achenbach and Craig S. Edelbrock, "The Child Behavior Profile: II. Boys Aged 12-16 and Girls Aged 6-11 and 12-16," *Journal of Consulting and Clinical Psychology* 47 (April 1979): 223-33.

rated. Such is not the case. In reality, there is on the one hand a body of research and theory concerning the course of normal development, and on the other hand a vast literature and an army of practitioners dealing with behavior problems. Rarely has the study of normal development been extended to the origin, course, and amelioration of behavior disorders. Establishment of a baseline from which to proceed therefore requires a synthesis of the disparate developmental and clinical traditions. This has been attempted elsewhere,[16] but it can be summarized by saying that the developmental tradition has contributed adaptations of the methodology of behavioral research to the study of normal developmental change,[17] documentation of developmental differences in behavior, and heuristic conceptualizations of the mechanisms of development. By contrast, the clinical tradition has contributed descriptions of particular disorders, a mixture of theory and experience concerning their nature and management, research on specific disorders, and technologies of intervention evolved by rival schools of thought.

Given this situation, we need programmatic research designed to place clinical problems into a coherent developmental framework. There is no single way to do this, but the following sections outline prerequisites for a more sophisticated infrastructure of knowledge and services.

TAXONOMIC RESEARCH

It is clear that prevention and treatment cannot advance without some notion of what is being prevented or treated. It is equally clear that no taxonomy constructed in our present stage of ignorance will either satisfy everyone or endure forever. Since some form of conceptual organization is nevertheless necessary to distinguish among young persons whose problems differ in etiology, prognosis, and appropriate treatment, the immediate question is not *whether* to classify but *how* to classify. The official psychiatric taxonomy has recently been placed on a firmer empirical footing with respect to the major adult categories of schizophrenia and affective dis-

16. Achenbach, *Developmental Psychopathology.*

17. Thomas M. Achenbach, *Research in Developmental Psychology: Concepts, Strategies, Methods* (New York: Free Press, 1978).

orders,[18] but has less of an empirical base with respect to disorders of childhood and adolescence. Neglect of these age groups has spurred efforts to identify empirical groupings of behavior problems through multivariate statistical methods, which have produced the convergent findings noted earlier.

Much remains to be done, however, by way of translating empirically derived groupings into taxonomies that may have etiological, prognostic, or theoretical significance. One approach is to categorize individuals according to the single behavioral syndrome they most resemble. A second approach is to score them on scales representing all the syndromes identified for their age and sex, and then to classify them according to their entire profiles of scores. This approach preserves more information about each individual's overall behavior pattern, and it has been found to yield categories of youth who are similar not only with respect to behavioral pattern but also with respect to changes in behavior following mental health contacts.[19] The ultimate value of this taxonomic approach will, of course, depend on how well its categories and their correlates guide research and practice, as compared to other taxonomic approaches.

NORMATIVE AND EPIDEMIOLOGICAL RESEARCH

Besides clarification of *what* is to be prevented or treated, we need better data on *how much* there is to prevent or treat, how it is *distributed* within the population, and what its typical *course* is. The most basic approach is through general population surveys of specific adaptive and maladaptive behaviors, and the assessment of differential incidence in relation to specific environmental, geographic, demographic, and referral variables.[20] Research of this sort need not wait upon definitive taxonomies, as taxonomic and

18. American Psychiatric Association, *Diagnostic and Statistical Manual of Mental Disorders.*

19. Craig S. Edelbrock and Thomas M. Achenbach, "A Typology of Child Behavior Profile Patterns: Distribution and Correlates in Clinically Referred 6-16 Year Olds," unpublished paper.

20. Thomas M. Achenbach and Craig S. Edelbrock, "Behavioral Problems and Competencies Reported by Parents of Normal and Disturbed Children Aged 4 through 16," *Monographs of the Society for Research in Child Development,* in press.

epidemiological research can each benefit from data gained through the other.

Knowledge of the distribution of specific behaviors in the general population can also help to rectify the preoccupation of clinical theory and practice with the end products of referral. By the time young people are actually seen in clinical settings, it is difficult to separate behavior problems characteristic of their developmental level from those that may have truly warranted referral and those that are by-products of the referral process. Unlike adults, youth rarely seek mental health services on their own and are often frightened or angered by referral, thus aggravating the pathological biases inherent in clinical assessment. This argues for longitudinal studies to trace the typical course of behavioral problems and competencies in samples drawn from the general population rather than exclusively from referred groups. It also argues for close study of adaptive and maladaptive behavior in nonclinical settings such as schools, homes, and neighborhood hangouts.

RESEARCH ON OUTCOMES

Whereas normative and epidemiological research is aimed at documenting the distribution and course of disorders in the general population, research on the outcome of interventions is needed to determine what approaches work best with what type of youth under what conditions. This requires studies designed to determine how client characteristics and treatment interact to shape outcomes. Unfortunately, little research of this sort has been undertaken with clients of any age. Existing research on outcomes has generally been designed either to answer the question, "Does treatment X work?" (as compared to a control condition), or, "Which of two treatments works better?" for a predefined group of clients.

Most efforts to answer the first question for traditional psychotherapy have failed to demonstrate significant benefits for children or adolescents.[21] Stimulant drug therapy for hyperactivity and behavior modification for a variety of focalized behavior problems have fared better, but the very few studies designed to compare

21. Donald P. Hartmann, Brenda L. Roper, and Donna M. Gelfand, "An Evaluation of Alternative Modes of Child Psychotherapy," in *Advances in Clinical Child Psychology*, ed. Benjamin B. Lahey and Alan E. Kazdin (New York: Plenum Press, 1977), pp. 1-46.

treatments have not shown unequivocal across-the-board superiority for a particular treatment modality with children or adolescents.[22] Instead, post hoc analyses have shown that the interactions of client characteristics, such as age and socioeconomic background, with treatment variables account for more variance in outcome than do the treatment modalities alone.[23] It is therefore essential that prognosis be viewed as a complex function of such variables as the individual's developmental level, behavioral pattern, social competence, and family background, on the one hand, and the type of intervention, on the other. Because some clinical approaches may be potentially as harmful to some people as they are helpful to others, it is especially important to compare no treatment and nonclinical interventions with clinical interventions.

RESEARCH ON HIGH-RISK POPULATIONS

The failure of nearly a century of research to reveal the etiology of adult schizophrenia and the frustration of seeing promising leads repeatedly exposed as by-products rather than antecedents of schizophrenia have led to new research strategies. One of these is the longitudinal study of early adolescents judged to be at statistically high risk for schizophrenia because they have schizophrenic mothers.[24] This strategy of studying a high-risk group longitudinally in order to identify the premorbid characteristics of those who eventually become afflicted has since been adopted for research on other disorders as well. Despite its difficulty, expense, and ethical intricacies, the high-risk strategy promises a more complete picture of the antecedents of particular disorders than almost any other approach. This is because it is the only way to separate antecedents of the disorders from the consequences of labeling, referral, treatment, and concomitant life-styles. When such studies include a sophisticated assessment of developmental course, as well as comparisons among groups varying in risk factors, they can be

22. Achenbach, *Developmental Psychopathology.*

23. Leonore Love and Jacques Kaswan, *Troubled Children* (New York: John Wiley and Sons, 1974); Lovick C. Miller et al., "Comparison of Reciprocal Inhibition, Psychotherapy, and Waiting List Control for Phobic Children," *Journal of Abnormal Psychology* 79 (June 1972): 269-79.

24. *Genetics, Environment, and Psychopathology,* ed. Mednick et al.

highly informative about a variety of adaptive and maladaptive patterns in addition to target disorders such as schizophrenia. The emergence in adolescence of new patterns of maladaptation makes the middle-school years a particularly favorable period for high-risk studies. It should be remembered, however, that the complexities of causal inference and the possibility that predisposing factors are rooted in much earlier development mean that such studies are more likely to yield a basis for improved prediction and theory than conclusive evidence on etiology.

Theories of psychopathology focus on etiology, and knowledge of specific etiologies would help to answer many other questions. Specific etiologies are unlikely to be found for most behavior disorders of early adolescence, however, until advances in the areas already outlined provide more precise formulations of etiological questions. It is perhaps ironic that such an enormous array of mental health services rests on unverified etiological notions, but the probable multidetermination of most behavior disorders means that sophisticated prognostic and outcome research may tell us more about how to deal with disorders than will research focused narrowly on etiology. In fact, with the exception of disorders having specific organic etiologies, efforts to enhance adaptive development in the face of adversity may be more effective than a preoccupation with etiological conceptions that point only backward to infinitely complex combinations of constitutional dispositions, environmental ambience, and accidents of fate that cannot be undone anyway.

Research Problems

A detailed discussion of research problems has been presented elsewhere,[25] but it is worth noting some obstacles to efforts at increasing our knowledge of behavior disorders. Probably the most publicized issue concerns the ethics of research with human subjects. From inadequate ethical guidelines, the pendulum has swung

25. Thomas M. Achenbach, "Psychopathology of Childhood: Research Problems and Issues," *Journal of Consulting and Clinical Psychology* 46 (August 1978): 759-76.

to an almost fanatical preoccupation with the protection of human subjects and the privacy of records. As a result of this concern, the National Commission for the Protection of Human Subjects of Biomedical and Behavioral Research was appointed to make recommendations for a uniform federal policy on research. These recommendations have been translated into regulations applicable to nearly all research. The regulations themselves are probably less of a threat to the conduct of research on behavior disorders than is the ponderous bureaucratic and legal machinery governing them. Following an inevitable period of frustration and adjustment, however, the most worthwhile research should still be feasible, although the burden and expense of regulation may increase institutional resistance where research is already less than welcome.

Unfortunately, schools and clinical agencies share many understandable reasons for resisting the research necessary to advance our knowledge and treatment of behavior disorders, especially during such an ostensibly volatile period as the middle-school years. Despite the fact that schools and clinical agencies both face demands for better documentation and evaluation of what they do, they are simultaneously facing fundamental threats to their autonomy, financial stability, and capacity to carry out bona fide documentation and evaluation. Under these conditions, research must be closely attuned to service needs in order to be feasible at all. This is not necessarily a disadvantage, however, as the ecological validity and the practical value of behavioral research would be enhanced by close links with educational and clinical systems. Given the applied goals of research on behavior disorders, well-validated instruments and procedures that can be shared by practitioners and researchers can benefit both practice and research.[26]

Summary and Conclusions

A skeletal framework has been presented for research on behavior disorders of the middle-school years. Such disorders are best understood within a developmental context that highlights the role of biological, cognitive, social-emotional, and educational variables. Although antisocial behavior, schizophrenia, and certain depressive

26. Achenbach, "The Child Behavior Profile: I"; Achenbach and Edelbrock, "The Child Behavior Profile II."

conditions begin to emerge in their adult forms during adolescence, there is no satisfactory clinical taxonomy for most disorders of the middle-school years. Alternatives to traditional psychiatric taxonomies include assessment of specific behavior problems and empirical identification of groupings of problems through multivariate statistical methods. The latter approach has produced considerable convergence in syndromes identified from behavior checklists filled out by parents, teachers, and mental health workers.

Despite the importance of viewing behavior problems in a developmental context, there is an unfortunate gap between research on normal development, on the one hand, and clinical research and practice on the other. To remedy this situation, certain research strategies deserve priority, including taxonomic research, normative and epidemiological research, outcome research, and research on high-risk populations. As these kinds of research clarify the nature, course, and distribution of behavior disorders, research on specific etiologies may become more productive. While the need for knowledge is clear and there are growing demands for better documentation and evaluation of mental health services, increasingly burdensome regulation of research, as well as institutional resistance to it, mean that research must be carefully tailored to service needs. Closer links between service and research, however, should benefit both enterprises in the long run.

CHAPTER XIV

School-based Research

CONRAD F. TOEPFER, JR. AND JEAN V. MARANI

As is the case at lower and higher school levels, junior high and middle schools almost incidentally serve as sites, and their students as subjects, for a variety of educational research studies. Many of these studies shed light on specific instructional and guidance practices and certain characteristics and problems of students. Because studies at this level are not replicated at the others, it is often impossible to determine which findings hold true for all ages and which ones characterize the middle grades. Moreover, the studies seldom generate a holistic view of the age group. In this chapter we suggest several kinds of needed studies and give particular attention to some promising naturalistic methods for studying transescents in the school setting.

Effects of Separate Organizational Units

Researching the educational effectiveness of the middle-school organization presents considerable difficulty, since there is much variation among middle schools as to purpose as well as to program. A lack of clarity about purposes also characterized their predecessors, the junior high schools.

In establishing a separate junior high school early in the twentieth century, the United States became the first modern nation to focus on the middle grades within a separate unit of school organization. The programs of these schools, however, varied markedly. In the early years of the junior high school a serious organizational dilemma had to be faced because of the Carnegie Unit requirement that graduation from high school must include subjects

---

EDITOR'S NOTE. The first sections of this chapter were written by Conrad F. Toepfer, Jr. Jean V. Marani is the author of the section on naturalistic studies, which begins on p. 276.

studied in grades nine through twelve. Although increasing numbers of school districts were reorganizing their secondary programs so as to include a junior high school comprising grades seven through nine and a senior high school consisting of grades ten through twelve, the program in the ninth grade remained tied to the subject requirements for graduation from the high school. The ninth-grade program was largely dictated by the Carnegie Unit requirements specifying the number of classes and the number of minutes of instruction per week in the various subjects.[1] Consequently, the early junior high school programs were actually little more than a seventh- and eighth-grade experience followed by a quite different ninth-grade experience. Often the ninth-grade program in a junior high school consisted merely of high school classes at the ninth-grade level that were housed separately from grades ten through twelve.

In 1913, a committee on the Economy of Time in Education recommended the establishment of a three-year junior high school comprising grades seven through nine.[2] By 1920, however, there were almost as many junior high schools that included only grades seven and eight as those that included grades seven through nine. It had become clear to many educators that a distinctive program suited to the needs of students in the three-year junior high school was largely impossible under the restrictions of the Carnegie Unit. Thus, the objectives of the committee on the Economy of Time in Education were largely unrealized.[3]

The features that consistently marked the junior high school in its early years were departmentalization, promotion by subject, a high-school time schedule, and exploratory experiences in the areas of foreign language, manual training, and cooking and sewing. A

1. Ellsworth Tompkins and Walter H. Gaumnitz, *The Carnegie Unit: Its Origin, Status, and Trends,* U.S. Department of Health, Education and Welfare Bulletin 1954, No. 7 (Washington, D.C.: U.S. Government Printing Office, 1954), p. 12.

2. *Report of the Committee of the National Council on Education on Economy of Time in Education,* James H. Baker, Chairman, U.S. Bureau of Education Bulletin 1913, No. 38 (Washington, D.C.: U.S. Government Printing Office, 1913), pp. 26-27.

3. Conrad F. Toepfer, Jr., "Evolving Curricular Patterns in Junior High Schools: An Historical Study" (Doct. diss., University of Buffalo, 1962), pp. 32-120.

unique curriculum, distinct from that found in the six-year secondary school, was never developed. The change was largely an administrative one that gave junior high schools independence through their own principals and staffs. While a few junior high schools attempted to develop a curriculum that was responsive to the needs of students in the middle grades, most of these schools were little more than a "junior edition" of the senior high school. This may account for the practice, still common today in many state departments of public instruction, of legally defining education in these grades as "early secondary education."

During the past twenty years, the concept of the middle school has represented an attempt to develop an educational program that is appropriate to the distinctive nature and characteristics of middle-grade learners, who differ significantly from elementary school children and from adolescents in the high school. The problem for research on the middle schools is to take on the difficult task of identifying how effectively those schools have succeeded in developing educational programs based upon such a commitment, particularly in comparison with the junior high school and other organizational patterns for the middle grades. This challenge is compounded because data on the success of the junior high schools were never effectively gathered or evaluated. As Kirby prophetically observed in 1927:

Changes in our American schools are frequent. Our assumption is that the change is an improvement but there are few instances where the condition before the change or after it was carefully enough evaluated so that progress or regression could be claimed with assurance. The junior high has been accepted with such alacrity that about two-thirds of the cities of the United States of one hundred thousand population have adopted it or are moving in that direction. To what extent is this new organization an improvement over the organization it displaced or is displacing? To what extent is it achieving the ends for which it was organized? Do results show that the enthusiastic supporters of this movement are justified in the extravagant claims which they have made?

It is time to begin taking stock while there still remains enough of the old to set over against the new.[4]

4. Thomas J. Kirby, "Preface," in Ralph A. Fritz, *An Evaluation of Two Special Purposes of Junior High School: Economy of Time and Bridging the Gap,* in *University of Iowa Studies in Education,* vol. 4, no. 5 (Iowa City, Ia.: University of Iowa, 1927), p. 3.

Kirby's admonition went unheeded. Data were not gathered to document the comparative effectiveness of the junior high school over the organizational patterns it was displacing. Had such data been available, it would have been more obvious that a similar data base should be established for the middle school when it, in turn, became part of the American educational scene. Indeed, it may well be that a good share of the early acceptance of the middle school stemmed from the fact that hard data could not be supplied on the effectiveness of the junior high school. Such data might have provided a standard against which the effectiveness of the middle school could be compared. In any event, the case for maintaining a separate educational unit for the middle grades has yet to be made, either by comparison with other organizational patterns or by evidence of the extent to which the middle school has achieved its own stated objectives.

There also was no research on the nature of the clientele of the junior high school. No term was supplied to replace the ubiquitous but ambiguous designation, "early adolescent." Experience with young people in the middle grades indicates that they have their own uniqueness as a group and that they cannot be adequately described as "early anything." Although there has been general acceptance of the data attesting to the wide variability in maturation between boys and girls and within each sex in the middle-school years,[5] educators have failed to agree upon a common term for this developmental period. We still have no widely accepted descriptor that communicates the unique nature of the clientele the middle school seeks to serve. Instead, we have characterized the middle school in terms of an academic function. Research that seeks to find evidence of the need for such a separate school unit must take into account the needs and characteristics of learners during this period. It must also recognize that individuals of this age range from being precocious to being late in their physical, social, and emotional development, but that they also have common needs that are unique to this developmental epoch.

The concept of "transescence," as defined by Eichhorn and re-

5. James M. Tanner, *Education and Physical Growth* (London: University of London Press, 1962); Allan Drash, "Variations in Pubertal Development and the School System," *Transescence* 6 (1976): 14-26.

fined in this yearbook, merits wider recognition as a descriptor communicating the nature and characteristics of learners in the middle grades. In defining the term, Eichhorn focused on the transformational tasks facing children as they approach pubescence and as they consolidate the new capacities that come with the middle-school years.[6]

Although many scholars who study the middle school, as well as practitioners, are confident that data will validate the enthusiasm they have for the institution, empirical confirmation is necessary. Continued failure to broaden the now limited data will leave the need for a separate middle unit of schooling in doubt and will seriously handicap further research needed on the middle school.

Using Primary Data Sources

The formulation of objectives and rationale for the junior high school did not precede the inauguration of the first junior high programs. Rather they were developed after the movement was well established. Authors of early textbooks on the junior high school assumed that there was a firm rationale, but their conclusions were drawn totally from secondary sources.[7] My research in communities where the early junior high schools evolved, in which I used minutes of school board meetings and other primary sources, contradicts these early texts. The initial move to junior high schools was for economic reasons, and the development of a rationale for the education of early adolescents in the new middle-grade unit was largely one of hindsight.[8]

Contemporary technology for gathering data will make research on the middle school much easier. A number of individual schools have gathered longitudinal data on the development and effectiveness of their programs. Analysis of these data will greatly facilitate the design of studies based upon primary data, which was not possible during the junior high school movement. If the middle school

6. Donald H. Eichhorn, *The Middle School* (New York: Center for Applied Research in Education, 1966), p. 3.

7. See, for example, Vernon G. Bennett, *The Junior High School* (Baltimore: Warwick and York, 1919) and Thomas H. Briggs, *The Junior High School* (Boston: Houghton Mifflin Co., 1920).

8. Toepfer, "Evolving Curricular Patterns in Junior High Schools," pp. 32-148.

is to succeed where the junior high failed, sources for primary data that stand the tests of external and internal validation must be identified.

Although there is little definitive research on education in the middle grades, there are some studies that are helpful. The Eight-Year Study, although not primarily concerned with the junior high school, furnished some comparative data on curriculum of different junior high school programs that gave support to the senior high schools included in that study.[9] Wright's comparative data on programs of general education in the junior high school provide an excellent background for similar investigations that could be undertaken in the middle school.[10] The Boyce Medical Study, in which the physical characteristics of the entire student population of the Boyce Middle School were investigated, resulted in detailed findings on each child that were then analyzed for both medical and educational implications.[11] This study provides significant primary data that have implications for continuing research on the middle school.

Epstein's research on brain growth periodization has opened up areas of research on curriculum development, learning characteristics, and expectations for intellectual and personal development.[12] Epstein has established that the brain undergoes age-linked periods of great growth as well as plateaus in growth that correlate highly with the findings of Piaget. The greatest of the plateaus occurs between the ages of twelve and fourteen—the middle-school years. I have been collaborating with Epstein to bring these data to the attention of the middle school educational community and to gather

9. Wilford M. Aiken, *The Story of the Eight-Year Study* (New York: Harper and Brothers, 1942).

10. Grace S. Wright, *Block-time Classes and the Core Program in the Junior High School*, U.S. Department of Health, Education, and Welfare Bulletin 1958, no. 6 (Washington, D.C.: U.S. Government Printing Office, 1958).

11. Donald H. Eichhorn, "The Boyce Medical Study," *Educational Dimensions of the Emerging Adolescent Learner*, ed. Neil Atkins and Philip Pumerantz (Springfield, Mass.: Educational Leadership Institute, 1973), pp. 19-23.

12. Herman T. Epstein, "Growth Spurts During Brain Development: Implications for Educational Policy," in *Education and the Brain*, ed. Jeanne S. Chall and Allan F. Mirsky, Seventy-seventh Yearbook of the National Society for the Study of Education, Part II (Chicago: University of Chicago Press, 1978), pp. 343-70.

additional data suggesting directions that the middle school could pursue to improve the learning and development of students at that level.[13] Data from pilot studies suggest that students in the period of low brain growth (ages twelve to fourteen) have difficulty initiating new cognitive skills and achieve more when the middle-school program is directed toward helping them mature and consolidate cognitive skills acquired in the preceding period of great brain growth (ages ten to twelve). It also appears that students between the ages of twelve and fourteen learn better when information is presented at cognitive levels that the students have acquired before entering the period of low brain growth.

A study now under way seeks to identify how students from ages twelve to fourteen learn when the instruction requires a level of cognitive skill previously achieved as compared with similar students who receive instruction that introduces new cognitive skills during this period. The study will also try to determine whether students in both groups who have a community-based out-of-school activity for affective as well as cognitive support will achieve differently from students who do not have access to such an activity.

Epstein's research suggests that inappropriate expectations for cognitive learning during the period of a plateau in brain growth (ages twelve to fourteen) could result in difficulties for students. I have attempted to examine the levels of success in cognitive achievement for high school students who experienced their first critical problems in cognitive achievement in the middle grades. Cumulative records for students completing their high school education between 1976 and 1978 were examined. Records were obtained for 1,000 students in each of the following ranges of intelligence quotients: 90-99, 100-109, 110-119, and 120 and above. All students selected for the study had to have achieved consistent success in elementary school. From this group, students who experienced their first serious problems in cognitive achievement at ages twelve to fourteen (grades seven and eight), as indicated by grade reports, were identified. A similar procedure was used to identify students who had continuing problems with cognitive achievement in high school.

13. Herman T. Epstein and Conrad F. Toepfer, Jr., "A Neuroscience Basis for Reorganizing Middle Grades Education," *Educational Leadership* 35 (May 1978): 656-60.

The most striking finding in this study of cognitive performance, as shown in table 1, was the high incidence of continuing problems in cognitive achievement in high schools revealed by students who first experienced such difficulties between ages twelve and fourteen. These data suggest that there is a need to study the degree to which

TABLE 1

PERCENT OF STUDENTS IN VARIOUS CATEGORIES OF ACHIEVEMENT, BY CATEGORIES OF INTELLIGENCE

ACHIEVEMENT CATEGORY	RANGE OF INTELLIGENCE QUOTIENTS			
	90–99 N = 1,000	100–109 N = 1,000	110–119 N = 1,000	120 AND ABOVE N = 1,000
Consistently successful in elementary school	100.0	100.0	100.0	100.0
Had achievement problems in middle school	24.3	34.2	35.8	29.8
Had continuing achievement problems in high school	18.1	28.1	31.2	22.1

existing programs in the middle grades may be overchallenging students during the plateau in brain growth at ages twelve to fourteen. It is possible that this overchallenging occurs because schools are providing learning inputs for which the children have not yet developed receptors. The numbers of students who experience initial difficulties in cognitive learning at those ages suggest the need for further research on educational programs in the middle school. The relatively low percent of students in the 90-99 IQ range experiencing achievement problems is surprising. While causality in all four categories must be investigated, one interesting hypothesis deserves comment. It may be that we do not challenge the students in the low range sufficiently, probably because we do not see them as potential college material. In that sense, we may be creating the least stressful learning environment for students in this category of ability.

Naturalistic Studies

Several promising approaches to learning more about the transescent age group can be classified as "naturalistic" methods. As the term suggests, these methods involve much gathering of data in the natural habitat of individuals in a group, such as their homes, their school, or their community. They emphasize unstructured direct observation of the day-by-day or even minute-by-minute flow of life in a particular setting. These features contrast sharply with the artificiality and control found in laboratory experiments and with the contrived stimuli and standardized conditions that characterize formal testing. Naturalistic studies bear some resemblance to the anecdotal record procedure, but differ in purpose in that they are directed at increasing understanding of an entire age group, not at providing a basis for counseling or teaching a particular individual.

Some of the distinguishing characteristics of naturalistic research are: (a) the setting is authentic and free from contrived variables; (b) the setting contains the regular and expected stimuli intrinsic to the situation; (c) the observer's behavior is not rigidly prescribed in advance; (4) the researcher is expected to record faithfully that which stands out in the situation.

Some limitations of the method are that it (a) does not lend itself to controlled replications, (b) does not focus on a single variable, (c) reflects the perspective of the observer, and (d) is subject to questions of validity and reliability.

Of the various types of naturalistic investigation, the "shadow study" may hold the greatest promise as a source of knowledge about transescents, but several others deserve mention, namely, observational, descriptive, and ethnographic studies. In their simplest form, observational studies are represented by such activities as measuring with a stopwatch an individual student's "time on task" in instructional situations or counting the frequency of participation of members of a discussion group. In more complex studies of this type, the observer is called upon to interpret behavior and classify responses, as in the use of instruments for interaction analysis, where it is necessary for the observer to be trained to discriminate among various degrees of indirectness in discourse. Since observational studies, in general, employ checklists or some other recording format, a certain amount of training is necessary to familiarize the observer with the classifications to be made, in order to reduce subjectivity as much as possible.

Descriptive studies differ from simple observation in that they involve verbatim or "shorthand" recording of behavior and utterances, rather than mere checkmarks or tallies, and frequently require much judgment and discrimination in deciding which instances should be recorded and how they should be categorized. Usually guidelines of some sort are provided to define categories and indicate the types of situation to be noted and recorded. Skillfully done, such descriptions can furnish much insight into the needs and characteristics of an age group, and if enough of them were made over a period of years, careful analysis should reveal trends worth noting.

Ethnographic research is basically a tool of anthropologists and other social scientists who attempt to describe and interpret their subjects through total immersion in their environmental setting. The researcher usually lives in the natural habitat and is enabled to examine minute details—artifacts, habits, customs, traditions, family and community structures—the entire range of experiences that have an impact upon behavior. Observations and analyses focus on the interplay between persons and their settings.

Of late, ethnographic methods have been applied to case studies in education in an effort to reveal the significance of a school setting and the meanings students or faculties ascribe to it. In a comprehensive review of ethnographic techniques in education, Wilson identifies the kinds of data examined through their use: (a) form and content of verbal interaction among participants; (b) form and content of verbal interaction with the observer; (c) nonverbal behavior; (d) patterns of action and nonaction; and (e) traces, archival records, artifacts, documents.[14]

Related to the above methods is the "shadow study" technique, in which the observer follows a subject like a shadow, recording what happens to the individual as well as how the individual responds to each situation encountered. When the technique is applied simultaneously to many individuals in many situations, and by different observers, a series of impressions emerges that provides a cross-section of what it is like to be a child or adolescent in a particular set of circumstances.

In the early 1940s, Barker and Wright employed the shadowing

14. Stephen Wilson, "The Uses of Ethnographic Techniques in Educational Research," *Review of Educational Research* 47 (Spring 1977): 255.

technique to tell the story of a day in the life of a seven-year-old boy. The whole day's record was included, from his getting up to his going to bed, minute by minute.[15] Ethnographic research also has that quality of detail and exactness, but the time-frame is considerably longer than one day. The shadow technique emphasizes the behavioral record, since the observer cannot infer the thought reactions of the subject.

Instead of focusing on a single individual, a study conducted in 1962 by Lounsbury and Marani engineered the simultaneous "shadowing" of a hundred eighth graders in junior high schools throughout the country. On a predesignated day, volunteer observers visited a neighboring school and followed a randomly selected eighth-grade student through that student's daily school routine, recording in ten-minute time segments what transpired between the subject and the total school environment. Observers reported the pupil's age and sex, parents' occupations, available test scores, and any additional significant information. They also noted certain features of the school, such as enrollment, grades included, grouping and scheduling practices, and sex ratios. At the close of the day, the observer posed two questions to the shadowed student: "What do you like best about this school?" and "What do you like least?" Finally, observers were urged to summarize their shadow log and formulate whatever conclusions seemed appropriate to them.[16]

Analysis and interpretation of the data were performed by the authors of the final report against several commonly accepted statements of learning principles. A series of generalizations were then formulated to sum up the state of the art of junior high school education in 1962. During the time it was in print, the report was a best-seller among pamphlets of the Association for Supervision and Curriculum Development.

In 1977, a similar shadow study, sponsored by the National Middle School Association, was coordinated by Lounsbury to provide a comparable picture of student life under that organizational

15. Roger S. Barker and Herbert F. Wright, *One Boy's Day: A Specimen Record of Behavior* (New York: Harper and Brothers, 1951).

16. John H. Lounsbury and Jean V. Marani, *The Junior High School We Saw: One Day in the Eighth Grade* (Washington, D.C.: Association for Supervision and Curriculum Development, 1964).

format—a revisit to the young adolescent after fifteen years. The directions to the volunteer observers for the day of the study read, in part, as follows:

You are one of some 150 observers who will be in the schools all across the country on that day. This study seeks to record a day's experience across the land for the seventh-grade transescent. What happens to him, is he getting individual attention, what is he asked to learn, how does he react? There is a related question—how goes the middle school movement itself? While not wholly a scientific study, the data, recorded events and dialogue, will yield a slice of the middle school movement on February 17, 1977.[17]

Observers were instructed to "be prepared to stay with the student from the beginning of the school day until the end," not to conduct the study in their own school "unless it is unavoidable," and to select randomly a seventh grader "in the regular program, excluding exceptionalities."[18] The instructions indicated that, while it was not necessary for teachers in the school to know the details of the observation, they should realize that it was not they who were being observed. If the student figured out that he was being followed (from the coincidence of the observer's being present in his every class), the problem was to be handled as seemed best to the observer, and the student should, in any event, be interviewed at the end of the day.

While the potential of the shadow study as a teacher-training device or as a data base for making instructional decisions is obvious, such studies also have a number of applications in educational research other than that of enriching our understanding of an age group. In accountability studies, conventional testing of pupils might be supplemented with shadow studies designed to identify factors contributing to high and low achievement. In studies of motivation, they might focus on factors in learning situations that serve as positive and negative reinforcers. Shadow studies could be conducted during site visits when schools or programs are being evaluated. They could also play a part in research on sexism and racism, if observers attended to the presence of appropriate role

17. John H. Lounsbury, "Middle School 'Shadow Study' Research Project," unpublished manuscript, 1977.

18. Ibid.

models, the nature of instructional materials, and the extent to which certain groups are "put down" in discussion. Also, although the quality of randomness would have to be sacrificed, it might be useful in studying the effects of mainstreaming to shadow handicapped children throughout a school day to see how they fare. Not least of the benefits of shadow studies are those accruing to the observers themselves, who, if teachers, gain a different perspective on classroom life, are helped to see a pupil as a whole person, and have the opportunity to contrast another school with their own.

Summary

The movement for the middle school will suffer if there is continued failure to validate the accomplishment of such schools, to gather data showing their results as compared with other patterns of education for the middle grades, and to identify needed changes and improvements. Well-conceived experiments must have priority in planning for research on the middle school, but other research methodologies can also be employed. Philosophical and historical investigations of the middle-school concept and program are urgently needed. Shadow studies and other naturalistic methods deserve serious consideration, both for learning more about the age group and for studying the effects of school practices on pupils. Case studies should also be undertaken, as well as normative and descriptive research. Foundation and governmental support should be enlisted to make possible large-scale studies on all facets of the middle-school experience. Only through such a research effort can we add significantly to the presently limited baseline data. If we need a charge to begin such an undertaking, we need only to recall the still unanswered questions raised by Kirby in 1927. While addressed to the junior high school over a half-century ago, they stand as cogent challenges to the middle school today.

CHAPTER XV

Investigating Intelligence in Early Adolescence

DAVID ELKIND

From the earliest days of psychology as a science there have been two rather different approaches to human intelligence. One of these, the developmental approach, has been concerned with adolescent thought as a special type of mental activity worthy of study in its own right. The other, the psychometric approach, has with few exceptions seen adolescent thought as continuous with intelligence in general and, therefore, undeserving of any special attention.

Before turning to the developmental approach, which will be the focus of concern for this chapter, we need to compare the two positions to put the developmental position in proper perspective. This is necessary because both the psychometric and developmental approaches employ the term "intelligence," although in quite different senses. It is important, therefore, to distinguish between these two conceptions of mental functioning in order to avoid purely semantic confusions and arguments.

Two Conceptions of Intelligence

THE DEVELOPMENTAL APPROACH

The developmental approach to intelligence, exemplified by the work of Jean Piaget,[1] starts from a general epistemological assumption that is shared by other psychologies. This assumption is that if anything exists, it exists in an organized fashion and that such organizations are characterized by sets of rules. Indeed, what differentiates psychologies that start from the same epistemological

---

1. Jean Piaget, *The Psychology of Intelligence* (London: Routledge and Kegan Paul, 1950).

assumption is the kind of rules they postulate as characterizing organizations. Gestalt psychology, for example, shares with Piagetian psychology the assumption that organization is the prime stuff of being.[2] But the principles of organization suggested by the Gestaltists are different from those postulated by Piaget.[3] Likewise, those who advocate a computer or information-processing psychology[4] also advocate different organizational principles than do either developmentalists or Gestaltists.

The principles of organization advocated by Piaget are those of structuralism. The criteria of a structural system are that it should (a) operate as a totality, (b) have rules of transformation, and (c) be self-regulational. In Piaget's view, these principles can characterize the organization of intelligence at different levels of development. That is to say, organizations at different levels of complexity can, nonetheless, reflect these same principles. To make this point concrete a couple of examples from Piaget's stage theory of intellectual development will be given.

At the end of the first stage in the Piagetian theory, the sensory motor stage, the infant has constructed a world of permanent objects. Even at this level the infant's thinking shows totality, transformation, and self-regulation. Consider an infant of two years who has seen a sweet hidden first under a cup then under a small box. The infant looks first under the cup then under the box. First, the child's actions form a totality in that they all deal with a particular goal, namely, finding the sweet. Secondly, the child is able to deal with a transformation, the displacement of the sweet from one hiding place to another. Finally, the system is self-regulational in the sense that when the sweet is obtained the child's search behavior comes to an end.

One can see the same rules operate at the higher level of mental organization, which appears about the age of six or seven and which Piaget speaks of as "concrete operations." These operations enable school-age children to deal with classes, relations, and numbers in

2. Wolfgang Köhler, *Gestalt Psychology* (New York: Liveright Publishing Corp., 1947).

3. Jean Piaget, *Structuralism* (New York: Basic Books, 1970).

4. Warren S. McCulloch, *Embodiments of Mind* (Cambridge, Mass.: M.I.T. Press, 1965).

a systematic way. Consider, for example, the child's grasp of class relationships. When children are reasoning about cars or children or numbers, they stay within the context of the class content. They do not reason from cars to children or the reverse. Their thinking is bounded and operates as a totality. Secondly, children know, say, that the class of children includes (can be transformed into) the class of boys and the class of girls. Finally, children also appreciate that the division of the class into boys and girls can be compensated by a new addition of the subordinate classes (boys and girls) to recreate the superordinate class (children). The system is reversible or self-regulational.

The structural principles of totality, transformation, and self-regulation thus distinguish Piagetian psychology from other psychologies that also see organization as the essence of human intelligence.

For purposes of discussion, I would like to use the term "forms" to refer to the organizations studied by developmentalists (or Gestaltists or information-processing theorists). Some general characteristics of forms should be noted. First, forms are generally regarded as genotypic or species characteristics that must be abstracted from the multiple phenotypic forms in which they appear as a consequence of sociocultural conditioning. For example, both Chomsky's language acquisition device (L.A.D.) and Jung's archetypes are proposed as universal forms of mental organization, although in any given individual they are heavily overlaid with sociocultural accretions.[5]

Second, in principle the form approach to mental functioning makes no assumptions about nature or nurture. The identification and descriptions of forms do not require any assessment of the contribution of these variables. This is important to keep in mind because theories of forms are often assumed to be "nativistic" and to be freighted with a lot of hereditary baggage. But as the term is used here, forms assume nothing whatsover in the way of nature-nurture contributions. Forms are descriptive, not causative.

The Piagetian psychology of forms is distinguished from other psychologies that stress organization by its developmental dimen-

5. Noam Chomsky, *Language and Mind* (New York: Harcourt Brace Jovanovich, 1968); Carl G. Jung, *The Archetypes and the Collective Unconscious* (Princeton, N.J.: Princeton University Press, 1959).

sion as well as by its rules. For the Gestaltists, the information-processing theorists, for Jung, Chomsky, and others, the organizations are not only universal; they are also more or less fixed, in the sense of being the same for individuals at all levels of intellectual development. What is unique to Piaget is the postulation of many layers of organization instead of just one. The organization of intelligence, from this perspective, must always be related to the individual's level of development. There are no organizations that characterize a given individual at all times in his or her life.

Because psychologies of form are concerned with species characteristics, individual differences in forms are regarded as a sort of "error" variance from which the more universal forms have to be extracted. Individual differences are thus not a major focus of form psychologies that are concerned with what is common to all members of the species. In a sense, form theories are at a higher level of abstraction than those concerned with individual differences. Accordingly, attempts to psychometrize Piagetian tasks to assess individual differences is a kind of category error, like dealing with the concepts of "fruit" and "pears" as if they were conceptually equal.

THE PSYCHOMETRIC APPROACH

Psychometricians, those concerned with mental tests, start from the assumption that if anything exists, it exists in some amount. Essentially the argument is that what characterizes human behavior is its dimensionality or measurability. A dimension is established when it can be measured with reliability and validity. Although all measures of dimensions must meet the criteria of reliability and validity, they can vary in the sophistication of scaling (ordinal, interval, ratio) and in content (intelligence, achievement, personality, interest, and so forth).

Although the dimensions studied by the psychometricians are regarded as universal, the universality is taken for granted and is not a prime focus of concern. Rather, for the psychometric position, individual or group differences upon a dimension are what matter most. From this perspective, error variance resides not in the individual as a totality, but in aspects of test-taking performance. Nonetheless, the individual is assumed to possess the trait in a fixed amount and the task of the psychometrician is to assess this quantity as accurately as possible.

Again, for purposes of discussion I propose to use the term "traits" to refer to dimensions studied by psychometricians. Traits are defined by their reliability and validity of measurement. Variability or change in the dimensions is accounted for by the theory of individual differences. While it is true that the study of traits is sometimes concerned with age-related changes, this is often an attempt to demonstrate the constancy of individual differences across maturational change.

Like the study of forms, the study of traits implies nothing directly about the role of nature and nurture. Whether a particular individual's position on a dimension is a function of heredity, or experience, or the interactions of the two is independent of the assessment and definition of traits, as it is in the assessment and definition of forms. Forms are qualitative and traits are quantitative, but neither rests on assumptions about nature and nurture.

This long discussion of forms and traits was necessary, or so it seemed to me, in order to shed some light on current issues in the study of adolescent intelligence. The confusion of forms and traits has sometimes led to statements about educational policy and programming that may be false and misleading. We will return to these issues at the end of the chapter. At this point we need to look at some procedures for the assessment of forms.

The Assessment of Forms

The way in which forms are studied depends in part upon the way in which they are defined. For example, information-processing models that define forms in terms of feedback, retrieval, and storage would probably use variations of memory or concept-formation procedures to study them. The method to be described here, however, derives from the Piagetian conception of forms. As noted earlier, according to Piaget,[6] mental forms or organizations are characterized by three qualities: wholeness, transformation, and self-regulation. To demonstrate the presence of forms one must show that all three criteria are operative.

It is because of the necessity of demonstrating all three of these

6. Piaget, *Structuralism*.

criteria that Piaget has devoted entire books to the study of children's conceptions of number, time, space, and so forth.[7] Each book contains a compilation of different investigations that speak to one or another of the criteria of forms. It is not my intention here to give a full description of Piaget's method of studying the forms of thinking that are characteristic of early adolescence.[8] All that is necessary to do is to highlight how these criteria are manifested in one type of formal operational task.[9]

Consider the following materials: four wooden discs, each of which is painted a different color—red, blue, green, and yellow. The subject's task, after instruction and example, is to arrange the discs in all possible combinations taking them one, two, three, and four at a time. Success on the task involves forming all of the sixteen possible combinations (including the null combination). Success shows totality because the subject is able to generate all the combinations that give evidence of a coordinated system. Reversibility is shown by the fact that the subject can combine, dissociate, and recombine the same elements. Self-regulation is shown by the fact that the subject stays within the system and does not, say, use order of permutations in making the arrangements.

Although the assessment of forms would seem to be straightforward, it in fact raises a number of problems. Perhaps the most serious is the performance-competence issue.[10] That is to say, if young persons fail a test of formal operations, are we to say that they lack those operations, or that they have failed to show what their abilities are on this particular task?

The problem is a very real one for the simple reason that formal

7. Jean Piaget, *The Child's Conception of Number* (London: Routledge and Kegan Paul, 1942); ibid., *The Child's Conception of Time* (New York: Basic Books, 1969); Jean Piaget and Bärbel Inhelder, *The Child's Conception of Space* (London: Routledge and Kegan Paul, 1955).

8. Jean Piaget and Bärbel Inhelder, *The Growth of Logical Thinking in Children and Adolescents* (New York: Basic Books, 1958).

9. David Elkind, Ralph Barocas, and Bernard Rosenthal, "Combinatorial Thinking in Adolescents from Graded and Ungraded Classrooms," *Perceptual and Motor Skills* 27 (December 1968): 1015-18.

10. John H. Flavell and Joachim Wohlwill, "Formal and Functional Aspects of Cognitive Development," in *Studies in Cognitive Development*, ed. David Elkind and John H. Flavell (New York: Oxford University Press, 1969), pp. 67-120.

operations are not automatically extended to all content areas. A young person must construct each content area on the formal operational plane, and this takes time and effort as well as interest. Sex differences in formal operational tasks suggest also that young men and women differentially apply their formal operational thinking skills.[11]

Accordingly, a subject's failure to succeed on a formal operational task does not provide an infallible index to the attainment of formal operations. Ideally, one would want to assess formal operations in many different domains before asserting that a subject had not attained this level of development. When ethnic and/or socio-cultural differences are involved as well, the diagnosis of lack of formal operations becomes even more precarious. In assessing formal operations, then, one has to be wary of false negatives. While success on a measure of formal operations provides an index of the presence of those skills, failure is no sure sign of their absence.

Before closing this discussion one more complication should be added. The distinction between performance and competence may well vary with the child's level of development. For example, during a cognitive growth cycle, when mental structures are in the process of formation, performance is very closely tied to competence.[12] At such times, young people are intrinsically motivated to perform at their very best. It is only after the structures have been formed and the intrinsic growth motivation has dissipated that performance becomes progressively dissociated from competence. In practical terms what this means is that the best time to assess formal operations is probably early adolescence when they are being formed. At that time young people are most likely to show the highest level of operativity of which they are capable.

Research Issues

When the development of intelligence is viewed as the pro-

11. David Elkind, "Quantity Conceptions in Junior and Senior High School Students," *Child Development* 32 (1961): 551-60; E. D. Hobbs, "Adolescents' Concepts of Physical Quantity," *Developmental Psychology* 9 (November 1973): 431; C. Tomlinson-Keasey, "Formal Operations in Females from Eleven to Fifty-four Years of Age," *Developmental Psychology* 6 (March 1972): 364.

12. David Elkind, *Child Development and Education* (New York: Oxford University Press, 1976).

gressive elaboration of more complex forms in relation to age, a number of different research issues are suggested. Many of these have been extensively explored, and all have relevance to educational practice. A brief review of some of these issues and how they bear on education is provided here.

THE UNIVERSALITY OF FORMAL OPERATIONS

By definition, forms are universal in the sense of being common to all members of the species. The age at which these forms appear, however, will vary with individual circumstances. Likewise, since the stages are hierarchical, not all individuals may attain the final stages because of either genetic or environmental limitations. Clearly, the older organism is more variable, due to social-cultural conditioning, than the young one. Hence one would expect greater variability of forms at the older age levels.

This, indeed, is what has been found. For example, I have shown elsewhere that volume conservation, a formal operational task, was not attained by a majority of young people of college age. I also found that boys were significantly more successful in attaining formal operations than were girls.[13] These differences have since been replicated by others.[14] There are at least three different interpretations of these findings (a) not all individuals of average ability attain formal operations, (b) all individuals of average ability attain formal operations but do not develop them in all content domains, (c) all individuals of average ability attain formal operations but at different times. Some individuals attain them much later than others.

The correct interpretation will, of course, have to wait upon further research data. In the meantime, however, the educational implication is clear cut. We cannot assume that all young people who are moving into junior high schools or middle schools have

13. David Elkind, "Quantity Conceptions in College Students," *Journal of Social Psychology* 57 (August 1962): 459-65.

14. L. G. Dale, "The Growth of Systematic Thinking: Replication and Analysis of Piaget's First Chemical Experiment," *Australian Journal of Psychology* 22 (December 1970) 277-86; Avis J. Graves, "Attainment of Conservation of Mass, Weight, and Volume in Minimally Educated Adults," *Developmental Psychology* 7 (September 1972): 223; Milton Shwebel, *Logical Thinking in College Freshmen*, Final Report, Project No. O-B-105 (New Brunswick, N.J.: Rutgers University, April 1972).

attained formal operations. And yet that is just what the curriculum at these levels assumes. The relation between curriculum and formal operations will be discussed more fully below. Here we need only stress that the difficulties some young people encounter when entering secondary schools may have to do with lack of fit between mental ability and curriculum.

A second research issue has to do with the relation between the attainment of formal operations and performance at lower levels. One approach to this problem is that of regression,[15] which assumes that circumstances can cause an individual to function at a lower level than that of which they are capable and than that called for by the task. But there is another way of looking at the problem. Are the formal operational subjects more or less able to shift their mental organization to suit the cognitive level of the task? Put differently, do formal operations enhance or impede a subject's mental flexibility and ability to deal with problems at different levels of complexity?

My colleagues and I have looked at this issue in several studies.[16] The question was whether adolescents were more ready than were children to shift their conceptual orientation in relation to the difficulty of the task. Concept-production tasks (the ability to produce concepts to particular stimuli) were employed, and children and adolescents were asked to produce concepts to objects, pictures, and words. By and large, adolescents produced the most concepts, regardless of the stimuli employed. They were able to shift their conceptual orientation in keeping with the conceptual level of the task much more easily than were children. These results suggest that formal operations facilitate rather than constrain mental flexibility in problem-solving situations.

15. David J. Bearison, "The Construct of Regression: A Piagetian Approach," *Merrill Palmer Quarterly* 20 (January 1974): 21-30.

16. David Elkind, "Conceptual Orientation Shifts in Children and Adolescents," *Child Development* 37 (September 1966): 493-98; David Elkind, Ralph Barocas, and Peter Johnsen, "Concept Production in Children and Adolescents," *Human Development* 12, no. 1 (1969): 10-21; David Elkind, Louis Medvene, and Anne S. Rockway, "Representational Level and Concept Production in Children and Adolescents," *Developmental Psychology* 2 (January 1970): 85-89.

FORMAL OPERATIONS AND CURRICULUM

From an educational perspective the domain that is wide open for systematic research relates to formal operations and the curriculum. Karplus and his colleagues have been active in this area, but primarily in the domain of science.[17] And there is considerable work being done at the college level, again primarily in the science domain. But there is relatively little work being done among early adolescents. The work of Epstein and Toepfer, while intriguing, is to my mind still very general and conjectural.[18]

What I have in mind is a more fine-grained analysis of the sort I have discussed elsewhere. Consider first the content of a subject such as algebra. The difficulty young people encounter in learning algebra derives in part from what I have called the logical substructure of the task. This logical substructure consists of the mental operations necessary to deal successfully with the material. The logical substructure of a task, however, is not obvious and usually has to be discovered empirically rather than by theoretical or conceptual analysis.

Consider a young man struggling with the equation $(a + b)^2 = a^2 + 2ab + b^2$. While he grasps that the equation works for two numbers, say 3 and 4, he cannot grasp that it holds for all numbers. In effect, he believes that the letters stand for specific numbers rather than any numbers. Nor does he grasp that a and b can both represent the same number. Formal operations, which enable young people to separate form from content and to recognize that a single form can represent many contents, are clearly required in order for a young person to understand algebra. As suggested earlier, formal operations cannot be assumed merely because a young person is a certain age or pubescent. Some assessment of formal operational ability should be made before young people are introduced to algebra.

A similar argument could be made for an interpretative approach to literature. Certainly young people should be encouraged

17. Robert Karplus, "Opportunities for Concrete and Formal Thinking in Science Tasks" (paper presented at the third annual meeting of the Jean Piaget Society, Philadelphia, 1973).

18. Herman T. Epstein and Conrad F. Toepfer, Jr., "A Neuroscience Basis for Reorganizing Middle Grades Education," *Educational Leadership* 35 (May 1978): 656-60.

to read good authors and poets and to think and to talk about what they have read. But it really does not help a young person to be asked "What did the author (poet) have in mind when he wrote this book (poem)?" Such a question goes beyond a grasp of the theme or symbolism of the work and asks the young person to hypothesize about intentions. For a young person moving into formal operations, understanding complex plots and metaphorical language presents problems enough without their having to speculate about a writer's intentions, and yet that is what many are asked to do.

Put somewhat differently, there are probably levels of understanding of literature. For preschool children, plots are simple, characters are one-dimensional, and much of the pleasure of the story or poem comes from the music of the language. Once children move into concrete operations, they can begin to appreciate more complex plots, one or more subplots, more rounded characters, and more variegated time and spatial frameworks. At adolescence, and if formal operations are attained, young people can deal with quite elaborately drawn characters, involved plots, and metaphorical language. But literary criticism and evaluation really have to wait upon the young person's having become comfortable with his or her new level of comprehension.

One can see a similar problem in science education. Basically, the attainment of formal operations is really a prerequisite to understanding experimental science. My own feeling is that young people are introduced to experimentation too early. The natural scientific activity for concrete operational children, as shown by their spontaneous hobbies, is collecting and classifying. Systematic collection is the natural base upon which any healthy science is founded. Rather than promote and capitalize upon this natural bent of school-age children, we try to teach them formal science. My guess is that many young people become disenchanted with science because they are presented with concepts and procedures that are far removed from what they can really understand or successfully execute.

Experimentation presupposes a rather broad conceptual base. First, it presupposes an understanding of quantification along one or many dimensions. Second, it involves an ability to analyze reality and to distinguish between reality and appearance—to recognize that two liquids of the same color can have different compositions or that a given substance is made up of many smaller elements called atoms and that the behavior of that substance depends upon the behavior of those atoms. In addition, young people have to grasp propositional logic that will enable them to understand how to test for effects by systematically varying quantities, materials, and so forth. Experimentation presupposes a sophistication of thought that many young adolescents simply do not possess.

These few examples should, perhaps, show the value of looking at curriculum materials from the standpoint of their logical and conceptual difficulty. The psychology of forms that Piaget has offered is really not a curriculum to be taught. It is, rather, a tool for curriculum analysis. This is important, because if we simply try to teach the Piagetian tasks, or to psychometrize them, we have lost their real value. The Piagetian forms do not tell us how or what to teach. They do tell us, once we know what we want to instruct young people in, how to do it most efficiently and effectively.

Summary and Conclusion

In this chapter I have attempted to present the developmental approach to the study of intelligence in young adolescents. The first section contrasted the developmental approach to the psychometric one. It was suggested that the developmental approach is concerned with intelligence as a form, an organization or succession of organizations that follow certain rules and that are characteristic of the species. In contrast, the psychometric approach is concerned with traits, dimensions upon which individuals can be assessed and arrayed. The psychology of forms sees adolescent intelligence as interesting in and of itself, while the psychology of traits sees it as continuous with the psychology of children and adults.

The next section briefly described the method used to assess formal operations, the form of adolescent intelligence. Assessment is complicated by the fact that not all individuals elaborate their formal operations in the same domains. Hence, a failure to show formal operations may only mean that the task content has not been conceptualized at that level, not that formal operations are lacking. It was suggested that the best time to assess formal operations is early adolescence, when the discrepancy between performance and competence is at a minimum.

Some of the issues in the study of formal operations have to do with their generality, with sex differences in their elaboration, and with their facilitation of thinking at different levels. A concluding section suggested a line of research that offers much promise. This line of research is the analysis of curriculum materials at the secondary level. The aim of such analysis is to bring the materials more closely into line with the mental abilities of the students they are designed for. In the end, the research and theory of Jean Piaget is best seen as providing tools for curriculum analysis and not a new curriculum.

CHAPTER XVI

Evaluative Studies

CAROL KEHR TITTLE

From a broad point of view, evaluation research has been a part of educational practice since the turn of the century.[1] The use of standardized tests or scales, however, had a longer history in education than the major concepts that presently inform the conduct of evaluation research. Early school surveys that resulted in changes in school practice were based on measuring individual differences in pupils' achievement. Although Tyler and later writers emphasized linking curricular objectives, instruction, and evaluation of pupils, they also expanded the conception of objectives to include the "higher mental processes" and a wide range of both cognitive and affective outcomes. These aspects of an educational program, however, are now being viewed differently in the practice of evaluation, with the result that evaluative research in education, in its best forms, will have more to offer researchers and practitioners concerned with understanding pupil growth and development in the early adolescent years.

1. Jack C. Merwin, "Historical Review of Changing Concepts of Evaluation," *Educational Evaluation: New Roles, New Means*, ed. Ralph W. Tyler, Sixty-eighth Yearbook of the National Society for the Study of Education, Part II (Chicago: University of Chicago Press, 1969), pp. 6-25. For the origins of evaluation research in the days of the Great Depression and the emergence of modern social research methodologies, see Howard E. Freeman, "The Present Status of Evaluation Research" in *Evaluation Studies Review Annual*, vol. 2, ed. Marcia Guttentag and Shalom Saar (Beverly Hills, Calif.: Sage Publications, 1977), pp. 17-51. An even broader perspective was taken by Hamilton, who traced the intellectual history of the ideas of scientific practice to John Stuart Mill and Francis Galton. See David Hamilton, "Making Sense of Curriculum Evaluation: Continuities and Discontinuities in an Educational Idea," in *Review of Research in Education*, vol. 5, ed. Lee S. Shulman (Itasca, Ill.: F. E. Peacock, 1977), pp. 318-347. Both Merwin and Hamilton consider the more formal beginning of evaluation in relation to the centralization of education and the cult of efficiency.

The purpose of this chapter is to contrast and compare evaluation research and educational research in general, and to identify major approaches and concepts that guide evaluation research studies. In the concluding section examples of evaluation studies that provide data about youth in early adolescence are presented.

It is well to note one caveat at the outset. The difficulty of gaining access to evaluation reports constitutes a major barrier to the use of evaluation research in contributing to fundamental knowledge in any area. Evaluation reports often contain data of interest to those concerned with youth in the middle grades, and such reports should be included as part of any review of the literature. Those reports may result in journal articles, which may readily be located through standard abstracting and indexing services, or they may appear in ERIC. Many reports of evaluations carried on at local, state, or even the federal level, however, never reach these sources of dissemination. The reports are disseminated to the funding source (local, state, or federal) and to those concerned with and involved in the evaluation. For the researcher or practitioner who wants to use this fugitive literature, the best procedure is to be alert to federal funding of programs that include studies of young adolescents and to contact the federal agency or the evaluation group for the reports. The examples included in this chapter are drawn from reports prepared for federal agencies and were requested from the evaluation group.

Lipsitz has provided an analysis of federal funding for research on adolescence.[2] Evaluation is included as one category of funding, and studies in that category showed decreasing percentages from fiscal year 1973 to fiscal year 1974. The estimates of 4 to 6 percent cited as the evaluation portion of total funding for research on adolescence in the fiscal year 1974 may be underestimates for later years, since there is continuing pressure at the federal level for evaluation of social programs.[3] It is to be hoped that these evaluations

2. Joan Lipsitz, *Growing Up Forgotten: A Review of Research and Programs Concerning Early Adolescence* (Lexington, Mass.: Lexington Books, 1977), pp. 56-74.

3. U.S. General Accounting Office, Program Analysis Division, *Evaluation and Analysis to Support Decision Making* (Washington, D.C.: Comptroller General of the United States, 1976). For comments on congressional use of program evaluation, which were made during hearings conducted by the Com-

will be increasingly seen as sources of basic information for researchers and practitioners concerned with early adolescence. This chapter provides evidence that evaluation research studies will contribute to our understanding, complementing those studies classified as basic or applied research.

The Programmatic Focus of Evaluation Studies

Definitions of evaluation are abundant and sometimes conflicting, yet there are commonalities in the discussions that are useful for identifying boundaries between evaluation research and other basic or applied research studies.[4] These boundaries can be described

mittee on Human Resources of the U.S. Senate on October 6 and 27, 1977, see "Hearings on the Cost, Management, and Utilization of Human Resources Program Evaluation," *Evaluation* (special issue, 1978) 8-30. Title VII of the 1974 Congressional Budget and Impoundment Control Act, "Program Review and Evaluation," empowers congressional committees to conduct, contract out, or request evaluations from government agencies. Also, the General Accounting Office was mandated to evaluate results of federal programs. Its reports provide information on evaluation research studies for the Office of Education Programs. See, for example, *Annual Evaluation Report on Programs Administered by the U.S. Office of Education, Fiscal Year 1976* (Washington, D.C.: Capitol Publications, 1977).

4. Research is broadly conceived here also, encompassing diverse ways of knowing and understanding human phenomena, and is not limited to the methods of knowing of the natural sciences. See, for example, Jurgen Habermas's critiques of the natural sciences as the model for the cultural sciences in *Knowledge and Human Interests* (Boston: Beacon Press, 1971). Paul Diesing distinguished between the holistic case-study approach and other methods in *Patterns of Discovery in the Social Sciences* (Chicago: Aldine-Atherton, 1971), and Severyn T. Bruyn examines the human character of the social sciences, with the resulting implications for theory and methods, in *The Human Perspective in Sociology: The Methodology of Participant Observation* (Englewood Cliffs, N.J.: Prentice-Hall, 1966). Glaser and Strauss provide an approach to developing theory that is reflected most directly in evaluation in Stake's discussion of "issues" as the focus of responsive evaluation. See Barney G. Glaser and Anselm L. Strauss, *The Discovery of Grounded Theory: Strategies for Qualitative Research* (Chicago: Aldine, 1967); and Robert E. Stake, "The Case Study Method in Social Inquiry," *Educational Researcher* 7 (February 1978): 5-8, and idem, "Program Evaluation, Particularly Responsive Evaluation," Occasional Paper No. 5 (Kalamazoo, Mich.: Evaluation Center, College of Education, Western Michigan University, 1975), pp. 9-15. The distinctions being drawn here are intended to assist the reader to understand the different context in which evaluation research is conducted. As other commentators have suggested, the differences are more conceptual than real when the skills required and methods employed in research and evaluation studies are examined in detail. See Jason Millman, *Selecting Educational Researchers and Evaluators*, T. M. Report No. 48 (Princeton, N.J.: ERIC Clearinghouse on Tests, Measurement, and Evaluation, Educational Testing Service, 1978). See also Scarvia B. Anderson and Samuel Ball, *The Profession and Practice of Program Evaluation* (San Francisco: Jossey-Bass, 1978), pp. 9-11.

in terms of the origin of the evaluation research study, the political and pragmatic nature of evaluation research, the program as the object of study, the role of the evaluator, the timing of studies, and the selection of variables for measurement. The boundaries also serve to identify benefits and limits to evaluation research as a source of basic information about early adolescence.

ORIENTATION TO PROGRAMS AND POLICY DECISIONS

The evaluation research study has its origin in a decision-oriented setting, where there are political concerns about the allocation of resources and power, and, therefore, a concern with efficiency and accountability of funded programs. Anderson and Ball have listed several major purposes for program evaluation: to contribute to decisions about program installation, modification, continuation, expansion, or certification; to obtain evidence to rally support for or opposition to a program; and to contribute to the understanding of basic psychological and social processes.[5] Except for the latter reason, these reasons for conducting an evaluation research study are in distinct contrast to the usual view of basic and applied research studies undertaken by individual investigators. Individual researchers are not decision oriented, except in the particular sense that their studies will contribute to the decisions about the next study to be undertaken, for example, decisions to eliminate variables from consideration or decisions that clarify the nature of relationships among variables of theoretical interest.

The "program," which may be a local school program on reading or a large-scale federally funded intervention, is the object of the evaluation study. The evaluation of a funded program in a decision-oriented setting is often perceived as placing the various constituencies of the program in the position of defending it. Whether or not the participants are accurate in their perceptions of a threat to the program, the result is a political setting in which the evaluator seeks to design, obtain consent for, conduct, and report a study from which the participants and administrators may

5. Anderson and Ball, *The Profession and Practice of Program Evaluation,* pp. 14-36.

have little to gain and much to lose.[6] The role of the evaluator, therefore, differs considerably from that of the investigator conducting research in which participants agree to the conditions of the study (or the conditions are negotiated) and participants do not view the research as a threat to the existence of any program.

Another difference is in the timing of the evaluation study and presentation of the results. The usefulness of the evaluation study is dependent on the results being available at the time decisions for funding are made; if the results are not available on schedule, decisions will still be made. Time pressures may necessitate compromises in design and measures. Other types of research studies do not face the pressure of external deadlines, and their results will be integrated into the research literature whenever they appear.

The selection of criterion or outcome variables for the evaluation research study also differentiates evaluation research from other research. Typically, outcome or process variables are not selected on the basis of a theoretical framework, but rather are determined by the goals and objectives of the program or the salient "issues" that emerge for evaluators, depending on the evaluator's approach.[7] Variables that may be of substantive interest to researchers may not be of interest to the sponsors of the program evaluation. Cost and resources available may also limit the type or number of variables measured.

A further difference that separates evaluation from other research relates to a concern with values. While individual researchers may be aware of the values that guide their choice of research topic and methods of research, the evaluator's role and the political setting do more than bring values to the level of awareness. There

6. Carol H. Weiss, "Evaluation Research in the Political Context," in *Handbook of Evaluation Research,* vol. 1, ed. Elmer L. Struening and Marcia Guttentag (Beverly Hills, Calif.: Sage Publications, 1975), pp. 13-26. Weiss clarifies the nature of the organizational setting of programs and the political implications of evaluation. The inherently political nature of evaluation of experimental programs is stressed by Gideon Sjoberg, "Politics, Ethics and Evaluation Research," in *Handbook of Evaluation Research,* vol. 2, ed. Guttentag and Saar, pp. 29-51, and by Richard A. Berk and Peter H. Rossi, "Doing Good or Worse: Evaluation Research Politically Reexamined," ibid., pp. 77-90.

7. Stake has distinguished between preordinate and responsive evaluation studies, the first emphasizing goals and objectives, and the second emphasizing issues as an organizing structure for planning and data collection. See Stake, "Program Evaluation, Particularly Responsive Evaluation."

is a growing concern with the values of different groups that have an interest in the outcomes of evaluation studies and with ways in which the interests of these groups may be represented in the evaluation. The writings of Stake, House, Guttentag, and Scriven particularly reflect this concern, although in different ways.[8]

BENEFITS AND LIMITATIONS OF THE PROGRAMMATIC FOCUS

One of the benefits of the programmatic focus of evaluation, particularly as evidenced in large-scale evaluations of federal programs, is that the evaluation studies may be interdisciplinary in orientation. The evaluators for one of the studies cited later in this chapter include social psychologists and specialists in communications and media, as well as curriculum and research specialists. The emphasis on clarifying and defining both goals and objectives leads to debate and to analysis of appropriate measures of outcomes. Evaluation sponsors will review the planned measures and often provide for critiques by other evaluators or subject-matter specialists. Similarly, more attention is likely to be paid to the reliability and validity of outcome measures in large-scale evaluations. If standard measures are not available, classroom observation and pupil measures are often developed and field tested for the particular evaluation study.

The limitations of evaluative studies for developing basic knowledge have been mentioned in contrasting research and evaluation. Limitations include the restrictions on the design and outcome measures due to the sponsor's purposes, the political compromises that may further weaken design and narrow consideration of measures used to collect data, and the fundamental limitations due to the practical rather than theoretical origin of the study.

Major Approaches to Evaluation Studies

The major approaches to evaluation studies are briefly mentioned here to demonstrate the potential use of these approaches in

8. See Robert E. Stake, "Objectives, Priorities, and Other Judgment Data," *Review of Educational Research* 40 (April 1970): 181-212. See also, David K. Cohen, "Politics and Research: Evaluation of Social Action Programs in Education," ibid., pp. 213-38; Harold Berlak, "Values, Public Policy, and Educational Evaluation," ibid., pp. 261-78; Ernest R. House, "Justice in Evaluation," in *Evaluation Studies Review Annual*, vol. 1, ed. Gene V Glass (Beverly Hills, Calif.: Sage Publications, 1976), pp. 75-100; Marcia Guttentag, "Subjectivity and Its Use in Evaluation," *Evaluation* 1, no. 2 (1973): 60-75; Michael Scriven, "Pros and Cons about Goal-free Evaluation," in *Evaluation in Education*, ed. W. J. Popham (Berkeley, Calif.: McCutchan Publishing Corp., 1974), pp. 34-43.

providing knowledge about youth aged ten to fifteen years who
are in transition between childhood and adolescence. In many of
the approaches, despite differences in terminology, there will be a
variety of methods used, including those that would be found in
basic or applied research. The approaches listed below are drawn
from analyses presented by Stake and by House.[9]

The institutional self-study by staff (and accreditation teams),
the blue ribbon panel, and the art criticism approaches to evaluation
have as their general purposes the review of staff and institutional
effectiveness and the key element is the use of professionals to review and observe the work of other professionals. Another group
of approaches emphasizes decision making and analyses of social
policy, the use of behavioral objectives and students' gains, and
sometimes instructional research (experimental methods). These
approaches emphasize definition of program goals (although un-
intended outcomes are also included) and subject objectives. Any
evaluation study of a program for early adolescents using these approaches may well include data that will be of basic interest. The
so-called adversary approach may also yield useful data, collected
for the quasi-legal procedures presenting the pros and cons of a
program.

The final approach to be mentioned here is the transaction/
responsive approach. This approach focuses on the transactions
(classrooms, schools, districts) in the educational process and is
likely to use the methodologies of participant observation and of
the case study. The approach is represented in *Case Studies in Science Education*, which is presented as one of the examples in the
next section of this chapter.

Most evaluation studies have the potential to include data of
interest to researchers concerned with early adolescence. The labels
used here to identify various approaches serve more to remind
evaluators of the complexities of evaluating educational phenomena
and of the emphasis in a particular evaluation study than to limit
evaluators' methodological or substantive interests, or their in-
genuity.

9. Stake, "Program Evaluation, Particularly Responsive Evaluation," p. 33;
Ernest R. House, "Assumptions Underlying Evaluation Models," *Educational
Researcher* 7 (March 1978): 4-12.

Major Concepts in Evaluation and Illustrative Studies

Along with the various approaches to evaluation mentioned thus far, a number of concepts have become prominent. Their definition will assist the reader to identify the type of information that may appear in an evaluation study. These concepts include: needs assessment; formative and summative evaluation; comparison groups (experiments and quasi-experiments versus naturalistic description and case studies); and secondary analysis and meta-evaluation. The formative and summative concepts, and the case study, will be used to illustrate the kinds of knowledge about the early adolescent age group that can be gained from evaluation studies.

NEEDS ASSESSMENT

"The process by which one identifies needs and decides upon priorities among them has been termed 'needs assessment'."[10] An example of needs assessment that included secondary pupil data, as well as opinions of principals, teachers, and central administrators, was a needs assessment in crime prevention and drug education, conducted by the Dallas Independent School District.[11] An inventory was used and the desired and actual levels of performance on program objectives were estimated. Thus, needs assessment data are likely to be obtained through surveys, respondents may include students as well as school staff, and these assessments frequently focus on other than the basic skills areas of the curriculum.

FORMATIVE AND SUMMATIVE EVALUATION

In making a distinction between the role and goals of evaluation, Scriven distinguished two roles: the role of formative evaluation is to discover deficiencies and successes in the intermediate versions of a new curriculum (or program), while the role of summative evaluation is to provide an overall, that is, terminal or outcome

10. Scarvia Anderson et al., *Encyclopedia of Educational Evaluation* (San Francisco: Jossey-Bass, 1975), p. 254.

11. C. LaVor Lyn, "Needs Assessment in Crime Prevention and Drug Education for 1975-76," in *Abstracts of Research and Evaluation Reports, 1975-76* (Dallas, Tex.: Dallas Independent School District, 1976), pp. 276-80. See also, "Results on the System-wide Survey of Drug Usage, 1973-74," ibid., pp. 281-83, which provides data for each of grades five through twelve for each of five years.

judgment of the merit or worth of a program (also called "impact evaluation").[12] An example of the formative role of evaluation is the evaluation directed by Williams of the Annenberg School of Communications for "Project Freestyle," a "Television Career Awareness" project sponsored by the National Institute of Education. The evaluator's reports to date are presented in an executive summary and in a technical report.[13]

The goal of the Television Career Awareness Project (TV CAP) is to expand career awareness by increasing knowledge and influencing attitudes and behaviors through an interrelated set of broadcast and nonbroadcast experiences for girls and boys of majority and minority backgrounds, ages nine through twelve. These experiences are designed to increase understanding of: [the] relationship of current interest and activities to educational progress and career development; career opportunities; [and] sex-role stereotyping, and ethnicity as it is affected by sex-role stereotyping.[14]

The curriculum is a series of television programs called "Freestyle." The programs can be shown as twenty-two fifteen-minute segments for classroom use or eleven half-hour programs for home broadcast. The series is accompanied by guides for teachers and parents, by supplementary comic books for pupils, and by community outreach activities and in-service training for parents and teachers.

The formative evaluation data were collected to assess the entry level beliefs, attitudes, and behaviors of pupils aged nine to twelve pertaining to career opportunities and particularly to sex-role stereotyping. The data also focused on gauging the pupils' reactions to

12. Michael Scriven, "The Methodology of Evaluation," in *Perspectives of Curriculum Evaluation*, ed. Ralph W. Tyler et al. (Chicago: Rand McNally, 1967), pp. 39-83.

13. Frederick Williams et al., *Project Freestyle National Evaluation Results: Executive Summary* (Los Angeles: University of Southern California, 1977); idem, *Technical Report of Formative Evaluation Baseline Studies on Children's Career Awareness and Sex-role Stereotypes for the Television Career Awareness Project* (Los Angeles: University of Southern California, 1978). For a review of the literature on career awareness covering ages three through twelve, see Aimée Dorr Leifer and Gerald S. Lesser, *The Development of Career Awareness in Young Children* (Washington, D.C.: National Institute of Education, 1976).

14. Williams et al., *Technical Report*, p. 1.

prototypical media. A panel of 666 upper-elementary school children was used. Grades four through six, boys and girls, and white, black, and Hispanic ethnic groups were represented, with the data being analyzed in a 3 × 2 × 3 design. Because of the groups represented in the sample, the number of measures related to careers and to sex-role stereotyping, and the construction of a typology of sex-role attitudes, these data will be of interest to researchers and practitioners concerned with the development of role expectations in activities and work, and with the nature of stereotyping in relation to sex roles. The nature of prejudices and of stereotypes seems to be an underresearched area in the literature on development, so that these data should be of considerable interest to those who work with children in the middle school.

Among the measures used were semantic differential scales on personality characteristics (perceptions of self and "most boys" and "most girls"), preferences for sex-typed play activities (with data that up-date preferences measured in 1960), preferences for activities used in a vocational choice instrument (John Holland's *Self-Directed Search*), aspirations for adult occupations, and attitudes toward the role of girls.

Data on television viewing habits were also included. Martin Fishbein's "expectancy value theory" was used to construct a measure of channels through which to reach important sources of social influence in the pupil's life (parents, teachers, peers). The data were used to suggest media content, for example, significant others to model.

Other researchers who are more interested in the media and attitude change will find much of interest in the data on pupil responses to the pilot television series, particularly since in the viewing sessions audience response devices were used to record data automatically for computer analysis. Items were constructed to measure pupils' responses to appeal, comprehension, message reception, character perceptions, and believability for each type of television format. Open-response interviews were also used to follow up the structured-choice questions.

The formative evaluation data led to major changes in the format of the television shows, and current shows bear little relationship to the cartoon, fast-paced, "Electric Company" format of the early pilots. Of particular interest are the effects on comprehension of attempts in the initial format to define and show examples of stereotyping directly. Items related to conceptual understanding ("What is stereotyping?") were least understood. Stereotyping presented in a rhythmic, fast-paced style with attractive main characters was not perceived negatively, and some children even thought stereotyping was when girls did "boy-things" or vice versa! The data provide valuable information for researchers concerned with these areas of early adolescent development. In addition to the formative evaluation data, the final television series itself would offer many opportunities for researchers to examine adolescents' responses to specific stimulus situations provided within the story format used for the broadcast series.

Another television series is also under development for young adolescents.[15] The National Science Foundation is sponsoring a series for eight- to twelve-year olds, and the development effort includes baseline and continuous evaluation studies, as in Project Freestyle. Again, these data will be of value in providing further knowledge about youth of this age group.

An example of the summative role of evaluation will be provided by the evaluation of Project Freestyle, directed by Johnston for the Institute for Social Research.[16] The evaluation will provide evidence of accountability (federal money spent for a product that meets the sponsor's specifications); consumer information (product information for potential decisions on adoption); policy guidance (evidence on the impact of an intervention such as "Freestyle"); and basic information (data on the nature of sex-role stereotypes and the possibilities or effects of intervening). The evaluation will examine school viewing, home viewing, and use of nonbroadcast materials and activities. The data, collected in the fall and winter of 1978-79, will provide further basic information about the age group.

"Program implementation" and "process" are concepts that are also of concern in summative evaluation. These terms call attention

15. Constance Holden, "Science Show for Children Being Developed for TV," *Science* 202 (November 17, 1978): 730-31.

16. Jerome Johnston, "Research Design for Summative Evaluation of 'Freestyle'" (Paper presented at the annual meeting of the American Educational Research Association, Toronto, March 1978).

to the degree to which planned program activities and processes are actually implemented and permit a better understanding of the relationship between actual program activities and effectiveness measures.

COMPARISON GROUPS

The term "comparison groups" is being used to represent the evaluation problem of providing meaningful comparative data, that is, how are evaluation data placed in perspective so as to be useful in making decisions pertaining to the worth of something? The traditional approaches have been to compare students' achievement against norm groups or against control groups of students, where the design for the control group ranges from a true experimental design to quasi-experimental designs using statistical adjustments to equate groups.[17] Another approach is through the use of naturalistic and case-study methods,[18] relying primarily upon participant observers who are knowledgeable enough about educational processes and their participants to identify salient issues and provide the final integration for an overall evaluation. Since the use of this methodology in evaluation is relatively recent, an example will be useful to illustrate its potential for providing basic information about young adolescents.

Stake and Easley directed a large-scale application of case study methodology to the evaluation of a program of science education (kindergarten through grade twelve) for the National Science Foundation.[19] Eleven high schools and their associated elementary and junior high schools were selected to provide diversity on such characteristics as rural-urban, geographic location, racial com-

---

17. For a recent discussion of these design considerations, see Thomas D. Cook and Donald T. Campbell, "The Design and Conduct of Quasi-Experiments and True Experiments in Field Settings," in *Handbook of Industrial and Organizational Psychology*, ed. Marvin D. Dunnette (Chicago: Rand McNally, 1976), pp. 223-326. For an expanded discussion, see idem, *The Design and Analysis of Quasi-Experiments in Field Settings* (Chicago: Rand McNally, 1979).

18. See footnote 4 for relevant references.

19. Robert E. Stake and Jack A. Easley, Jr., *Case Studies in Science Education* (Urbana, Ill.: Center for Instructional Research and Curriculum Evaluation, University of Illinois, 1978). The publication consists of twelve case-study booklets, an overview, three booklets of findings, and an executive summary.

position, socio-economic level, and innovative and traditional schools. Field observers prepared case studies of the eleven sites, a national survey of science-related questions was conducted, and the results were integrated on the basis of major "issues" for the National Science Foundation on the status of science education and its improvement.

The major findings, ranging across kindergarten through grade twelve, were that: (a) science education is being affected by the back-to-basics movement across the country; (b) the teaching of science content is preempted often by the socialization aim of teachers (and their concern with student motivation); (c) teaching is predominantly text-bound, with student recitation, particularly at the junior high school level; (d) there is a lack of articulation of science and mathematics content for schools at different levels, and even at the same level within districts; and (e) there is a generally low priority for science education. Particular concerns at the junior high school level relate to reading skills, student motivation for school work, and, as at the high school level, the mainstreaming of classes, and dealing with the children who engage in disruptive behavior.

The value of the case study is apparent in the detailed case material in the site studies. Most provide extensive transcripts of interactions of teachers and students in junior high school classes in mathematics or science. Walker's poignant descriptions of individual students in a small community "in the heart of Dixie" also suggest the use of the evaluation case studies as potential sources of research hypotheses about students in this period of transition.[20] Walker makes it clear that understanding the student in the junior high school in many instances involves understanding the educational part of the total environment with which students interact as part of their developmental process. The socialization efforts of teachers, parental attitudes toward education, issues of desegregation and prejudice, and the small-town environment need to be understood for their role in the socio-emotional and vocational development of young adolescents. The case study descriptions hint at the potential contribution of this evaluation approach.

20. Rob Walker, *Case Studies in Science Education: Pine City*, Booklet VI (Urbana, Ill.: Center for Instructional Research and Curriculum Evaluation, University of Illinois, 1977).

SECONDARY ANALYSIS AND META-EVALUATION

Secondary analysis is concerned with the reanalysis of data from a primary study. A classic example is found in the reanalyses of data in the Coleman report on equality of educational opportunity.[21] Cook and others provide another example in their reanalysis of the data from the evaluation of "Sesame Street" conducted by Ball and Bogatz.[22]

Meta-evaluation, as discussed by Stufflebeam,[23] may include secondary analyses of primary evaluation data, but goes beyond that. Meta-evaluation includes setting criteria to evaluate plans for evaluation and establishing criteria to evaluate completed studies with respect to the goals of the evaluation, the evaluation design, the processes of evaluation, and the evaluation results. Questions of cost effectiveness may also be examined. While some secondary analyses may be of concern to basic understanding, a meta-evaluation is likely to be of most interest to other professional evaluators, unless reanalyses of data indicate inaccuracies in the data and/or in the interpretations of those data.

Summary

Evaluation research is broadening its scope, both in the variety of methods and basic concepts that provide the paradigm or framework within which evaluators work. In this chapter some of the differences between evaluation research and other basic or applied research have been described, some current approaches and major concepts of the current framework have been presented, and types of information that may contribute to basic knowledge in other fields have been illustrated. These examples have focused on the early adolescent age group with which readers of this yearbook

21. Frederick Mosteller and Daniel P. Moynihan, *On Equality of Educational Opportunity* (New York: Vintage Books, 1972).

22. Samuel Ball and Gerry Ann Bogatz, *The First Year of "Sesame Street": An Evaluation* (Princeton, N.J.: Educational Testing Service, 1970); idem, *The Second Year of "Sesame Street": A Continuing Evaluation*, 2 vols. (Princeton, N.J.: Educational Testing Service, 1971); Thomas D. Cook et al., *"Sesame Street" Revisited: A Case Study in Evaluation Research* (New York: Russell Sage Foundation, 1975).

23. Daniel L. Stufflebeam, "Meta-Evaluation," Occasional Paper No. 3 (Kalamazoo, Mich.: Evaluation Center, Western Michigan University, 1974).

are concerned. Researchers and practitioners who become aware of the contributions of evaluation research to basic knowledge will be in a position to make full use of its potential.

SECTION FOUR

EPILOGUE

CHAPTER XVII

Tasks for the School in the Middle

MAURITZ JOHNSON

In this yearbook, authorities in a variety of scholarly and professional specializations have examined various aspects of the stage of development encompassing pre- and early adolescence, to which we have occasionally and somewhat hesitantly applied the label "transescence." Whether this term will ever become widely accepted cannot be predicted, but it should not be misconstrued. It connotes the period that begins when the first members of an age-cohort become pubescent and ends when the last ones finally reach puberty. It does not imply that the period itself is merely transitional, for it is far too important in its own right; nor does it suggest that each individual is undergoing a transition throughout, for those occasions are relatively brief. But unlike all other times in life, when one can count on one's age-mates to be like oneself, whether children, adolescents, or adults, this period of four to five years' duration is one in which each individual, whatever his or her own development status, must continuously deal with a mixed and shifting configuration among classmates and friends. It is not an easy task.

As a yearbook in education, this volume is particularly pertinent to the concerns of those associated professionally with the "school in the middle." One of its principal messages, however, is how extremely important it is that all adults who deal with members of this age-group be aware of the totality of their life-space and of the efforts of others to intervene in their behalf. It is, of course, impossible within the covers of one book to include all facets of development, all aspects of the environment, all efforts at intervention, all subgroups with special problems. Omission of certain topics in no way implies that they are unimportant.

Nevertheless, it is paradoxical that, while far too much is known about this age-group to be included in a single volume, what we do *not* know is even more impressive. Hence, even at the expense of other important topics, the final section was devoted to a few promising approaches to the research that is so badly needed. Clearly, however, we already know more than we act upon in our various efforts to educate, socialize, protect, and bring up our children as they approach and enter adolescence.

The contributors to the yearbook, writing from different vantage points and without communicating with each other, have some-times echoed and sometimes contradicted each other, confirming some things we have long known, exploding some of our myths, providing some new insights, and reviving some old controversies. In this seventieth anniversary year of the earliest junior high schools, it is reassuring to find that some of the things our counterparts of 1910 knew about transescence are still valid today. What new knowledge and insights we have are in part the results of con-tinuing inquiry, but in part they merely serve to remind us that times have changed since then. Our adult recollections of what it was like to be growing up can be deceptive if we fail to keep in mind that to one degree or another all of us adults grew up in another world.

Still, there is a distinction between what is no longer true and what never was the case. To disabuse ourselves of myths may be one of the most constructive things we can do. Discovering truth and keeping up with change are by no means easy, however, and in the face of conflicting evidence, honorable people often disagree on what is and is not true. In many apparent controversies, both sides are correct in certain respects and under certain cir-cumstances. Our task should be to determine those respects and circumstances, keeping in mind that even when they do agree on the facts, well-meaning people often differ as to the best course of action in the light of them.

Moreover, courses of action that are wise for certain individuals under certain conditions can be unwise in other situations. Par-ticularly with a diverse and changing age-group, there is always the danger of expecting or demanding either too much or too little, of exposing some individuals to experiences beyond their level of maturity, while stultifying others through childish treatment and unchallenging requirements. The sensitiveness and sensibleness required of parents, teachers, counselors, physicians, police, judges, social workers, group leaders, and others in dealing with this age-group make it hazardous to draw any general conclusions from the vast amount of material presented here. What rules can be offered when what is appropriate for one individual may not be for the next and what was last week appropriate for either of them may not be today?

But if the yearbook does not offer prescriptions, it does raise many questions that deserve to be discussed within, among, and beyond our various collegial groups. Some pertain to the society as a whole, some to schools in particular, some to everyone who works with transescents. Society in general must, for example, consider whether the "marginal role" currently assigned adolescents is the best one we can devise, whether status offenses ought to be deinstitutionalized, and whether we are going to insist on the separation of young offenders and older criminals in our detention facilities. The responsibility for initiating and pursuing discussions of these and other issues falls on all who are concerned with this age-group. Similarly, all concerned institutions and agencies need to consider what readjustments will be required in view of the fact that successive age-cohorts approaching adolescence in the United States are getting smaller; what steps can be taken to reverse the rising rate of admission to mental institutions at this age level; what it means for sex education that this is the only age-group in which the birth rate is increasing; and whether, in view of the observation that young adolescents now respond to experiences that a decade ago would have been associated with youth three to five years older, efforts should be directed at resisting and reversing the tendency or at adjusting programs to accommodate it.

All concerned parties should also consider whether the greater increase in arrests among girls in this age-group is to be dismissed as an inevitable consequence of "liberation" or viewed as an indication that the traditional underserving of girls by both schools and youth agencies needs to be rectified. Discussions might explore the significance of such apparently unrelated observations as that most status offenders are girls, that television viewing declines during transescence, that the 45 rpm record and the entire pop music industry exist primarily for girls making the transition from dolls to boys, and that the parents of many children of this age are confronting a mid-life transition of their own. In addition, the usefulness of a number of concepts employed in the volume merits some discussion by workers at this level: imaginary audience, taste culture, the dual integrations of sexuality and intimacy and of peer and parent norms, a generalized empathic distress capability as a basis for moral behavior, and the personal fable, with its implicit danger of construing one's uniqueness as immunity from consequences that befall other human beings.

Other concepts are of particular significance to teachers in middle and junior high schools: the three "metas"—metacognition, metalinguistic awareness, and metaphoric ability; the reality and cooperative principles in the communication process; the "ten to twelve shift" to semiformal operations; the student as a legal person with education as a property right; and the many constructs associated with meaningful verbal learning, such as cognitive structure, nonarbitrary and substantive relatability, progressive differentiation, ideational anchorage, and obliterative subsumption. Serious discussions among educators are needed on such topics as how the schools can become more sensitive to mental growth plateaus, which were first reported during the 1950s and are now confirmed by brain periodization studies; how frustration and the fear of failure in school can be reduced, in view of their serious emotional consequences and association with juvenile delinquency; and what alternative to the grade organization of middle and junior high schools might be more consistent with the realities of development at that stage.

School personnel also ought to consider what can be done to promote a sense of optimism and determination among transescents from lower socioeconomic backgrounds, who begin at this time to view the future as hopeless and school as useless, while their more favored peers are growing in self-confidence and see life as promising; what help minority children can be given in dealing with the conflicting expectations of school and neighborhood at the same time that they are negotiating the transition to adolescence; and what the implications are of the finding that this is the only period in which being in an integrated classroom does not appear to enhance the achievement of black pupils. The matter of reading also warrants special attention, for while linguistic competence increases during this period, interest in reading tends to decline, probably due to such factors as competition from other activities, its association with adults and the higher socioeconomic and intelligence levels, the stigma of seeming antisocial that attaches to any solitary pursuit, and the fact that no admired models are ever seen engaged in reading. Yet, the age-group does read its special magazines, science fiction, movie paperbacks, and the books of selected authors, such as Judy Blume, along with listening to recordings of "pube" rock. What significance, if any, does all this have for the methods and materials of instruction?

Perhaps the most fruitful and interesting discussion of all would be one in which parents, teachers, and everyone else concerned about the age-group contemplated how we would act differently if we abandoned all of our erroneous assumptions about it, if we could avoid viewing as typical those tendencies that only represent an increase over earlier stages or former generations. What changes would occur in our practices, for example, if we reminded ourselves frequently that for most children this is not a period of great storm and stress; that most do not experience a serious "identity crisis"; that for most there is no serious "generation gap"; that rebelliousness, while more common than at earlier ages, is not typical; that despite its critical importance the peer group is not really "tyrannical," its influence being limited for the most part to trivial matters; that most teenagers continue to maintain close relationships with their parents and value their advice on important questions; and that few students at this age level become fully functional cognitively at the stage of formal operations?

Beyond discussing the many questions raised by the yearbook, we need to do three things: act wisely, learn more, and work together. It will help us in acting wisely to adopt the stance of "authoritative parenting," in which we recognize that although we may not know as much as we would like about this age-group, we do know something and we have a moral obligation to use all the wisdom our experience has given us in our interventions in their behalf. It is possible to avoid both the arrogant authoritarian assumption that adults know everything and the pusillanimous permissive position that they know nothing about what is in the best interest of children during the transescent years.

At the same time we need to learn more about this period of development. Transescence has been a neglected area of research, within which a large number of scholars in a variety of disciplines should be encouraged to undertake carefully designed studies both in schools and in other contexts. Those of us who do not do research have the obligation to cooperate in such studies and to use our influence to see that they are supported.

Finally, we need to work together in our intervention efforts. Readers whose field is education may have been surprised to learn of the existence of a National Collaboration for Youth and a National Juvenile Justice Program Collaboration. Both of these coalitions provide for a sharing of information about transescents; both promote a comprehensive system of community services and a sharing of resources; both reach out to the schools in one way or another. Do the schools reach back, or even recognize that other agencies know and care about children in this age-group and work with them and their families? The school has its distinctive functions and problems, but both are intertwined with those of other agencies. Teachers, counselors, and administrators in middle and junior high schools should take the lead in creating in every locality in the country a mechanism for coordinated community action in behalf of their clientele. By the year 2000, we should not only have learned more and acted wisely, but have found a way of working together.

Name Index

Subject Index

Accidents, during adolescence, 159-60

Adolescence: changes in attachment to parents during, 36-38; common health problems during, 151-59; definitions of, 11-13; disorders of sexual development during, 150-51; federal funding of research on, 296-97; major tasks of, 141-43; misconceptions about, 20-22; physical changes during, 136-39; rebelliousness during, 37-38. See also Adolescents, Early adolescence, Early adolescents, Transescence

Adolescents: age segregation of, in school and society, 29-30; attitudes of, toward race, 27; attitudes of, toward intimacy and sexuality, 45-48; concerns of, relating to sexuality, 142-43; depression and suicide among, 158-69; lack of homogeneity among, 20-21; myths pertaining to, 20-22; numbers of, in U.S., 10-11; nutritional requirements of, 143-45; requirements for healthy development of, 30-31; unemployment among, 28. See also Adolescence, Early adolescence, Early adolescents, Transescence

Advance organizers, as pedagogic devices, 246

Advertising, responses of children to, 91

American Psychiatric Association, 258

American Red Cross, 98, 107

Assimilation theory, 233-36

Association for Supervision and Curriculum Development, 279

Association of Junior Leagues, 105

Authoritarianism, in early adolescence, 19

Authoritative parents: achievement-oriented behavior of children in relation to, 48-49; authoritarian and permissive parents in contrast to, 34-35, 54-55

Autonomy: variations among adolescents in development of, 41-42; relative effects of peers and families on development of, 42-45

Bill of Rights protections, 187, 189, 191, 194

Behavior disorders: alternative approaches to research on, 262-66; findings of survey of, in children aged ten through fifteen (table), 259; importance of developmental context in relation to, 253; obstacles to research on, 266-67; patterns in, 260-61

Boy Scouts of America, 95, 97, 102

Boyce Medical Study, 274

Boys' Clubs of America, 101, 106, 111

Brain function, implications of research related to, 70-71

Brain growth: educational implications of studies of, 275-76; hiatus in, from ages twelve to fourteen, 64, 274

Brown v. Board of Education of Topeka, 188-201

Camp Fire Girls, Inc., 95, 97, 102, 111

Carnegie Unit, influence of, on junior high school programs, 269-70

Case study methodology, in evaluation studies, 306-7

Center for Youth Development and Research (University of Minnesota), 110

Childhood, changes in concept of, in relation to legal rights, 186-87

Cognition, changes in, related to changes in linguistic skills, 206-24

Cognitive conflict, in relation to moral development, 170-74, 182

Cognitive development: implications of study of periods of low brain growth for, 63-65; variations in, among students in middle schools, 63

Cognitive structure, of learners: idiosyncratic nature of, 236-37; role of, in acquiring new learnings, 233-49;

INFORMATION ABOUT MEMBERSHIP IN THE SOCIETY

From its small beginnings in the early 1900s, the National Society for the Study of Education has grown to a major educational organization with more than 4,000 members in the United States, Canada, and overseas. Members include professors, researchers, graduate students, and administrators in colleges and universities; teachers, supervisors, curriculum specialists, and administrators in elementary and secondary schools; and a considerable number of persons who are not formally connected with an educational institution. Membership in the Society is open to all persons who desire to receive its publications.

Since its establishment the Society has sought to promote its central purpose—the stimulation of investigations and discussions of important educational issues—through regular publication of a two-volume yearbook that is sent to all members. Many of these volumes have been so well received throughout the profession that they have gone into several printings. A recently inaugurated series of substantial paperbacks on Contemporary Educational Issues supplements the series of yearbooks and allows for treatment of a wider range of educational topics than can be addressed each year through the yearbooks alone.

Through membership in the Society one can add regularly to one's professional library at a very reasonable cost. Members also help to sustain a publication program that is widely recognized for its unique contributions to the literature of education.

The categories of membership, and the dues in each category for 1980, are as follows:

> *Regular.* The member receives a clothbound copy of each part of the two-volume yearbook (approximately 300 pages per volume). Annual dues, $15.
>
> *Comprehensive.* The member receives clothbound copies of the two-volume yearbook and the two volumes in the current paperback series. Annual dues. $28.
>
> *Retirees and Graduate Students.* Reduced dues—Regular, $12; Comprehensive $24.
> The above reduced dues are available to (a) those who have retired or are over sixty-five years of age and who have been members of the Society for at least ten years, and (b) graduate students in their first year of membership.

Life Membership. Persons sixty years of age or over may hold a Regular Membership for life upon payment of a lump sum based upon the life expectancy for their age group. Consult the Secretary-Treasurer for further details.

New members are required to pay an entrance fee of $1, in addition to the dues, in their first year of membership.

Membership is for the calendar year and dues are payable on or before January 1. A reinstatement fee of $.50 must be added to dues payments made after January 1.

In addition to receiving the publications of the Society as described above, members participate in the nomination and election of the six-member Board of Directors, which is responsible for managing the business and affairs of the Society, including the authorization of volumes to appear in the yearbook series. Two members of the Board are elected each year for three-year terms. Members of the Society who have contributed to its publications and who indicate a willingness to serve are eligible for election to the Board.

Members are urged to attend the one or more meetings of the Society that are arranged each year in conjunction with the annual meetings of major educational organizations. The purpose of such meetings is to present, discuss, and critique volumes in the current yearbook series. Announcements of meetings for the ensuing year are sent to members in December.

Upon written request from a member, the Secretary-Treasurer will send the current directory of members, synopses of meetings of the Board of Directors, and the annual financial report.

Persons desiring further information about membership may write to

KENNETH J. REHAGE, Secretary-Treasurer
National Society for the Study of Education

5835 Kimbark Ave.
Chicago, Ill. 60637

PUBLICATIONS OF THE NATIONAL SOCIETY FOR THE STUDY OF EDUCATION

1. The Yearbooks

NOTICE: Many of the early yearbooks of this series are now out of print. In the following list, those titles to which an asterisk is prefixed are not available for purchase.

*Fifteenth Yearbook, 1916, Part II—*The Relationship between Persistence in School and Home Conditions.* Charles E. Holley.

*Fifteenth Yearbook, 1916, Part III—*The Junior High School.* Aubrey A. Douglass.

*Sixteenth Yearbook, 1917, Part I—*Second Report of the Committee on Minimum Essentials in Elementary-School Subjects.* W. C. Bagley, W. W. Charters, F. N. Freeman, W. S. Gray, Ernest Horn, J. H. Hoskinson, W. S. Monroe, C. F. Munson, H. C. Pryor, L. W. Rapeer, G. M. Wilson, and H. B. Wilson.

*Sixteenth Yearbook, 1917, Part II—*The Efficiency of College Students as Conditioned by Age at Entrance and Size of High School.* B. F. Pittenger.

*Seventeenth Yearbook, 1918, Part I—*Third Report of the Committee on Economy of Time in Education.* W. C. Bagley, B. B. Bassett, M. E. Branom, Alice Camerer, J. E. Dealey, C. A. Ellwood, E. B. Greene, A. B. Hart, J. F. Hosic, E. T. Housh, W. H. Mace, L. R. Marston, H. C. McKown, H. E. Mitchell, W. V. Reavis, D. Snedden, and H. B. Wilson.

*Seventeenth Yearbook, 1918, Part II—*The Measurement of Educational Products.* E. J. Ashbaugh, W. A. Averill, L. P. Ayers, F. W. Ballou, Edna Bryner, B. R. Buckingham, S. A. Courtis, M. E. Haggerty, C. H. Judd, George Melcher, W. S. Monroe, E. A. Nifenecker, and E. L. Thorndike.

*Eighteenth Yearbook, 1919, Part I—*The Professional Preparation of High-School Teachers.* G. N. Cade, S. S. Colvin, Charles Fordyce, H. H. Foster, T. S. Gosling, W. S. Gray, L. V. Koos, A. R. Mead, H. L. Miller, F. C. Whitcomb, and Clifford Woody.

*Eighteenth Yearbook, 1919, Part II—*Fourth Report of Committee on Economy of Time in Education.* F. C. Ayer, F. N. Freeman, W. S. Gray, Ernest Horn, W. S. Monroe, and C. E. Seashore.

*Nineteenth Yearbook, 1920, Part I—*New Materials of Instruction.* Prepared by the Society's Committee on Materials of Instruction.

*Nineteenth Yearbook, 1920, Part II—*Classroom Problems in the Education of Gifted Children.* T. S. Henry.

*Twentieth Yearbook, 1921, Part I—*New Materials of Instruction.* Second Report by Society's Committee.

*Twentieth Yearbook, 1921, Part II—*Report of the Society's Committee on Silent Reading.* M. A. Burgess, S. A. Courtis, C. E. Germane, W. S. Gray, H. A. Greene, Regina R. Heller, J. H. Hoover, J. A. O'Brien, J. L. Packer, Daniel Starch, W. W. Theisen, G. A. Yoakam, and representatives of other school systems.

*Twenty-first Yearbook, 1922, Parts I and II—*Intelligence Tests and Their Use.* Part I—*The Nature, History, and General Principles of Intelligence Testing.* E. L. Thorndike, S. S. Colvin, Harold Rugg, G. M. Whipple, Part II—*The Administrative Use of Intelligence Tests.* H. W. Holmes, W. K. Layton, Helen Davis, Agnes L. Rogers, Rudolf Pintner, M. R. Trabue, W. S. Miller, Bessie L. Gambrill, and others. The two parts are bound together.

*Twenty-second Yearbook, 1923, Part I—*English Composition: Its Aims, Methods and Measurements.* Earl Hudelson.

*Twenty-second Yearbook, 1923, Part II—*The Social Studies in the Elementary and Secondary School.* A. S. Barr, J. J. Coss, Henry Harap, R. W. Hatch, H. C. Hill, Ernest Horn, C. H. Judd, L. C. Marshall, F. M. McMurry, Earle Rugg, H. O. Rugg, Emma Schweppe, Mabel Snedaker, and C. W. Washburne.

*Twenty-third Yearbook, 1924, Part I—*The Education of Gifted Children.* Report of the Society's Committee. Guy M. Whipple, Chairman.

*Twenty-third Yearbook, 1924, Part II—*Vocational Guidance and Vocational Education for Industries.* A. H. Edgerton and others.

*Twenty-fourth Yearbook, 1925, Part I—*Report of the National Committee on Reading.* W. S. Gray, Chairman, F. W. Ballou, Rose L. Hardy, Ernest Horn, Francis Jenkins, S. A. Leonard, Estaline Wilson, and Laura Zirbes.

*Twenty-fourth Yearbook, 1925, Part II—*Adapting the Schools to Individual Differences.* Report of the Society's Committee. Carleton W. Washburne, Chairman.

*Twenty-fifth Yearbook, 1926, Part I—*The Present Status of Safety Education.* Report of the Society's Committee. Guy M. Whipple, Chairman.

*Twenty-fifth Yearbook, 1926, Part II—*Extra-Curricular Activities.* Report of the Society's Committee. Leonard V. Koos, Chairman.

*Twenty-sixth Yearbook, 1927, Part I—*Curriculum-making: Past and Present.* Report of the Society's Committee. Harold O. Rugg, Chairman.

*Twenty-sixth Yearbook, 1927, Part II—*The Foundations of Curriculum-making.* Prepared by individual members of the Society's Committee. Harold O. Rugg, Chairman.

*Twenty-seventh Yearbook, 1928, Part I—*Nature and Nurture: Their Influence upon Intelligence.* Prepared by the Society's Committee. Lewis M. Terman, Chairman.

*Twenty-seventh Yearbook, 1928, Part II—*Nature and Nurture: Their Influence upon Achievement.* Prepared by the Society's Committee. Lewis M. Terman, Chairman.

Twenty-eighth Yearbook, 1929, Parts I and II—*Preschool and Parental Education,* Part I—*Organization and Development.* Part II—*Research and Method.* Prepared by the Society's Committee. Lois H. Meek, Chairman. Bound in one volume. Cloth.

*Twenty-ninth Yearbook, 1930, Parts I and II—*Report of the Society's Committee on Arithmetic.* Part I—*Some Aspects of Modern Thought on Arithmetic.* Part II—*Research in Arithmetic.* Prepared by the Society's Committee. F. B. Knight, Chairman. Bound in one volume.

*Thirtieth Yearbook, 1931—*The Status of Rural Education.* First Report of the Society's Committee on Rural Education. Orville G. Brim, Chairman.

Thirtieth Yearbook, 1931, Part II—*The Textbook in American Education.* Report of the Society's Committee on the Textbook, J. B. Edmonson, Chairman. Cloth, Paper.

*Thirty-first Yearbook, 1932, Part I—*A Program for Teaching Science.* Prepared by the Society's Committee on the Teaching of Science. S. Ralph Powers, Chairman.
*Thirty-first Yearbook, 1932, Part II—*Changes and Experiments in Liberal-Arts Education.* Prepared by Kathryn McHale, with numerous collaborators.
*Thirty-second Yearbook, 1933—*The Teaching of Geography.* Prepared by the Society's Committee on the Teaching of Geography. A. E. Parkins, Chairman.
*Thirty-third Yearbook, 1934, Part I—*The Planning and Construction of School Buildings.* Prepared by the Society's Committee on School Buildings. N. L. Engelhardt, Chairman.
*Thirty-third Yearbook, 1934, Part II—*The Activity Movement.* Prepared by the Society's Committee on the Activity Movement. Lois Coffey Mossman, Chairman.
Thirty-fourth Yearbook, 1935—*Educational Diagnosis.* Prepared by the Society's Committee on Educational Diagnosis. L. J. Brueckner, Chairman. Paper.
*Thirty-fifth Yearbook, 1936, Part I—*The Grouping of Pupils.* Prepared by the Society's Committee. W. W. Coxe, Chairman.
*Thirty-fifth Yearbook, 1936, Part II—*Music Education.* Prepared by the Society's Committee. W. L. Uhl, Chairman.
*Thirty-sixth Yearbook, 1937, Part I—*The Teaching of Reading.* Prepared by the Society's Committee. W. S. Gray, Chairman.
*Thirty-sixth Yearbook, 1937, Part II—*International Understanding through the Public-School Curriculum.* Prepared by the Society's Committee. I. L. Kandel, Chairman.
*Thirty-seventh Yearbook, 1938, Part I—*Guidance in Educational Institutions.* Prepared by the Society's Committee. G. N. Kefauver, Chairman.
*Thirty-seventh Yearbook, 1938, Part II—*The Scientific Movement in Education.* Prepared by the Society's Committee. F. N. Freeman, Chairman.
*Thirty-eighth Yearbook, 1939, Part I—*Child Development and the Curriculum.* Prepared by the Society's Committee. Carleton Washburne, Chairman.
*Thirty-eighth Yearbook, 1939, Part II—*General Education in the American College.* Prepared by the Society's Committee. Alvin Eurich, Chairman. Cloth.
*Thirty-ninth Yearbook, 1940, Part I—*Intelligence: Its Nature and Nurture. Comparative and Critical Exposition.* Prepared by the Society's Committee. G. D. Stoddard, Chairman.
*Thirty-ninth Yearbook, 1940, Part II—*Intelligence: Its Nature and Nurture. Original Studies and Experiments.* Prepared by the Society's Committee. G. D. Stoddard, Chairman.
*Fortieth Yearbook, 1941—*Art in American Life and Education.* Prepared by the Society's Committee. Thomas Munro, Chairman.
Forty-first Yearbook, 1942, Part I—*Philosophies of Education.* Prepared by the Society's Committee. John S. Brubacher, Chairman. Cloth, Paper.
Forty-first Yearbook, 1942, Part II—*The Psychology of Learning.* Prepared by the Society's Committee. T. R. McConnell, Chairman. Cloth.
*Forty-second Yearbook, 1943, Part I—*Vocational Education.* Prepared by the Society's Committee. F. J. Keller, Chairman.
*Forty-second Yearbook, 1943, Part II—*The Library in General Education.* Prepared by the Society's Committee. L. R. Wilson, Chairman.
Forty-third Yearbook, 1944, Part I—*Adolescence.* Prepared by the Society's Committee. Harold E. Jones, Chairman. Paper.
*Forty-third Yearbook, 1944, Part II—*Teaching Language in the Elementary School.* Prepared by the Society's Committee. M. R. Trabue, Chairman.
*Forty-fourth Yearbook, 1945, Part I—*American Education in the Postwar Period: Curriculum Reconstruction.* Prepared by the Society's Committee. Ralph W. Tyler, Chairman.
Forty-fourth Yearbook, 1945, Part II—*American Education in the Postwar Period: Structural Reorganization.* Prepared by the Society's Committee. Bess Goodykoontz, Chairman. Paper.
*Forty-fifth Yearbook, 1946, Part I—*The Measurement of Understanding.* Prepared by the Society's Committee. William A. Brownell, Chairman.
*Forty-fifth Yearbook, 1946, Part II—*Changing Conceptions in Educational Administration.* Prepared by the Society's Committee. Alonzo G. Grace, Chairman.
*Forty-sixth Yearbook, 1947, Part I—*Science Education in American Schools.* Prepared by the Society's Committee. Victor H. Noll, Chairman.
*Forty-sixth Yearbook, 1947, Part II—*Early Childhood Education.* Prepared by the Society's Committee. N. Searle Light, Chairman. Paper.
Forty-seventh Yearbook, 1948, Part I—*Juvenile Delinquency and the Schools.* Prepared by the Society's Committee. Ruth Strang, Chairman. Cloth.
Forty-seventh Yearbook, 1948, Part II—*Reading in the High School and College.* Prepared by the Society's Committee. William S. Gray, Chairman. Cloth, Paper.
Forty-eighth Yearbook, 1949, Part I—*Audio-visual Materials of Instruction.* Prepared by the Society's Committee. Stephen M. Corey, Chairman. Cloth.
*Forty-eighth Yearbook, 1949, Part II—*Reading in the Elementary School.* Prepared by the Society's Committee. Arthur I. Gates, Chairman.
*Forty-ninth Yearbook, 1950, Part I—*Learning and Instruction.* Prepared by the Society's Committee. G. Lester Anderson, Chairman.
Forty-ninth Yearbook, 1950, Part II—*The Education of Exceptional Children.* Prepared by the Society's Committee. Samuel A. Kirk, Chairman. Paper.
Fiftieth Yearbook, 1951, Part I—*Graduate Study in Education.* Prepared by the Society's Board of Directors. Ralph W. Tyler, Chairman. Paper.
Fiftieth Yearbook, 1951, Part II—*The Teaching of Arithmetic.* Prepared by the Society's Committee. G. T. Buswell, Chairman. Cloth, Paper.
Fifty-first Yearbook, 1952, Part I—*General Education.* Prepared by the Society's Committee. T. R. McConnell, Chairman. Cloth, Paper.

Fifty-first Yearbook, 1952, Part II—*Education in Rural Communities.* Prepared by the Society's Committee. Ruth Strang, Chairman. Cloth, Paper.

*Fifty-second Yearbook, 1953, Part I—*Adapting the Secondary-School Program to the Needs of Youth.* Prepared by the Society's Committee: William G. Brink, Chairman.

Fifty-second Yearbook, 1953, Part II—*The Community School.* Prepared by the Society's Committee. Maurice F. Seay, Chairman. Cloth.

*Fifty-third Yearbook, 1954, Part II—*Mass Media and Education.* Prepared by the Prepared by the Society's Committee. Edgar L. Morphet, Chairman. Cloth, Paper.

Fifty-third Yearbook, 1954, Part II—*Mass Media and Education.* Prepared by the Society's Committee. Edgar Dale, Chairman. Paper.

*Fifty-fourth Yearbook, 1955, Part I—*Modern Philosophies and Education.* Prepared by the Society's Committee. John S. Brubacher, Chairman.

Fifty-fourth Yearbook, 1955, Part II—*Mental Health in Modern Education.* Prepared by the Society's Committee. Paul A. Witty, Chairman. Paper.

*Fifty-fifth Yearbook, 1956, Part I—*The Public Junior College.* Prepared by the Society's Committee. B. Lamar Johnson, Chairman.

Fifty-fifth Yearbook, 1956, Part II—*Adult Reading.* Prepared by the Society's Committee. David H. Clift, Chairman. Paper.

Fifty-sixth Yearbook, 1957, Part I—*In-service Education of Teachers, Supervisors, and Administrators.* Prepared by the Society's Committee. Stephen M. Corey, Chairman. Cloth.

Fifty-sixth Yearbook, 1957, Part II—*Social Studies in the Elementary School.* Prepared by the Society's Committee. Ralph C. Preston, Chairman. Cloth, Paper.

Fifty-seventh Yearbook, 1958, Part I—*Basic Concepts in Music Education.* Prepared by the Society's Committee. Thurber H. Madison, Chairman. Cloth.

Fifty-seventh Yearbook, 1958, Part II—*Education for the Gifted.* Prepared by the Society's Committee. Robert J. Havighurst, Chairman. Paper.

*Fifty-seventh Yearbook, 1958, Part III—*The Integration of Educational Experiences.* Prepared by the Society's Committee. Paul L. Dressel, Chairman. Cloth.

Fifty-eighth Yearbook, 1959, Part I—*Community Education: Principles and Practices from World-wide Experience.* Prepared by the Society's Committee. C. O. Arndt, Chairman. Cloth, Paper.

*Fifty-eighth Yearbook, 1959, Part II—*Personal Services in Education.* Prepared by the Society's Committee. Melvene D. Hardee, Chairman. Paper.

*Fifty-ninth Yearbook, 1960, Part I—*Rethinking Science Education.* Prepared by the Society's Committee. J. Darrell Barnard, Chairman.

Fifty-ninth Yearbook, 1960, Part II—*The Dynamics of Instructional Groups.* Prepared by the Society's Committee. Gale E. Jensen, Chairman. Cloth, Paper.

Sixtieth Yearbook, 1961, Part I—*Development in and through Reading.* Prepared by the Society's Committee. Paul A. Witty, Chairman. Cloth, Paper.

Sixtieth Yearbook, 1961, Part II—*Social Forces Influencing American Education.* Prepared by the Society's Committee. Ralph W. Tyler, Chairman. Cloth.

Sixty-first Yearbook, 1962, Part I—*Individualizing Instruction.* Prepared by the Society's Committee. Fred T. Tyler, Chairman. Cloth.

Sixty-first Yearbook, 1962, Part II—*Education for the Professions.* Prepared by the Society's Committee. G. Lester Anderson, Chairman. Cloth.

Sixty-second Yearbook, 1963, Part I—*Child Psychology.* Prepared by the Society's Committee. Harold W. Stevenson, Editor. Cloth.

Sixty-second Yearbook, 1963, Part II—*The Impact and Improvement of School Testing Programs.* Prepared by the Society's Committee. Warren G. Findley, Editor. Cloth.

Sixty-third Yearbook, 1964, Part I—*Theories of Learning and Instruction.* Prepared by the Society's Committee. Ernest R. Hilgard, Editor. Paper, Cloth.

Sixty-third Yearbook, 1964, Part II—*Behavioral Science and Educational Administration.* Prepared by the Society' Committee. Daniel E. Griffiths, Editor. Paper.

Sixty-fourth Yearbook, 1965, Part I—*Vocational Education.* Prepared by the Society's Committee. Melvin L. Barlow, Editor. Cloth.

Sixty-fourth Yearbook, 1965, Part II—*Art Education.* Prepared by the Society's Committee. W. Reid Hastie, Editor. Cloth.

Sixty-fifth Yearbook, 1966, Part I—*Social Deviancy among Youth.* Prepared by the Society's Committee. William W. Wattenberg, Editor. Cloth.

Sixty-fifth Yearbook, 1966, Part II—*The Changing American School.* Prepared by the Society's Committee. John I. Goodlad, Editor. Cloth.

Sixty-sixth Yearbook, 1967, Part I—*The Educationally Retarded and Disadvantaged.* Prepared by the Society's Committee. Paul A. Witty, Editor. Cloth.

Sixty-sixth Yearbook, 1967, Part II—*Programed Instruction.* Prepared by the Society's Committee. Phil C. Lange, Editor. Cloth.

Sixty-seventh Yearbook, 1968, Part I—*Metropolitanism: Its Challenge to Education.* Prepared by the Society's Committee. Robert J. Havighurst, Editor. Cloth.

Sixty-seventh Yearbook, 1968, Part II—*Innovation and Change in Reading Instruction.* Prepared by the Society's Committee. Helen M. Robinson, Editor. Cloth.

Sixty-eighth Yearbook, 1969, Part I—*The United States and International Education.* Prepared by the Society's Committee. Harold G. Shane, Editor. Cloth.

Sixty-eighth Yearbook, 1969, Part II—*Educational Evaluation: New Roles, New Means.* Prepared by the Society's Committee. Ralph W. Tyler, Editor. Paper.

Sixty-ninth Yearbook, 1970, Part I—*Mathematics Education.* Prepared by the Society's Committee. Edward G. Begle, Editor. Cloth.

Sixty-ninth Yearbook, 1970, Part II—*Linguistics in School Programs.* Prepared by the Society's Committee. Albert H. Marckwardt, Editor. Cloth.

Seventieth Yearbook, 1971, Part I—*The Curriculum: Retrospect and Prospect.* Prepared by the Society's Committee. Robert M. McClure, Editor. Paper.

Seventieth Yearbook, 1971, Part II—*Leaders in American Education.* Prepared by the Society's Committee. Robert J. Havighurst, Editor. Cloth.
Seventy-first Yearbook, 1972, Part I—*Philosophical Redirection of Educational Research.* Prepared by the Society's Committee. Lawrence G. Thomas, Editor. Cloth.
Seventy-first Yearbook, 1972, Part II—*Early Childhood Education.* Prepared by the Society's Committee. Ira J. Gordon, Editor. Cloth. Paper.
Seventy-second Yearbook, 1973, Part I—*Behavior Modification in Education.* Prepared by the Society's Committee. Carl E. Thoresen, Editor. Cloth.
Seventy-second Yearbook, 1973, Part II—*The Elementary School in the United States.* Prepared by the Society's Committee. John I. Goodlad and Harold G. Shane, Editors. Cloth.
Seventy-third Yearbook, 1974, Part I—*Media and Symbols: The Forms of Expression, Communication, and Education.* Prepared by the Society's Committee. David R. Olson, Editor. Cloth.
Seventy-third Yearbook, 1974, Part II—*Uses of the Sociology of Education.* Prepared by the Society's Committee. C. Wayne Gordon, Editor. Cloth.
Seventy-fourth Yearbook, 1975, Part I—*Youth.* Prepared by the Society's Committee. Robert J. Havighurst and Philip H. Dreyer, Editors. Cloth.
Seventy-fourth Yearbook, 1975, Part II—*Teacher Education.* Prepared by the Society's Committee. Kevin Ryan, Editor. Cloth.
Seventy-fifth Yearbook, 1976, Part I—*Psychology of Teaching Methods.* Prepared by the Society's Committee. N. L. Gage, Editor. Cloth.
Seventy-fifth Yearbook, 1976, Part II—*Issues in Secondary Education.* Prepared by the Society's Committee. William Van Til, Editor. Cloth.
Seventy-sixth Yearbook, 1977, Part I—*The Teaching of English.* Prepared by the Society's Committee. James R. Squire, Editor. Cloth.
Seventy-sixth Yearbook, 1977, Part II—*The Politics of Education.* Prepared by the Society's Committee. Jay D. Scribner, Editor. Cloth.
Seventy-seventh Yearbook, 1978, Part I—*The Courts and Education,* Clifford P. Hooker, Editor. Cloth.
Seventy-seventh Yearbook, 1978, Part II—*Education and the Brain,* Jeanne Chall and Allan F. Mirsky, Editors. Cloth.
Seventy-eighth Yearbook, 1979, Part I—*The Gifted and the Talented: Their Education and Development,* A. Harry Passow, Editor. Cloth.
Seventy-eighth Yearbook, 1979, Part II—*Classroom Management,* Daniel L. Duke, Editor. Cloth.

Yearbooks of the National Society are distributed by

UNIVERSITY OF CHICAGO PRESS, 5801 ELLIS AVE.,
CHICAGO, ILLINOIS 60637

Please direct inquiries regarding prices of volumes still available to the University of Chicago Press. Orders for these volumes should be sent to the University of Chicago Press, not to the offices of the National Society.

2. The Series on Contemporary Educational Issues

In addition to its Yearbooks the Society now publishes volumes in a series on Contemporary Educational Issues. These volumes are prepared under the supervision of the Society's Commission on an Expanded Publication Program.

The 1980 Titles

Minimum Competency Achievement Testing: Motives, Models, Measures, and Consequences (Richard M. Jaeger and Carol K. Tittle, eds.)

Collective Bargaining in Public Education (Anthony M. Cresswell, Michael J. Murphy, with Charles T. Kerchner)

The 1979 Titles

Educational Environments and Effects: Evaluation, Policy, and Productivity (Herbert J. Walberg, ed.)

Research on Teaching: Concepts, Findings, and Implications (Penelope L. Peterson and Herbert J. Walberg, eds.)

The Principal in Metropolitan Schools (Donald A. Erickson and Theodore L. Reller, eds.)

The 1978 Titles

Aspects of Reading Education (Susanna Pflaum-Connor, ed.)

History, Education, and Public Policy: Recovering the American Educational Past (Donald R. Warren, ed.)

From Youth to Constructive Adult Life: The Role of the Public School (Ralph W. Tyler, ed.)

The 1977 Titles

Early Childhood Education: Issues and Insights (Bernard Spodek and Herbert J. Walberg, eds.)

The Future of Big City Schools: Desegregation Policies and Magnet Alternatives (Daniel U. Levine and Robert J. Havighurst, eds.)

Educational Administration: The Developing Decades (Luvern L. Cunningham, Walter G. Hack, and Raphael O. Nystrand, eds.)

The 1976 Titles

Prospects for Research and Development in Education (Ralph W. Tyler, ed.)

Public Testimony on Public Schools (Commission on Educational Governance)

Counseling Children and Adolescents (William M. Walsh, ed.)

The 1975 Titles

Schooling and the Rights of Children (Vernon Haubrich and Michael Apple, eds.)

Systems of Individualized Education (Harriet Talmage, ed.)

Educational Policy and International Assessment: Implications of the IEA Assessment of Achievement (Alan Purves and Daniel U. Levine, eds.)

The 1974 Titles

Crucial Issues in Testing (Ralph W. Tyler and Richard M. Wolf, eds.)

Conflicting Conceptions of Curriculum (Elliott Eisner and Elizabeth Vallance, eds.)

Cultural Pluralism (Edgar G. Epps, ed.)

Rethinking Educational Equality (Andrew T. Kopan and Herbert J. Walberg, eds.)

All of the above volumes may be ordered from

McCutchan Publishing Corporation
2526 Grove Street
Berkeley, California 94704

The 1972 Titles

Black Students in White Schools (Edgar G. Epps, ed.)

Flexibility in School Programs (W. J. Congreve and G. L. Rinehart, eds.)

Performance Contracting—1969–1971 (J. A. Mecklenburger)

The Potential of Educational Futures (Michael Marien and W. L. Ziegler, eds.)

Sex Differences and Discrimination in Education (Scarvia Anderson, ed.)

The 1971 Titles

Accountability in Education (Leon M. Lessinger and Ralph W. Tyler, eds.)

Farewell to Schools??? (D. U. Levine and R. J. Havighurst, eds.)

Models for Integrated Education (D. U. Levine, ed.)

PYGMALION *Reconsidered* (J. D. Elashoff and R. E. Snow)

Reactions to Silberman's CRISIS IN THE CLASSROOM (A. Harry Passow, ed.)

The 1971 and 1972 titles in this series are now out of print and are no longer available.

TOWARD ADOLESCENCE:
THE MIDDLE SCHOOL YEARS